INKED

Harvard East Asian Monograph Series 461

INKED

Tattooed Soldiers and the Song Empire's Penal-Military Complex

Elad Alyagon

Published by the Harvard University Asia Center
Distributed by Harvard University Press
Cambridge (Massachusetts) and London 2023

Printed in the United States of America

The Harvard University Asia Center publishes a monograph series and, in coordination with the Fairbank Center for Chinese Studies, the Korea Institute, the Reischauer Institute of Japanese Studies, and other faculties and institutes, administers research projects designed to further scholarly understanding of China, Japan, Vietnam, Korea, and other Asian countries. The Center also sponsors projects addressing multidisciplinary and regional issues in Asia.

Library of Congress Cataloging-in-Publication Data

Names: Alyagon, Elad, author.
Title: Inked : tattooed soldiers and the Song Empire's penal-military complex / Elad Alyagon.
Other titles: Harvard East Asian monographs ; 461.
Description: Cambridge, Massachusetts : Harvard University Asia Center, 2023. | Series: Harvard East Asian monographs ; 461 | Based on the author's thesis (Ph. D—University of California, Davis, 2016). | Includes bibliographical references and index. |
Identifiers: LCCN 2022049729 | ISBN 9780674291287 (hardcover)
Subjects: LCSH: Convict soldiers—China—History—To 1500. | Tattooing—China—History—To 1500. | China—History, Military—960–1644. | China—History—Song dynasty, 960–1279. | China—Social life and customs—960–1644.
Classification: LCC DS750.74 .A49 2023 | DDC 951/.02—dc23/eng/20230110
LC record available at https://lccn.loc.gov/2022049729

Index by Anne Holmes

Printed on acid-free paper

Last figure below indicates year of this printing
32 31 30 29 28 27 26 25 24 23

For my parents, Dalya and Oded Alyagon, and for Lulu

Contents

Illustrations

Acknowledgments

Beverly Bossler taught me how to write history. I am grateful to her for long years and countless hours of guidance and mentorship, for many amazing dinners (thank you, too, James!), and for providing me with an inspiring role model as both a scholar and a person. I owe a great debt of gratitude to Mark Halperin and Paul Smith for their mentorship and advice in the years I was developing this project. Don Price was a wonderful teacher and a true *mensch*, and I was fortunate to enjoy Don and Nancy's hospitality many times. Susan Mann taught me my first class at UC Davis, and I still remember with great fondness that introduction into American academic life. In the years that passed since, I continue to learn from her. A true privilege.

I first set foot on this path at the Hebrew University in Jerusalem. Lin Qian introduced me to the Chinese language, and she made learning Chinese beautiful. I miss our funny conversations and drinking cheap and much-too-sweet hot chocolate from the vending machine. Natan Ofek was a brilliant scholar and the kindest of souls. I will always remember classes at his house on chilly Jerusalem evenings, talking about Walter Benjamin, and his long sighs whenever he wondered about Laozi's straw dogs. May he rest in peace.

Rachel Reeves and Jordan Scavo read many versions of this work and helped me more than any friend should. I could not have done this without their support. Sarah Schneewind, Pat Ebrey, and two anonymous readers offered thoughtful and sincere comments that greatly changed and improved this book. I am deeply grateful to Robert Graham and Kristen Wanner from the Harvard University Asia Center for believing in this book and for helping to make it a reality. Big thanks to Michelle Asakawa for copyedits, Angela Piliouras for seeing the book to print, and Anne Holmes for indexing.

During research and writing, I was fortunate to enjoy the support of the UC Davis Department of History, the Center for Chinese Studies in Taipei, the Chiang Ch'ing-kuo Foundation, the Zvi Yavetz School of Historical Studies in Tel Aviv University with the kind hosting of Asaf Goldschmidt, and the Henry Luce Foundation/ACLS Program in China Studies. Their support made this work possible.

I owe a great debt of gratitude to many friends and colleagues for their support along the way. My Chinese History and Asian Studies colleagues during graduate school provided me with strong intellectual and emotional support: my big sister Wu Yulian, Sean Marsh, Nicole Richardson, Zhou Yi, and D Dayton. My little sister Lin Shan taught me much about Chinese history and provided camaraderie along this lonely path. Gumu pai forever! Iiyama Tomoyasu, Lincoln Tsui, and Zhou Huanqing helped me gain access to much-needed literature. Ren Baihua provided me with great insights on Song paintings. Special thanks go to Neel Amin, TJ Hinrichs, Rajbir Judge, Christopher Mayo, Carlotta Sparvoli, Wu Yating, and Elsa Yang.

Brenda Medina-Hernandez, thank you for being my friend. I kept your comments on the manuscript, and I tried to follow them to the best of my ability. I learned so much from you, and your spirit lives in these pages and in everything I do. I'm sure you keep the party going up there in Heaven. See you on the other side one day, my friend.

I would not be where I am without the support of many nonhuman friends that did not live to see the end of this project: the dogs Lola, Shibboleth, and Suki; the cats Dror, Ktato, and Nesikhon; and Pip the rabbit. The cat Nicki and the dogs Ludi, Marco, and Rocket are still with us. May they live ten thousand years!

I am eternally grateful to my partner, Griseyda Vargas-Alyagon, for staying by my side despite all that I do. We lived through some long nights these past few years, but you were always there. May the next chapter of our lives be filled with light. I love you very much.

E. A.

Note on Romanization and Dates

Chinese terms are transcribed according to the Hanyu Pinyin romanization system. Superscript is used to distinguish between terms that share the same romanization (Yizhou, Yizhou^{1}); readers may refer to the glossary to locate their corresponding Chinese characters. Dates are usually converted to the standard modern system. Traditional dates and reign periods are used for citing traditional sources when required and in cases where the exact year of events is unclear.

Repudiating the virtues of your world,
criminals hopelessly agree to organize a forbidden universe.
They agree to live in it.
The air there is nauseating: they can breathe it.

—Jean Genet, *The Thief's Journal*
(translated by Bernard Frecthman)

INTRODUCTION

As it is told today, the rise and fall of the Song dynasty (960–1279) is a story of triumph and tragedy. It is the triumph of benevolence and intellectual inquiry, of social mobility and economic growth, of the worthy over the highborn, and of scholar-officials over military officials. The story of the Song dynasty is also told as a great tragedy: of factional strife between reformers and conservatives that shook that empire to its foundations, threw its political institutions into disarray, and pitted the empire's officials against one another. The tragedy of the Song was also that of the military destruction of the Chinese state and the humiliation, extortion, and slaughter of the Chinese people by foreigners.

The story of the Song dynasty has another side, one that has been hidden in plain sight. That is the story of the penal-military complex, the Song empire's vast system for the extraction of labor, social control, and warfare. Millions of men and women lived under the shadow of the military institutions of the Song state. For these millions, the state was a violent, predatory entity. Economic growth meant exploitation and servitude, while war provided new opportunities for escape, revenge, and glory. At the heart of this group stood the tattooed soldiers of the Song military, and this is their story.

This story begins in the ninth century, during the last century of the Tang period (618–907). It ends with the Mongol conquest of the Song dynasty, close to five centuries later. These five centuries fall within a time frame that scholars often refer to as the Chinese Middle Period. No clear standards exist for this period. It can commence with the decline of the early Chinese empire in the third century and end as late as the Ming Commercial Revolution of the sixteenth century, over a thousand years later. Here, the Middle Period refers to the time stretching from the early eighth century (high Tang period) to the fourteenth century (early Ming).

Between the eighth and tenth centuries, the nature of military service in the Tang empire changed significantly. In the preceding centuries, commoner households provided the state with soldiers as a form of tax or obligation to the state. By the middle of the eighth century, professional soldiers who worked for a salary had emerged as a new social class.[1] During the ninth century, in one region of the Tang empire, the three provinces of the Hebei region (Youzhou, Chengde, and Weibo), soldiers came to form a strong political lobby. They intervened in the appointments of their superiors, protected the soldiers' salaries, and acted to keep their comrades in the registers even in old age.[2] The professional soldiers of the ninth century had another unique trait: many of them were tattooed. The Song state would take this practice to new heights, making the time between the tenth and thirteenth centuries the highpoint of penal and military tattoos in East Asian history.[3]

One of the most outstanding traits of the Song empire was the huge scale of its military system. The Song empire experienced steep population growth, reaching over a hundred million people by the end of the twelfth century.[4] The military, too, was growing, and it soon became a meaningful component of Song society. The early Song military numbered about 400 thousand during the late 970s, and it grew to 660 thousand twenty years later. By 1020 it had reached a size of 900 thousand, with

1. Graff, *Medieval Chinese Warfare*, 212, 216, 239; Huang Qinglian, "Tangmo Wudai de qingzu," 147.

2. Graff, *Medieval Chinese Warfare*, 212, 216, 239; Graff, "China, The Tang: 600–900," 227–28; Zhang Guogang, "Transformations of the Tang Military," 305–6; Tackett, *Destruction of the Medieval Chinese Aristocracy*, 151.

3. For more about Middle-Period tattoos see Ceresa, "Written on Skin and Flesh"; Chen Yuanpeng, "Shenti yu huawen"; Huang Qinglian, "Tangmo Wudai de qingzu"; Lei, "Blood-Stained Text in Translation"; Ning Ke, "Shibing cizi"; Reed, "Early Chinese Tattoo"; Reed, "Tattoos in Early China"; Sogabe Shizuo, "Sōdai no shi-hai ni tsuite"; Zhu Ruixi, "Songdai cizi he wenshen xisu."

4. Ge Jianxiong, "Songdai renkou xinzheng."

half of the troops being combat troops and the other half labor troops. During the wars with the Tanguts of the mid-eleventh century, the military reached a size of 1.4 million, of which about 800 thousand were combat troops. The Southern Song state, having lost the northern part of the empire, numbered only about 65 million people in its early years. However, at the end of the thirteenth century, during their wars with the Mongols, the Song military once again reached its former size of around 1.4 million.[5] The size of the Song armies made military tattoos a massive phenomenon, and there were at least hundreds of thousands of tattooed men at any given time over the course of three centuries. In times of great wars, over a million men had military tattoos, whether those were facial tattoos (tenth and eleventh centuries) or arm tattoos (twelfth and thirteenth centuries).

In the Song empire, the systems of the military, state labor, penal justice, and law enforcement were all intertwined. People moved through various parts of this world—labor, prison, workshop, military fort, and marketplace—but remained within the same social universe, even after their formal discharge from military service. I use the term "penal-military complex" to refer to both the formal aspects of the Song state's military organization and the social world generated by the military system. Like the United States' military-industrial complex, the Song empire's penal-military complex was a collection of organizations, policies, relationships, political and financial interests, and physical and social spaces. Without officially existing, its influence permeated all of Song society and its institutions.

Despite the size and power of the Song military, the lives of Song-era soldiers were obscured by the Song elite, a group often referred to as scholar-officials. They produced the textual legacy of the Song period that survives to the present day, because these texts were the ones deemed worthy of preserving. Naturally, these texts reflect the concerns and values of a small segment of society—elite society. The rise of this group to prominence and the texts they left for us have shaped the great narratives that dominate the modern memory of the Song period: the restraining of military power, the rise of a nonhereditary elite, and the clash between

5. Cheng Minsheng, "Songdai bingli bushu kaocha"; Tan Su-cheng, "Songdai zhi jundui," 7.1a; Ge Jianxiong, "Songdai renkou xinzheng."

people of different ethnicities. The history of soldiers and their social world that I want to tell brings to light alternative themes and narratives, changing and broadening our understanding of Song history in the process.

The First Narrative: Restraining Military Power

In the middle of the eighth century, the Tang dynasty reached the height of its power and glory under Emperor Xuanzong (r. 712–756). During this time, however, fatal flaws in the Tang government came to light. Military power flowed into the hands of military governors (*jiedushi*) in the border regions. One of those governors, the general An Lushan (703–757), started a rebellion that greatly weakened the Tang state. Those who fought for the Tang cause won the day, but the central government never regained its former hold on large parts of the empire.[6] The Tang survived until 906, followed by a succession of short-lived dynasties that ruled the north, while the south broke up into more stable and smaller independent states. This period, known as the Five Dynasties period (907–960), lasted for about half a century, and it was marked by a high degree of political instability as power changed hands quickly in a cycle of fledgling dynasties and usurpations. The monarchs of the Five Dynasties rose to power and maintained that power through their control of the military.

During the mid- to late tenth century, the last monarchs of the Five Dynasties period and the founding emperors of the Song who succeeded them took steps to centralize military administration and bend it to the government's will in order to increase political stability. These gains came at the cost of losing some of their war-making capacity.[7] They concentrated large numbers of troops near the capital, stripped the old generals of their commands, and placed military officials under the supervision

6. For more on the decline of the Tang's central government see Wang Gungwu, "Military Governors and the Decline of the T'ang"; Pulleyblank, "An Lu-shan Rebellion in Late T'ang China"; Tackett, *Destruction of the Medieval Chinese Aristocracy*.

7. For studies of Five Dynasties developments and military systems, see Wang Gungwu, *Structure of Power in North China*; Mu Jing, "Wudai bingzhi kaolun."

of civil officials. The policies of the Song founders later became known as "strengthening the root and weakening the branches" (*qianggan ruozhi*) and "cherishing the civil and restraining the martial" (*chongwen yiwu*).

The premodern terminology of *wen* and *wu* (the "civil" and the "martial") is an important prism through which Chinese history has been analyzed in modern times. Modern-day scholars of Song history especially tended to follow the binary view of a world split between civil and military officials.[8] More recently, this view has become more nuanced as scholars point out that a binary analysis does not accurately reflect Song life.[9] However, debates about the martial-civil divide tend to focus on civil and military officials within the state bureaucracy, a relatively small part of the population.

From the perspective of soldiers, who were at the bottom of the social hierarchy, the more important split was not between civil and military officials but rather between the world of the elites and the military underclass, between those who wrote and those whose bodies were inscribed. Soldiers and their families lived in a world dominated by a martial ethos, where status was built around the body and where violence played an important part in everyday life. They formed the core of a larger group that included militia members, convicts, the poor, and their family

8. For example, see Chen Feng's *Wushi de beiai*.

9. Zhao Dongmei offers a more nuanced view of Song military bureaucracy with a study of another service track that was positioned between the civil and military realms (*Wen wu zhi jian*); Fang Cheng-hua explains how the division between the military and the civil came about gradually ("Power Structures and Cultural Identities"). Don Wyatt uses case studies of men who led Song armies to demonstrate that *wu* was not restricted to military men, nor was *wen* restricted to civil officials ("Unsung Men of War"); the career paths of civil officials also led them through the military realm (Huang Kuan-chong, "Jia She shigong shuping"). Civil officials were interested in and intervened in military affairs, and they also called for military strengthening (Fan Xuehui, "Songren benchao junzheng tizhi"; Fu Libai, "Songdai shumiyuan de shishi"). Robert Hymes suggests looking at office holding as one out of several characteristics of elite status that included a prefectural-level degree, donations to temples, donations to public projects, leadership of military organizations, and master-student relationship or affinal kinship to one of the previous. Hymes argues that this makes the distinction between civil and military positions less meaningful (Hymes, *Statesmen and Gentlemen*, 6–11). Other scholars have pointed out continuities between the Five Dynasties period and the Song in terms of leadership and military institutions (Lorge, *Reunification of China*, 278–86; Huang Kuan-chong, "Tang Song jiceng wuli," 3).

members. The Song state and its agents, ruling over a militarizing world, were always preoccupied, even obsessed, with the control of this marginal yet highly important group.

The Second Narrative: The Rise of the Scholar-Official and a New Elite

The founding of the Song state saw the culmination of a process that transformed the society, economy, and culture of the Sinitic-script world between the eighth and eleventh centuries. Modern scholars refer to this process as the Tang-Song Transition.[10] The rise of a new nonhereditary elite whose status was based on the civil-service examination system stands at the center of this transition. The civil-service examination system had already been in place under the Tang dynasty, but the Song founders opened the examinations to a much larger group of men, creating new opportunities for social mobility. The ethos of this new elite changed from one of high birth to one of skill, hard work, and morality. Most elite men did not hold office or an examination degree, but many studied for the examinations, and the examination system became a pillar of elite culture and society.[11] The scholar-officials of the Song were the heroes of that world, and the Song period was their golden age. Modern-day scholars, perhaps imagining themselves as the counterparts of Song-period intellectuals, described the Song period as a time of social mobility in which meritocratic and benevolent rule prevailed. For them, it was a society founded on the humanist values and ideals of the ancient classics.

The elites who made passing the examinations and entering public service central aspects of their lives dominated the Sinitic-script world for

10. The concept of the Tang-Song transition was pioneered by the Japanese scholar Naitō Torajirō. For a summary of Naitō's work and the debate it sparked in Japan, see Miyakawa, "Outline of the Naitō Hypothesis." Zeng Ruilong and Zhao Yule summarize the literature on the Tang-Song transition from the perspective of military administration (Zeng and Zhao, "Tang Song junzheng biange").

11. For the rise of the examinations system and its culture, see Chaffee's *Thorny Gates of Learning*. For the new ethos of Song elites, see Beverly Bossler's *Powerful Relations*.

almost a millennium, long after the fall of the Song state. In that sense, the rise of scholar-officials was one of the most meaningful developments in Chinese history. This new elite that emerged in the Song period has sparked a long debate among modern scholars about the definition of elite status and the permeability of elite lines. Scholars agree on a few basic facts: More people came to enjoy elite status. Social mobility based on merit became an accepted and respected notion. The examination system was the most famous and prestigious symbol of this meritocratic ideal.[12]

The men who studied for the examinations were only a small component of Song society. These men were a minority even within their own households. Next to them were their female kin, and below them, men and women who served them. Gender scholars highlighted this fact, that elite households contained nonelite members, women who had been purchased by elite households, while still emphasizing the growing possibilities offered to women by economic growth.[13] One consequence of economic growth, however, was the rise of the sex trade and the selling of females to serve as concubines or courtesans. Courtesans used to be equivalent to slaves, or dependents of the state or powerful households, but by the ninth century economic growth had led to the expansion of the consumer base. More people had money, and more households could purchase courtesans and concubines. These courtesans and concubines no longer came from hereditary courtesan households. Instead, they came

12. Kracke argues that the Song period saw the rise of a larger merit-based elite through the civil service examinations (*Civil Service in Early Sung China*). Hartwell argues for the emergence of a national elite during the Northern Song and a more local elite during the Southern Song (Hartwell, "Demographic, Political, and Social Transformations"). Hymes shows the diverse strategies used by Southern Song elites to maintain their status (Hymes, *Statesmen and Gentlemen*). Richard L. Davis studies the ways a family rose to elite status and maintained it over generations through success in the examinations (Davis, *Court and Family in Sung China*).

13. Scholars found that Song-period women had relatively strong property rights, could remarry, and played important roles in financial management and education within their households. Finally, kinship networks with women's birth families were crucial for maintaining their married families' elite status over generations. For important studies on women's property and marriage rights during the Song period, see Ebrey, *The Inner Quarters*; Birge, *Women, Property, and Confucian Reaction*. For more on women's roles in elite social networks, see Bossler's *Powerful Relations*.

from households in financial need.[14] Many of those households were families of soldiers.

Modern scholars interpreted the sex trade as a vehicle for upward social mobility. Growing commercialization and the creation of markets for courtesans and concubines brought women of lower-class backgrounds into elite social-cultural circles (in brothels) and elite households (as concubines), and some of them gave birth to children who would be part of the elite.[15] However, when we view this phenomenon from the perspective of lower-class women and their natal households, rather than elite men and their households, the market in female bodies looks like a vicious, predatory, and abusive practice, a great destroyer of life and human dignity. The women who appeared in elite social spaces had been taken away, often against their will, from their natal families to provide sexual services, labor, and companionship to elite men. Property rights, marriage rights, maintenance of elite status—all of these could mean very little from the perspective of those whose bodies were sold.

Even if one sets aside the severe trauma caused to the women sold through the sex trade, the concept of social mobility can be misleading. In a society structured like a pyramid, most people stay in place. There were individual cases of success during the Song period, but most people did not move up in life. Most lower-class women did not find themselves in elite households or brothels, just as most soldiers did not rise to fame and fortune through military service. A large part of Song-period lower-class households lived at the intersection of different systems of oppression: the military and the sex trade.[16] Both of these systems exerted great pressure on soldiers' households, often pulling the males and the females toward different worlds and different life trajectories—the females toward the sex trade, and the males toward a life of labor, servitude, and warfare. The social truth of their world lies not with those who had climbed

14. Bossler, *Courtesans, Concubines, and the Cult of Female Fidelity*, 418–19.

15. Bossler, "Shifting Identities"; Bossler, *Courtesans, Concubines, and the Cult of Female Fidelity*.

16. Intersectional theory looks at class and gender as interlocking systems that need to be analyzed in light of each other. Intersectional analysis was originally applied to the study of Black women's dual oppression within the American Civil Rights Movement and the Feminist Movement. For important studies of intersectionality see Collins, *Black Feminist Thought*; Angela Davis, *Women, Race, and Class*.

up but with those who stayed behind and continued to live their lives within the penal-military complex.

The Third Narrative: A Clash of Ethnicities?

The Song dynasty rose to power in a world with other well-established non-Chinese political entities. Following the conquest of the south, the early Song state fought its major campaigns against the Khitan Liao state to the north. War erupted again in 1038 with the Tangut Xia state in the northwest. Wars with the Tanguts flared again and again until 1127, when the Jurchens conquered the northern half of the Song empire and drove the remnants of the Song imperial house to the south, where they founded a new capital in Hangzhou. The location of the capital gave this second half of the Song period the name Southern Song. At this point, the Jurchens became the Song state's new mortal enemy for a century. Finally, during the thirteenth century, the Mongols destroyed the Southern Song over the course of decades of warfare.

The Chinese Song state's wars against a succession of strong and aggressive non-Chinese states on its northern borders became one of the most famous and powerful narratives of Song history. Despite superior resources, technology, and manpower, the Song's military record was littered with epic defeats. Denied victories, the Song court chased peace through less glorious means, by paying off rival states and recognizing the equal status—or even supremacy—of neighboring rulers. Whereas the Tang dynasty had dominated the region, the Song empire was a powerful state but only one of a few within the multistate landscape of the era.[17]

The question of military weakness became a crucial problem in twentieth-century Song historiography due, in part, to the important role of nationalism in historical analysis. Scholars identified the Song military crisis with the painful transformation of the Qing empire (1644–1911) into a modern Chinese nation-state during the nineteenth and twentieth centuries, when China suffered under the yoke of Western and Japanese

17. For more on the Chinese empire's unique position under the Song, see Rossabi, *China among Equals*; Wright, *From War to Diplomatic Parity*.

imperialism.[18] From this perspective, the Song's military history becomes a cautionary tale that needs to be studied so that national humiliation can be prevented in the future. Underlying the narrative of military weakness is the assumption that the natural and positive state of affairs is a strong centralized Chinese state that governs all territories considered Chinese, where the Han people and their culture rule hegemonic over the non-Han people.

The association of the Song state with a Chinese national identity continues to exert a strong influence on our understanding of that world, brushing out fault lines within Song society, projecting modern Han ethnic identity onto the Song period, making ethnicity the most meaningful component in identity formation, and assuming that such Han or Chinese identity was widely shared.[19] The Song state became the representative of all the Han people: rich and poor, officials and commoners, male and female. In the process, the nationalist narrative silenced the voices of groups without power.[20] Western scholars, too, view the Song empire as a Chinese empire, populated mostly by Han people.[21] The historical records available to us, produced by members of the literate elite,

18. James Liu explains that Japanese imperialism had a great impact on how Chinese scholars analyzed peace and war in the Song dynasty, specifically in the context of the general Yue Fei. See Liu, "Yüeh Fei," 44–45; Liu "Yue Fei." For more about Yue Fei, see chapter 7. The association of Middle-Period Song soldiers with modern China's political instability took hold in the West as well. In *Warlord Soldiers*, Diana Lary describes the soldiers of the Warlord Period (1911–1937) as badly trained and undermotivated, many of them forced to join the army out of despair and hunger. Lary uses the term "bad iron," a term often used to refer to Song soldiers, as the title for one of her chapters.

19. See Wang Zengyu's work on Song military history and the general Yue Fei: *Huangyin wudao Song Gaozong* and *Jinzhong baoguo.*

20. Prasenjit Duara's *Rescuing History from the Nation* highlights the problematic relationship between history and the state, and the ways it silences a multiplicity of voices and identities. Whereas Duara was focused on the Qing-dynasty-based Chinese nation-state, my study focuses on the Song period, about seven hundred years earlier.

21. For example, Von Glahn's study of the southwestern frontier analyzes the population in terms of the plain culture of Han settlers and the forest culture of indigenous people (Von Glahn, *Country of Streams and Grottoes*). The broad usage of terms such as "Song China" and "Chinese" in titles of historical literature about the Song period is another example of the assumption that the people who lived within the Sinitic-script empire shared a Chinese identity.

put great limitations on our ability to recover voices that challenge these notions.

More recently, scholars have argued that the transition to a more "national" or "modern" state during the Middle Period was still at an early phase. Even though Song elites increasingly thought of themselves as members of a larger group bound together with a common cultural heritage—represented by the Song state and closely associated with a defined territory—this vision was shared among a relatively small group of people.[22] The broader group that modern scholars refer to as Han was highly fractured and diverse, with people who lived in completely different climates, who spoke a variety of languages, and who had their own cultural practices.[23] "Confucian" or "Classical" culture was not shared throughout Song society, or, at least, these terms held different meanings for different social groups. Military people had their own non-Confucian world, one of potentially many other non-Confucian worlds in the Song empire that together formed the group that modern people often refer to today as "Han" or "Chinese."[24]

22. Abramson shows the importance of the discourse of ethnic identity during the Tang period (Abramson, *Ethnic Identity in Tang China*); Yang Shao-yun discusses the interplay between culture and ethnic identity in Tang and Song elite discourse (Yang, *Way of the Barbarians*); Standen's study of the Song-Liao border during the early Song period argues that loyalty was defined by people's location, not by their ethnic identity (Standen, *Unbounded Loyalty*). Tackett argues that the Song period's geopolitical environment brought about the rise of a "nationalist" identity among the Song empire's scholar-officials (Tackett, *Origins of the Chinese Nation*). According to Kim Sung Kyu, the Song state exhibited some of the traits of a modern nation-state, and the terms "state" and "territory" came close to their modern meanings (*Sōdai no seihoku mondai to iminzoku seisaku*, 1–11).

23. Hugh Clark points out the great ethnic diversity that existed within what came to be termed a Chinese world (Clark, "What's the Matter with 'China'?"). In his study of local religion and ancestral cult in Fuzhou during the Late Imperial period, Michael Szonyi argues that there was great diversity in cultural praxis across the empire, both among local elites and below the elite level (Szonyi, "Making Claims about Standardization").

24. Susan Mann treats the world of elite women in Late Imperial China as non-Confucian (Mann, *Male Bond in Chinese History*). The same holds true for the Song period's penal-military complex.

The Lost Voices of Song Soldiers

In the grand drama of Song history, reflected in the writings of Song-period scholars, the Song's scholar-officials made themselves into the only legitimate power brokers. As for the role of villains, that history cast a few senior officials in the role of "evil ministers," accusing men like Cai Jing (1047–1126), Qin Gui (1090–1155), and Jia Sidao (1213–1275) of persecuting good officials, of selling out the country to its enemies, and of accumulating power and riches for themselves and their cronies. Modern scholars followed this interpretation that the actions of "evil ministers" exposed the Song empire to external non-Chinese enemies: Khitans, Tanguts, Jurchens, and Mongols, who could then destroy the Chinese Song civilization through military conquest.[25] If the scholar-officials cast themselves as the heroes of the Song age, soldiers were not even fit to be the villains. In the historical narrative, soldiers bore the blame for the Song's decimation due to being lazy, violent, and cowardly. Song scholars ascribed very little moral agency to common soldiers, and the soldiers had no voice in the conversation. Yet, soldiers were a resource to be managed, controlled, and disciplined.

Present-day Chinese-language scholarship on Song dynasty military history is abundant, but it tends to approach history from the state's point of view.[26] In this context, the lives of soldiers were no more relevant than issues of topography or the supply of war horses.[27] Even where the current scholarship does pay attention to Song soldiers, those studies tend to place the state at the center, by discussing, for example, whether soldiers had a positive or negative impact on the state, or whether soldiers

25. For important examples of this narrative, see Wang Zengyu's works on Emperor Gaozong and the general Yue Fei: *Huangyin wudao Song Gaozong*, and *Jinzhong baoguo*.

26. Important classic studies include Deng Guangming's biography of Yue Fei, *Yue Fei zhuan*; Wang Zengyu's comprehensive history of the Song military system, *Songchao junzhi chutan*; and Huang Kuan-chong's study of local forces during the Southern Song, *Nansong difang wuli*.

27. For debates on military weakness, see Qian Mu, *Zhongguo lidai zhengzhi deshi*, 105–13; Chen Feng, *Wushi de beiai*; Chen Feng, "Shilun Song chu wujiang jingshen"; and Chen Feng, *Beisong wujiang qunti*. 348–352.

carry the blame for the Song state's military weakness.[28] Scholars acknowledge mismanagement and mistreatment of soldiers, but their goal remains the same: diagnosing the weakness of the state and prescribing its possible remedies.[29]

Japanese scholars have begun to place the Song state's system of military manpower management in a larger social and legal context, but military institutions stand at the center of their inquiries. Most notably, for more than fifty years Koiwai Hiromitsu has studied various aspects of the Song military that pertain specifically to the lives of common soldiers: income, food storage, and the issue of aging soldiers. Tsuji Masahiro studied the punishment of assigning convicts to military service and the criminalization of Song soldiers. More recently, Saitō Tadakazu wrote about the ways Song military institutions, especially the reserves (*shengyuan*), also functioned as social welfare providers for soldiers, thereby supporting social stability within the Song empire.[30]

Prior to the twenty-first century, Song military history received relatively little attention in the West.[31] The work of military historian Peter Lorge on the Song dynasty challenged the marginal position of military affairs in Chinese history by showing the crucial role military men played

28. In their study of the postal-station soldiers, Wang Yunhai and Zhang Dezong point out the harsh conditions of service and treatment, the large criminal component among the soldiers, and the problems of desertion and banditry ("Songdai de youdipu bing"). Huai Jianli's work on the prefectural armies of the Song military goes beyond institutional history to study living conditions in the prefectural armies, and looks at their social functions (Huai, *Songchao xiangjun yanjiu*). Fang Cheng-hua's study of the rationalization of the Song's recruitment system argues that making war was not the priority of the Song military and shows how it was also a tool for carrying out a social agenda (Fang Cheng-hua, "Yangbing weimin").

29. For examples, see Qian Junling, *Songdai jundui shangfa zhidu*, I–II; Liu Jin, *Songdai zhengguijun junshi xunlian*.

30. See Koiwai, *Sōdai heiseishi no kenkyū*; Tsuji, "Sō-hatsu no hairu to hai-gun"; Saitō, *Sōdai boheisei no kenkyū*.

31. Important studies of Song military history produced in the United States during the 1970s and 1980s include Kaplan, "Yueh Fei and the Founding of the Southern Sung"; McGrath, "Military and Regional Administration"; Labadie, "Rulers and Soldiers"; Forage, "The Sino-Tangut War." Wong Hon-chiu's study of state expenses demonstrates the great weight of military affairs within the Song administration, but also sheds light on issues of individual livelihood ("Government Expenditures in Northern Sung China").

during the early Song and the importance of military institutions and technologies in the centuries that followed. Lorge's analysis portrays the Song as a powerful and dynamic state from a military perspective. Rather than a failed military organization, the Song military was the pioneer that laid the foundations for the Military Revolution ascribed to European powers centuries later.[32] Lorge's work on the Song military, like the work of social, legal, and economic historians of this period, paints the Song as a positive moment in history, a moment pregnant with possibilities, a Chinese Renaissance. Lorge demonstrates this through military technology, whereas other social and legal historians paint the Song as a period of dignity for humankind.

Was the Song a Confucian, Pacifist Civilization?

In the West, scholars have generally characterized the Chinese empire as a Confucian pacifist civilization in which soldiers and military culture played little part. Even though the Song state had a sizable army, the world it inhabited was supposed to be Confucian and nonviolent.[33] Present-day scholars of government and political science argue that despite its moral rhetoric, the imperial Chinese state's turn to war and violence was driven by practical considerations of *realpolitik*.[34] Scholars

32. Parker's *The Military Revolution* is a classic study of the military aspect of "the rise of the West." Lorge wrote on a variety of topics: strategy, campaigns, military thought, and military institutions. For Lorge's work, see *War, Politics and Society*; "From Warlord to Emperor"; *Asian Military Revolution*; "Military Institutions as a Defining Feature."

33. Higham and Graff explain that military history has been neglected by scholars of Chinese history, and although works on Chinese history tend to emphasize the Confucian/pacifist aspects of Chinese civilization, warfare played an important role in Chinese history and society (Higham and Graff, "Introduction"). Kuhn titled his book on the Song *The Age of Confucian Rule*, alluding to its civil reputation. Mote described the Song empire as pursuing pacifist policies despite having a swollen military organization (Mote, *Imperial China*. 115). See also Di Cosmo, "Introduction."

34. Johnston's *Cultural Realism* separates the Ming state's moralist rhetoric from its behavior, arguing that *realpolitik* was a more useful term for analyzing the behavior of the Ming dynasty. Wang Yuan-kang extends that argument to the Song state, but he argues that Chinese bureaucracy and society were still dominated by a single pacifist culture (Wang, *Harmony and War*, 1–10). Hu Shaohua maintains that the idea of Chinese pacifism has some merit: Chinese philosophy and religion tended to be pacifist,

assigned an important role to violence in Chinese society, especially at the local level.[35] Modern scholars of the Middle Period also came to recognize violence as an important concept for analyzing Middle Period state and society, and they found that Chinese society could be as violent as the societies of Inner Asian peoples, both in terms of degree and the specific forms of violence employed.[36]

Violence played a central role in the lives of soldiers and their relationships with the state and its agents, as well as in soldiers' interactions with the elite. As the Song military absorbed lower-class commoners, it became an increasingly brutal space, both in the form of the exploitation and degradation of soldiers and the violent reactions of those disaffected.[37] Military skills and knowledge were widespread in the northern areas of the Northern Song empire, and they spread ever more broadly in the Song empire during the Southern Song period.[38] Beyond the moralist rhetoric of the historical sources, violence was an important part of local life. Violence, often and in generous amounts, maintained the power of both the social elite and the state over the population. Classical literacy did not abolish violence from a person's life, but it meant an individual was more likely to inflict violence than to receive it. This type of violence was part of everyday life, and it was associated with upholding law and order and sustaining the growing marketplace for human labor and human bodies. This type of violence

Chinese society was inward-looking and generally not inclined to warlike attitudes, historically China's wars tended to be defensive, and this defensive posture was determined by its geopolitical position vis-à-vis its nomad neighbors to the north (Hu, "Revisiting Chinese Pacifism").

35. ter Haar, "Rethinking 'Violence' in Chinese Culture," 123. For a study on the prevalence of violence in local society during the Ming period, see David Robinson's *Bandits, Eunuchs, and the Son of Heaven.* Fried argues that themes of military affairs and violence hold great sway over Chinese audiences (Fried, "Military Status in Chinese Society").

36. Di Cosmo explains that the notion of Inner Asian people and societies as being particularly violent has become more nuanced (Di Cosmo, "Violence in Inner Asian History"); Standen describes how during the Five Dynasties people living on the Chinese side and the Liao side of the border engaged in the same raiding practices (Standen, "Raiding and Frontier Society").

37. Don J. Wyatt calls this process the plebianization of *luan,* or "chaos." (Wyatt, "Conspirators in Violence").

38. Lorge, "State, Society and Trained Violence."

often goes unseen, and when it is seen, it is regarded as natural and necessary.[39]

A social analysis of the Song military world highlights the technologies of power that form the dark side of the Chinese Renaissance. The same Song civilization that celebrated the humanity of some denied it to millions of others. The Song Renaissance came at a price, much like slaughter, enslavement, and colonial expansion in the Americas were an intrinsic part of the European Renaissance.[40] I set aside questions of military strength in favor of social issues: I wish to examine more closely the military sphere as a setting of exploitation, resistance, and inward-facing violence. Whereas Lorge focuses on weapons technology, I look to technologies of power and social control: tattooing, counting, and registering. And even though a social history of the military focuses its attention on everyday life, it still offers important insights into the behavior of soldiers in combat.[41]

Placing Soldiers at the Center of the Story

In this book I analyze military institutions and military people to study the lower echelons of society at an imperial scale. Recent studies in other periods of premodern Chinese history that also analyze military people

39. Slavoj Žižek refers to this as "objective violence," in opposition to "subjective violence," which is seen as irrational, a disturbance of the natural nonviolent and peaceful state of affairs (Žižek, *Violence*, 2).

40. Walter D. Mignolo's *Darker Side of the Renaissance* demonstrates the close relationship between colonialism and the European Renaissance.

41. In his classic and influential study *The Face of Battle*, the military historian John Keegan analyzes the battlefield from the point of view of the fighting men to understand their behavior and performance. Keegan describes the field of battle as a scene of great confusion and uncertainty, where only a few factors keep fighting men from collapsing: training, fear of violent punishment from their superiors, and the will to live (because solidarity provides them with the best chances of survival). Keegan puts himself in the soldier's shoes: he envisions the smoke and noise on the battlefield, the weapons he carried and those aimed at him, the threat of violence from his enemies and from his own superiors. Yet soldiers also brought with them to the battlefield memories, relationships, and values that determined, to a great extent, their behavior in combat. This larger social context is crucial for understanding the political and military events of the Song period.

and military institutions in their social contexts have a more local focus. Andrew Chittick's study of patronage networks formed by military men in Xiangyang during the fifth and sixth centuries shows that local identity was highly fragmented, and it argues that vertical ties of patronage formed through military service were stronger than any class, gender, or local identities.[42] Michael Szonyi's local-institutional study of military families in the southeast, particularly Fujian, during the Ming period (1368–1644) focuses on strategies employed by military households when interacting with the Ming military system. Most of the members of Ming military households did not serve in the military, and for them military service was a tax, a duty that had to be negotiated or avoided by "gaming the system."[43] My choice to focus on the whole of the Song empire stems partly from the shape of the sources, but I also want to examine the historical documents through the lens of social class, because class is a crucial prism for understanding the rationale of Song military institutions.

Because the Song state assigned convicts to the military and also used soldiers for law enforcement, the story of the penal-military complex is also a story of law and order. Scholars find proof in the Song's legal code for moderation and benevolence, two values that reflect a "Confucian" spirit.[44] Brian McKnight's definitive English-language study of Song legal history describes a legal system founded on Confucian ideas whose goal was combating crime and disorder. His analysis relies on both specific and universal assumptions. Specifically, McKnight accepts the moralist rhetoric of the law, which was often an ideal form rather than a reality. Universally, McKnight sees legal systems as necessary and good for human societies.[45] In *Inked*, I study the law in practice, as a reflection of power relations in society. As Michelle Alexander's *The New Jim Crow* demonstrates, a legal system needs to be interpreted in the context of the larger social project governing it. A law can never be

42. Chittick, *Patronage and Community in Medieval China*.

43. Szonyi, *Art of Being Governed*.

44. Lü Zhixing argues that the Song's penal system displayed the Confucian spirit of mercy through its relatively moderate punishments (*Songdai peixing zhidu tanxi*). According to Dutton, over the course of two thousand years, from the Han to the Qing, there was a gradual move away from punishments causing pain to the body to punishments of shaming and exclusion (*Policing and Punishment in China*, 55–93).

45. Two important works by McKnight are *Law and Order in Sung China* and *The Quality of Mercy*.

applied equally when not all humans are considered equally human.[46] Song soldiers were not.

Warfare was but one of several important functions of the Song military. Others included a labor system, a penal system, law enforcement, and social control. The story of soldiers extends far beyond the battlefield: it threads through the forts and camps, the workshops, the relentless marches on the roads of the empire, the boat-dragging against the down-water pull of the canals, the conscriptions and press gangs, the disciplining cane and the tattooing needle, and the courts and the prisons. These institutions and spaces of war and justice and labor constituted the penal-military complex, which was itself embedded in a culture of violence and anger. When we place the soldiers at the center of our narrative, their world becomes more tangible and visible. Soldiers and militia men, their wives and children, their brothers and neighbors, bandits and convicts, beggars and loafers: all together, these millions of men and women lived under the gaze of the military register.

Recovering Soldier's Voices: Tools and Methods

Texts produced during the Song dynasty do not lend themselves naturally to the study of soldiers. Analyzing them for that purpose demands that one read the sources "against the grain." That means collecting the many fragments of evidence of soldiers' lives, detaching them from their original textual context, and reassembling them into a new narrative where soldiers occupy the central position, both as objects of control and as fully human independent subjects. For that purpose I have used a wide range of textual genres, including official political histories, poems, edicts, and gazetteers. Accounts of soldiers are often highly fragmented—a detail here, a number there. But this need not be an obstacle. If one treats the entire body of texts from the Song period as a reflection of the psyche of the elite rather than a collection of the disparate thoughts of many individuals, these fragments coalesce into something much greater, a grim collage of the Song empire's lower class. Many small in-

46. Alexander, *The New Jim Crow.*

stances of justice come together to create one long chronicle of injustice and suffering.

Writing a social history of the Song military requires that we treat the scholar-officials of the Song, on whose testimonies scholars rely, as hostile witnesses. As such, even when they tell the truth, they are complicit in a narrative meant to justify a certain distribution of power and to condemn those who were its victims.[47] *Biji* (compilations of random musings and anecdotes) have proven to be especially useful for decoding the social rationale of Song elites. The gossipy and informal nature of many *biji* allows us to see how scholar-officials felt about soldiers. After all, it is in the gossip column (the marginal space within a news source) that the truth of politics resides. Anecdotes in *biji* amply demonstrate that for scholar-officials, soldiers were a savage, lazy, criminal lot. Any kind of decision, edict, policy debate, or law promulgated needs to be understood in the context of these social attitudes.

Decoding elite social attitudes provides us with the compass necessary to navigate Song texts, to "reverse engineer" them into the many components that tell a story: facts, themes, concepts.[48] By placing all the discourse of the scholar-official class in one big pile and treating it as representative of the Song elite's state of mind, many contradictions come to light. These contradictions represent the cognitive dissonances in terms of how the elite framed the place of soldiers in their world. Using that social logic, that cognitive dissonance, as a guide for the interpretation of individual cases, I reassembled those fragments to create a new story with soldiers at its center.

Military institutions and laws open a window into both the elite's ways of thinking and the lower classes' ways of life. James Scott analyzes the tensions between a group's public portrayal of itself (or its communications with other groups) and its more private or internal communications,

47. Howard Zinn, writing about American history, treats government officials not as neutral referees but as participants, and he argues that the social order they upheld needs to be analyzed in the context of their social background and economic interests (Zinn, *People's History of the United States*, 97).

48. Inga Clendinnen encountered a similar problem when she used Spanish sources for a history of the indigenous people in the Yucatan during the Spanish conquest. The few extant indigenous writings served as her guide for extracting the indigenous point of view from Spanish texts (*Ambivalent Conquests*).

what he terms "public transcripts" and "hidden transcripts."[49] For the Chinese Middle Period, perhaps even more than for the more recent place-times Scott focuses on, there are no records of the "hidden transcripts." It is still possible, however, to reveal some of the "hidden transcripts" of elites and soldiers. Soldiers made their "hidden transcripts" public when they rose against their superiors in mutiny, a common occurrence during the Song. Elites spoke their truth about the lower classes through the promulgation and operation of a system of laws meant to control, degrade, and exploit large numbers of human beings.

Tattoos play a central role in this study because they represent texts, practices, and lived experiences. Branding and mutilating millions of people through tattooing is the smoking gun that contradicts the supposed civility and benevolence of the Song dynasty. Woodblock printing, an important technology of the Song period, had a sinister and common counterpart.[50] At any given time in the Song period, hundreds of thousands of people were tattooed; collectively, their tattoos string together a script that cut across multiple generations and thousands of miles. The tattoos themselves were composed of illuminating texts and images worthy of analysis as sources for sociopolitical history. Tattooing in the Middle Period was a social and political tool, a generator of a martial subculture, and a textual layer through which the reality of life in the penal-military complex can be deciphered.

Despite the Song's civilian and literary reputation, military issues were a top priority of the Song government, and they appear in great quantity in all Song sources: history, literature, letters, and poetry. Because the Song period was heavily militarized, an examination of the lives of Song soldiers offers insights that may not be visible through the study of poor commoners or other subordinate groups. Soldiers were a social-military-political issue, a rhetorical device in stories and court debates, and the background characters to the stories of others. Their marginal position in conventional historical records, coupled with their ubiquitous presence in Song life, makes soldiers both unavoidable and peripheral at the same time, uncredited actors just beyond the spotlight of historical analysis.

49. Scott, *Domination and the Arts of Resistance.*

50. For more on the history of the book in Middle-Period China, see Chia, *Printing for Profit*; McDermott, *Social History of the Chinese Book.*

A strange thing happens when one focuses the historical lens directly on these soldiers. The historical record, seemingly quiet about the lives of soldiers, blossoms in quantity and clarity. Through the right lens, individual faces of soldiers stare back. They remain mostly nameless, but they are marked and recorded nonetheless. In the records one can see the ugly and mutilated faces of men who led a miserable existence. They cursed and brawled, stole and murdered, loved and rebelled in a realm ruled by violence and conflict. In this world, benevolence and harmony were like the moral exhortations George Bernard Shaw saw on signs in a prison, hanging on the external wall where the prisoners could not see them.[51]

Soldiers are ubiquitous in Song texts, and they were very much present in the lives of officials. Soldiers guarded and served officials, interacting with them daily. Their peripheral position in those interactions offers some advantages for the historian. First, it is often in our peripheral vision, where our mind is not focused, that the unedited truth resides. Second, the treatment of subordinate populations is very telling of the thoughts and values of those who govern them, for it is in how people at the bottom of society are treated that the true character of its power brokers is exposed.

Reconstructing the voices and points of view of those who left no records of their own demands a special attention to the texts we have. One method of investigating texts is to treat them like photographs taken at a crime scene.[52] In our position as detectives, we can zoom in, noticing details that seemed trivial or unimportant to the author. We can also zoom out, seeing those details in the context of a larger pattern created by hundreds and thousands of texts, a pattern the individual authors could not have seen. By combing through Song sources and piecing together these details, it is possible to see beyond the authors' individual inten-

51. Shaw, "Preface," xli.

52. In this sense, my approach resembles Henry Bond's analysis of crime-scene photos using Lacan's psychoanalytic theory. Bond finds that the key to understanding a crime is hidden in small and banal details. These details are often overlooked by the individuals who produce these sources (the photographers). But once the truth locked within those details is extracted, a new narrative emerges, and our understanding of the main narrative of these photos (the murder) changes as well. See Bond's *Lacan at the Scene*.

tions and discover unintended truths. Upon doing so, a narrative of benevolence and justice is replaced with the cold and violent reality of life in the orbit of the penal-military complex.

Writing this kind of history comes with its own challenges and qualifications. The sources themselves do not always make the distinctions between different types of units, between convict-soldiers and volunteers, or between fighting troops and labor troops. The sources do not allow for in-depth research into a specific soldier or even a battalion. Nor are the sources complete enough to allow for accurate statistical analysis. It is unclear when some of these stories took place, or whether they all really took place. Because most of the texts produced during the Song period did not survive, there is also the question of representation. For some phenomena, only a few examples exist, sometimes only one. The methodology described above was designed to overcome some of these challenges. Even though little is known about each one single fragment, it is still possible to put them together to create a coherent picture. Once we look at the picture, we can go back and see its many individual components in a new light.

The Scope of This Study

Largely due to the shape of the historical sources, much of this study focuses on the Northern Song period. The primary sources left to us from the Song period contain far more details about Northern Song military institutions than do those of the Southern Song. This is further complicated by the different military reality of the Southern Song state. Still, some of the basic organizing principles of the military persisted throughout the Song period. I also deal with the social rationale behind the military institutions and policies. In this aspect, strong continuities existed between the Northern and Southern Song.

This study of soldiers tells a story that stretched across the Song empire, but it was more relevant in some places than others. With large militias and hundreds of thousands of regular soldiers stationed there on a regular basis, the circuits that lay on the northern border zones became highly militarized. The military stationed hundreds of thousands of soldiers close to the Northern Song capital, less so in the Southern Song capital of Hangzhou. Troops in other areas of the empire also numbered in the hundreds of thousands. They provided labor and took charge of law enforcement and local defense. Although much of the story of the penal-military complex takes place in the militarized border zones and in the capital region, military spaces existed in other towns and cities of the empire, as well as on the roads and canals that connected them.

Much of this study focuses on the social rationale at the base of the Song military system. Rather than providing a full institutional history of the military during the Song period, one of my goals is to make the case for the importance of the interplay between developments within military institutions and social change. If for that purpose I have sometimes painted the picture of Song military institutions with too broad a brush, I ask for the reader's patience and forgiveness.

Key Terms

The term "class" stands at the center of this study. Although the Song period had not yet seen the emergence of modern class identity, social groups in Song times still bear some proximity to the term. For this study, class will be defined as a social group whose members were tied together to varying degrees through a cluster of properties: material situation, culture, education, official rank, social prospects, family networks, and social prospects of their offspring.

Marks of membership in the elite (or upper classes) included a high level of literacy, values and ideals that emanated from a shared body of texts, property, patterns of consumption, high social status, access to the examination system or to people who had access to it, access to agents of the state, marriage and other kinship ties to people who displayed one or more of these traits, and the ability to grant one's descendants one or more of these traits.

The marginal groups caught in the orbit of the Song state's penal-military complex constituted a distinct class. Among some of their common traits one can find low or no literacy; a martial culture distinct from that of the elites; common physical traits for adult males (military tattoos);

little or no property; weak relationships to the land; small nuclear families; strong relationships to the state, often through a salary; and similar social prospects for their offspring.

In the context of this study, the term "Confucian" refers to a body of teachings, values, traditions, and practices linked to a number of core classical texts and the exegesis and study of these texts. Individuals could be linked to the Confucian world in varying degrees through education, scholarship, practices of consumption, and/or social networks. Classical literacy was a key component in Confucian identity. That degree of literacy was limited to elite circles.

Very little is known about the ethnic or cultural identity of the great majority of Song-period commoners. I use the term "Han" as an administrative category, to refer to the population that was fully incorporated into the Song state's system of registration, taxation, and labor. I treat the Song state as a "Sinitic-script state," a state governed through Sinitic script, the center of a larger Sinitic-script world stretching across large areas of East Asia and Southeast Asia. The elites of that state were the main producers and consumers of Sinitic-script texts and Confucian culture. Other groups who lived within the Song empire had a weaker relationship to the Sinitic-script state and Confucian culture. The greater their autonomy, the less the Song state knew about them, and the further removed they were from the "Han" world. I refer to those groups as "non-Han."

Structural Outline of the Book

The first chapter describes the breaking of the political and social power of soldiers through the transformation of the military into a tiered organization with a hierarchy of status, duties, and pay during the Northern Song. This new hierarchy turned soldiers into laborers and servants, and their social status was below that of commoners. The Rotation System brought elements from the penal system into the management of the fighting troops, separated soldiers from their localities, and prevented soldiers from forming roots in a single location.

Chapter 2 goes back to the late Tang period to tell how military tattoos arose and were eventually transformed into the symbol of the degraded soldier-convicts of the Northern Song period. A system of military tattoos altered the bodies of soldiers and separated them from clear-skinned commoners. Soldiers, rootless and demeaned, became mutilated as well. Military tattoos became one of the hallmarks of the Song military system and Song civilization.

Who were the tattooed soldiers of the Song army, and where did they come from? They were convicts, refugees, men of the border zones, the poor, non-Han groups, and press gangs. Chapter 3 looks at the army as a mechanism for the extraction of labor from marginal populations and for the mapping of the Song's spatial and social borderlands through conscription and tattooing. The social groups that dominated the lower ranks of the military all contributed to the formation of the tattooed soldiers' identity, marking soldiers as criminal, homeless, poor, and wild. By the beginning of the twelfth century, press gangs had become a common phenomenon, demonstrating the diminishing control of the state over the management of military manpower.

Chapter 4 follows the journey of soldiers in the army from conscription through demotion and discharge, once infirmity and old age took their toll. The soldier's body stood at the center of the army's evaluation and transfer criteria. Notwithstanding the remarkable cases of generals who rose from the rank and file, the gradual deterioration of the body through time meant a trajectory of downward social mobility for most common soldiers. The state evaluated and administered soldiers through their bodies, and Confucian values were irrelevant within the penal-military complex.

Chapter 5 charts the physical and social landscape of the military camps and of the families who inhabited them. Small nuclear families relied on the military salaries of one or more members for survival over generations. The families served as a semi-official extension of the military force, and the state used them as replacements for soldiers, as sources for additional labor, and as hostages. The picture that emerges is one of entire families waging a struggle for survival in the shadow of poverty, abuse, and war.

Life in the military was bitter. Commoners did not wish to join, and soldiers did not wish to remain. Chapter 6 studies resistance to the state's military policies and institutions, both by commoners in local militias and by soldiers in the regular armies. Commoners and soldiers used a variety of strategies to resist the Song military authorities: desertion, deceit, self-mutilation, and mutiny. Their efforts to organize and resist came at a steep personal price, but they also forced the state to negotiate with them and to even relax some of its policies, cut back on tattooing, raise soldiers' pay, and address problems of abuse and mismanagement.

Chapter 7 demonstrates how the first Song-Jin War during the twelfth century gave rise to another conflict, that between the agents of the state and the tattooed soldiers of the Song. The outbreak of war allowed for two phenomena that greatly troubled the Song state's officials: the diminished power of the state allowed tattooed soldiers to climb through the ranks and become powerful generals, while other soldiers utilized tattoos declaring loyalty to the dynasty to undermine the state and rise in arms against it.

The final chapter covers the ending of the first Song-Jin War (mid-twelfth century) to the destruction of the Song at the hands of the Mongols in the late thirteenth century. As the military crisis of the first Song-Jin War abated, the Song government began to reestablish its dominion over the bodies of soldiers. However, the Song state never regained the same level of centralized control over the military and society as it once had; this can be seen in the growing diversity of military tattoo forms and the emergence of an urban underclass culture of tattooing during this time period.

Inked focuses on social attitudes and analyzes institutions, laws, and policies in the context of those attitudes. It treats soldiers as representatives of a larger social group with its own distinct culture. Military tattoos stand at the center of this investigation as the link between the law, state institutions, the individual body, and the person who resided within that body.

CHAPTER I

A New Military Hierarchy and the Rise of the Penal-Military Complex

They say the fate of the world was sealed over a cup of wine. It was the middle of the tenth century. Zhao Kuangyin, the first emperor of the Song dynasty, held a banquet in his palace for his top generals. Zhao Kuangyin, himself once a general who had taken the throne through a military coup, grew suspicious of his former colleagues. Now that he had the throne, would his generals try to steal it from him? But the emperor was merciful, and instead of a massacre he allowed his generals an early retirement to a life of riches and pleasure, including marriage ties between their families and the imperial family. How benevolent the Song dynasty! The power of great generals was broken not in war and violence, but over a cup of wine. Or so, at least, the story goes.[1]

The story of the banquet reflects a much longer, bloodier process that involved millions of people.[2] After all, generals were only powerful if they had soldiers who were loyal and brave. Therefore, down at the bottom of the world, the breaking of the power of generals was accompanied by the breaking, or rather taming, of the rank and file through the restructuring and reimagining of military manpower, a process that reached its

1. *Song shi*, 250.8810.

2. Studies of the significance of the story of the feast and the institutional transition it reflected focus on the roles played by the first emperor, his officials, and the generals (Fan Xuehui, "Guan yu 'beijiu shi bingquan'"; Lorge, "Entrance and Exit of the Song Founders").

culmination during the late tenth century. The reconfiguring of military organizations was one of the most meaningful developments of the tenth century, and it provided one of the institutional foundations for the rise of the penal-military complex, a great state project that dramatically changed the lives of millions of men and women for centuries to come. For them, this was no age of benevolence, but one of servitude. This chapter will tell that story.

A New Military Hierarchy (10th Century–1127 CE)

When the Tang dynasty finally collapsed in the beginning of the tenth century, its territory disintegrated into many different political units, each with its own military force.[3] Local officials and warlords created military units bound to them with personal ties of loyalty. Hungry for fighters, they offered pay and a fresh start for those on the run from a criminal past, a gambling debt, or crushing poverty. War, political chaos, and a commercializing world drove men into the ranks of salaried armies.[4] However, volunteers failed to show up in sufficient numbers, and the rulers had to find additional sources for manpower. Local militias provided them with a relatively simple and cheap solution. The militia system divided communities into groups of households (often seven or ten), and each group had to provide one soldier and his equipment for part-time service in the area.[5] Hard pressed for men, rulers of the early tenth century also used their prerogative to simply command all available able-bodied men into full-time service in their armies. This allowed the creation of large military units almost instantly. Morale, however, was low.[6] Faced with high rates of desertion, the armies resorted to marking soldiers with facial tattoos, and deserters were executed.[7]

3. For overviews of the Tang period military system, see Graff, *Medieval Chinese Warfare*; Graff, "China, The Tang: 600–900"; Zhang, "Transformations of the Tang Military System."

4. Mu Jing, *Wudai bingzhi kaolun*, 89–93.

5. Mu Jing, *Wudai bingzhi kaolun*, 86–87.

6. Mu Jing, *Wudai bingzhi kaolun*, 87–89.

7. More on facial tattoos in chapter 2.

The salary-based pacts between Five Dynasties rulers and their professional troops did not lend stability to the political system. Whatever loyalty the soldiers felt for their rulers tended to die with them. Guo Wei (Zhou Taizu, r. 951–954), the founder of the Later Zhou state, solidified his position by creating new, strong military units that fell under his direct control.[8] When a general overthrew the Later Zhou in a military coup and founded the Song dynasty, he had to repeat the process, elevating one unit while allowing the previous units to exist in diminished form.[9] This process led to the formation of a hierarchy of fighting strength and loyalty in the units close to the emperor. As the system matured, this hierarchy also functioned as a military checks-and-balances system, preventing one military unit from having too much power. The Song dynasty was founded through a military coup, but it would not end in one.

The Song state continued to reorganize the military around the empire according to a new hierarchy, not just of fighting strength but of the duties and treatment of the different units as well. The soldiers considered strongest and fittest were transferred into units considered more dependable and charged with warfare. The elite fighting forces were referred to as the imperial armies (*jinjun*). The units drained of their best men, named prefectural armies (*xiangjun*), were charged with labor. The prefectural troops were paid less and treated worse than the imperial soldiers. The higher numbers of convict-soldiers in their ranks contributed to their poor treatment.

Below the regular armies, both imperial and prefectural, were local military forces, organized, paid, and commanded by the state and placed in charge of law enforcement. Archers (*gongshou*), commanded by county defenders (*xianwei*) and police chiefs (*xunjian*), operated on the level of the subprefecture, making them the armed representatives of the centralized

8. Zhou Taizu created new military units in the capital to increase his own personal power over the army. The imperial Bodyguard (Shiwei qinjun) was split into its infantry and cavalry components and was gradually eclipsed by the newer Palace Army (Dianqian jun). See Tan, *Songdai zhi jundui*, 2a; Fan Xuehui, "Liang Song sanya kao," 123–25; Worthy, "Founding of Sung China," 101–36.

9. Xue Jixuan, *Lang yu ji*, 16.5a.275; Wang Yinglin, *Yuhai*, 139.7a-b.661. For more on this process see Worthy, "Founding of Sung China," 137–211; Yang, *Emperor's Generals*, 27–32, 40–45; Wang Zengyu, *Songchao junzhi chutan*, 6–42.

state at the lowest administrative level.[10] These archers, local men who served for a lifetime, took charge of law enforcement, fought illegal trade and gambling, and captured bandits. Households were divided into five ranks. The first two ranks supplied the leadership, and households of the third rank provided the rank and file. In theory, men of the poorest households were not supposed to serve as archers. However, it appears that during the first century of the Song period, the burden of service gradually shifted to weaker social groups. Officials and local powerful people used archers to collect taxes and terrorize other local people, likely of a lower social standing.[11] In addition to archers, the Song state used other forces like the Local Troops (Tubing), a local armed organization active in the northwest border region and in Guangnan in the south.[12] Local Troops, like archers, tended to come from weaker social groups.

Northern Song Imperial Soldiers

The Northern Song's very best military units were the Palace Guards (Banzhi), placed in charge of the protection of the emperor. This was a relatively small force, numbering several thousand men.[13] Below them came the Four Superior Armies (Shangjun), the elite units of the imperial armies: Exalting the Sun (Pengri), Heavenly Martial (Tianwu), Dragon Guards (Longwei), and Spirit Guards (Shenwei). Each of the Four Superior Armies contained thirty to forty battalions, each battalion numbering five hundred men at full strength, putting each army at about fifteen to twenty thousand men.[14] Below the Four Superior Armies were the Middle Armies (Zhongjun) and Lower Armies (Xiajun). Those armies

10. Wang Zengyu, *Songchao junzhi chutan,* 101–4; Wang Zengyu, "History of the Sung Military," 218. County defenders were part of the civil bureaucracy, whereas police chiefs served in the military bureaucracy. These positions were ranked eight and below in the bureaucracy.

11. Huang Kuan-chong, "Tangsong jiceng wuli."

12. Wang Zengyu, *Songchao junzhi chutan*, 98–101; Wang Zengyu, "History of the Sung Military," 218.

13. Wang Zengyu, *Songchao junzhi chutan*, 16–17.

14. Wang Zengyu, *Songchao junzhi chutan*, 43.

formed the bulk of the Northern Song's fighting troops, numbering in the hundreds of thousands.

The Northern Song state stationed most of its fighting troops in the north of the empire: around the capital and in the threatened border zones to the north and northwest. Although the Song state sometimes signed peace treaties with its neighbors and even maintained a relatively long-lasting peace with the Liao state, tensions on the border never really subsided. The northern borders of the Northern Song remained highly militarized throughout the period.[15] The troops in the capital region, numbering a couple hundred thousand, defended it from foes, both foreign and domestic.[16] Their presence was a counterweight to the fighting armies on the border. The troops of the border zones, while in total more than double the number of troops in the capital, were divided into a few administrative circuits, making the capital army stronger than those of any given border circuit. This aspect of the Song military system, traditionally named "inner and outer controlling each other" (*nei wai xiangzhi*), formed an important element of the Song state's "checks-and-balances" system, preventing any single general or official from commanding too strong a military force.[17]

The Rotation System and the Criminalization of the Fighting Troops

A man who had committed a crime of a certain degree (theft, assault) in the Song empire was flogged, tattooed on his face, and then assigned to the military, usually to a labor unit in the prefectural armies. In the early Song (second half of the tenth century) convicts had to first march to the capital, where the emperor would pronounce their judgment, and then

15. For more on the border, see Tackett, "The Great Wall." Cheng Long's *Beisong xibei zhanqu* demonstrates the great effort necessary for supplying the military units in the northwestern border. For a discussion of the Song empire's southwest border, see James Anderson, "Treacherous Factions."

16. At one point during the reign of Renzong (1022–1063) there were 476 battalions of imperial soldiers in the capital, Kaifeng (Wang Zengyu, *Songchao junzhi chutan*, 43).

17. Wang Zengyu, *Songchao junzhi chutan*, 66.

were banished to remote places like Shamen Island in Shandong (about eight hundred kilometers from the capital) or Guangnan in the south (about two thousand kilometers from the capital).[18] The monetary and human costs of this system were high enough for the government to curtail some of its excesses, and in 1017 convicts began to serve their sentences closer to their home region.[19] The punishment of the convict was partially shared by his guards—soldiers who had been assigned to escort him to his place of exile and who also suffered greatly from a journey their bodies and purses could ill afford.[20]

The Song state extended the principle of forced marches as a tool for discipline into its fighting armies by creating the Rotation System (Gengshufa). This system aimed to sever the ties between generals and their troops by rotating the soldiers between different camps and different commanders, thereby decreasing the ability of generals to turn their units into their own personal power bases.[21] This policy had been put in place by the Song state's founding emperor, and his brother who inherited the throne followed it even more closely.[22] Later on, in 1017, when the state spared convicts the longer marches, it did not extend the same mercy to the fighting troops, who continued to be rotated as usual.

The Rotation System was not limited to the fighting troops of the Northern Song, the imperials. Soldiers in the prefectural armies, normally deployed to perform labor, could also be subject to rotations.[23] Even though prefectural soldiers posed a lesser military threat to the state, being unarmed and untrained for battle, they could still pose a threat on the local level: groups of convicts and other dissatisfied military workers

18. Tsuji, "Sō-hatsu no hairu to hai-gun," 338–40. For more on Shamen Island, see McKnight, "Maximum Security in the Sung."

19. Tsuji, "Sō-hatsu no hairu to hai-gun," 345–46.

20. Su Shi, *Dongpo quanji*, 52.12a-b.723.

21. *Chang bian*, 143.21.3452.

22. *Song shi*, 188.4627.

23. "As for the imperial and prefectural armies in the various circuits, they also all rotate" (*Song shi*, 196.4894). "At first the two armies [imperial and prefectural] were both rotated. Those in Liangzhe were rotated to Guangnan, while those in Jiangnan were rotated to Liangzhe. The purpose was to make them used to hardship and forget their attachments [to family and friends]" (Luo Jun, *Baoqing siming zhi*, *juan* 7.5.5070). "The prefectural soldiers were tied to the various circuits. They did only labor, and in between they were also rotated" (Zhang Ruyu, *Qunshu kaosuo xuji*, vol. 938, 44.5a.555).

concentrated in the towns and marketplaces, complaining, threatening, and extorting other commoners and local business owners.[24]

The Rotation System created a huge fiscal burden—an impediment to imperial defense—and it took a heavy toll on soldiers and their families.[25] Soldiers who had been rotated had to adjust to unfamiliar climates. Feeding the soldiers on the road home was a costly venture, and many died on the way.[26] By one account, only about half of the soldiers rotated to Guangnan made it back alive to their camp in Fuzhou.[27] It was only in the 1070s, during the New Policies (1069–1086) reform effort, that the Song state decided to abolish the Rotation System. During the reforms, Emperor Shenzong replaced the Rotation System with the Area-Generals System (Jiangbingfa). According to the new system, soldiers were permanently assigned to their generals, and they were no longer rotated.[28] However, not all troops were spared rotation even after the formal abolition of the Rotation System.[29]

The ending of the Rotation System gave officials a cause for concern, but their reservations were not purely for military reasons. In 1086 Sima Guang, the leader of the opposition to the reforms, warned that after being in place for close to a decade, the Area-Generals System hurt the military in several ways. It made military officials stronger than local officials at the local level, but it harmed the discipline among the rank and file in the military camps by allowing soldiers to "eat their fill and reside in peace," thereby becoming arrogant and lazy, difficult to deploy, and more likely to rise in mutiny.[30] The *Song shi* echoes Sima Guang's reasoning

24. *Song shi*, 97.2399.

25. McGrath, *Military and Regional Administration*, 149. More on the human toll of the system in chapter 4.

26. In 1071 the Bureau of Military Affairs reported that soldiers were sent from around the empire to do labor in the capital. They had problems adjusting to the climate. There were high death tolls on the journey home, especially among soldiers from Jiangnan and Huainan. Providing food for the journey was a considerable expense (*Chang bian*, 228.8.5541; also in *Song shi*, 189.4644).

27. Cai Xiang, *Duanming ji*, 26.6b.545.

28. Ma Duanlin, *Wenxian tongkao*, 153.13b.438. See also *Song shi*, 188.4627.

29. Wang Zengyu, *Songchao junzhi chutan*, 68.

30. The Song military suffered from a high rate of soldier mutinies. Sima Guang mentioned the uprisings of Li Shun (d. 994), Wang Lun (d. 1043), Wang Jun (d. 1000), and Wang Ze (d. 1048) (*Chang bian*, 379.41.9216–17).

when it states that the long marches between different military camps were supposed to make soldiers used to hardship and prevent them from becoming arrogant and lazy.[31]

Sima Guang's stance on the Rotation System, although it was voiced in a specific political context, stands as a testament to his social position. When it came to his personal life, Sima Guang was an austere man. He was a staunch defender of the poor, sensitive and compassionate to his servants' plight, and an opponent of the sex trade.[32] Yet soldiers were not deemed worthy of the same protections that commoners received by law and custom. The dehumanization of the residents of the penal-military complex was a project led by the state, but it was widely supported by the elite.

Questions of war and peace were also a matter of social position. The Song state emerged out of a century and a half of political instability and warfare. Even as the international situation was becoming more stable, the Song state put in place a system that simulated the suffering of war among soldiers, not to make them stronger but to make them weaker. The Rotation System routinely produced managed chaos for the rank and file, even in times of peace. In the eyes of the Song scholar-officials, peace was good for the country but bad for the soldiers.

Laborers, Soldiers, and Servants: The Prefectural Armies

The draining of the stronger manpower from the prefectural armies during the mid-to-late tenth century greatly diminished their fighting power, leaving them with the "weak and weary" (*pi ruo*).[33] Instead of disbanding them altogether, the Song state placed its prefectural troops in charge of the labor system with the aim of having prefectural soldiers

31. *Song shi*, 188.4627.

32. Sima Guang demonstrated his view on the sex trade when he refused to have a concubine (Shao Bowen, *Shaoshi wenjian lu*, 11.121–22).

33. Zhang Ruyu, *Qunshu kaosuo houji*, 41.3b.569; Anon., *Qunshu huiyuan jiejiang wang*, 13.27b.177.

perform labor that previously had been commoners' corvée duty to the state.[34] Reports of early Song labor projects show soldiers performing a broad range of duties: repair, construction, and transport—with the declared intention that soldiers take charge of all labor, leaving commoners to their own affairs.[35] As a result of their special duties, the prefecturals had a different pattern of troop distribution, with a large concentration in the southeast, compared to imperial armies, who were dominant in the northern border regions.[36]

The ideal of having regular troops take charge of all state-organized labor was never fully realized, as the state continued to also call upon commoners for labor duty. The Song state continued to grapple with this issue, most famously under the New Policies (1069–1086). One element of the New Policies, the *mianyifa* reforms, allowed for commoners to substitute payment for corvée duty. Other attempts to divert more labor to soldiers continued at least until the early Southern Song (mid-twelfth

34. *Yaolu*, 95.1824; Ma Duanlin, *Wenxian tongkao*, 12.27a.292, 156.42b.502.

35. In 968, officials who organized "repair and construction without disturbing the commoners" were rewarded with a promotion (*Chang bian*, 9.1.200); in 971 a thousand prefectural troops were sent to the capital to work on the tomb of the emperors of the previous dynasties. According to the received account, "it was ordered not to mobilize the commoners again. From this day on, when there is repair work, the labor should be assigned to the prefectural soldiers" (*Chang bian*, 12.11.264). In 982 an edict declared: "When Eastern and Western Chuan [in modern Sichuan] provide transport duty to the court, many of the adult males on the way are mobilized for transport. When convicts are delivered in shackles to the capital, commoners are mobilized to carry those among them who fall sick on the road. On the *yihai* day it was decreed that when Western Chuan, Lingnan [in modern Guangdong], Jinghu [in modern Hunan and Hubei], and Shaanxi send silk every year, there should be no more disturbance of commoners [by making them] do transport work. They should be replaced by soldiers dedicated to that purpose" (*Chang bian*, 23.5.514). In 1006 Emperor Zhenzong (r. 997–1022) had the people of Beizhou (in modern Hebei) who were working on the city walls replaced with prefectural soldiers to avoid disturbing the commoners (*Chang bian*, 62.26.1390); in the same year, the men working on the walls of the Tianxiong military prefecture were replaced by soldiers from ten neighboring prefectures (*Chang bian*, 63.28.1414). In 1012 soldiers replaced commoners in construction (*Song shi*, 177.4296). In 1016 Cao Wei (973–1030) was rewarded for leading a great construction project in a large series of forts without using commoners and instead using only families of the forts and prefectural soldiers (*Chang bian*, 87.22.1992).

36. Zhao Ruyu, *Song mingchen zouyi*, 147.23a.890.

century).[37] The *mianyifa* reforms, a reflection of the monetization of labor in the Song state, were founded on over a century of experience—from the Song state's founding during the middle of the tenth century to the New Policies of the late eleventh century—in operating hundreds of thousands of salaried labor soldiers whose labor had a clear monetary cost.

The labor duties of the prefectural armies included a wide range of activities. One of the important ones was the transportation of grain for other armies, a huge logistical challenge considering the size of the Song military. Transportation of grain depended in large part on water transport, and the Song labor system focused much of its energy on the rivers and waterways.[38] Duties on the rivers included river dredging and the dragging of boats.[39] The vast amounts of labor demanded for operating the waterways made the official Fan Chunren (1027–1101) proclaim in 1088 that "the corvée on the great rivers is tied to the joy and sorrow of half the people of the world."[40]

The work of prefectural troops extended into many other areas: the postal service system, agriculture, shipyards and felling trees, wine production, construction, horses, working metal, artisanal work, and temple service.[41] A list of names of prefectural army battalions from the Xining reign period (1068–1077) reflects the variety of their tasks: Wine Monopoly (Quegu), Water and Land Transportation (Shuilu yunsong), Opening Roads (Tongdao), Precipitous Mountains (Shanxian), Bridges (Qiaoliang), Mail Delivery (Youchuan), Horse Pastures (Mamu), Embankments (Difang), and Dams (Yandai).[42] Although prefectural troops specialized in labor, they also came to be used in defense throughout the Song period, up until the last days of the Southern Song state.[43]

37. In 1141 Emperor Gaozong decided to use prefectural soldiers for construction so as "not to disturb the commoners in the villages" (*Yaolu*, 162.3086).

38. For more on prefectural soldiers on the waterways see Huai, *Songchao xiangjun yanjiu*, 139–89.

39. Qian Ruoshui, *Song Taizong shilu*, 26.9; Su Shi, *Dongpo quanji*, 57.7b.800.

40. *Chang bian*, 415.28.10090.

41. Liang Kejia, *Chunxi sanshan zhi*, 5.2.7828; *Chang bian*, 328.20.7894, 341.3.8204; Luo Jun, *Baoqing siming zhi*, 9.8.5072; Li Gang, *Liangxi ji*, 104.5a.281; Wang Shipeng, *Wang Shipeng quanji*, 4.637; Ouyang Xiu, *Ouyang Xiu quanji*, 26.185; *Song huiyao, zhiguan*, 16.13; Gao Cheng, *Shiwu jiyuan*, 10.10a-b.

42. *Song shi*, 189.4644.

43. In 986, after a failed Song campaign against the Liao, the Liao went on a counter assault. When the Song's fighting troops failed, the official Zhang Qixian

Many soldiers worked as servants in the personal service of officials. Those could be either prefectural soldiers or imperial soldiers who were demoted to the reserves. When officials went on missions, soldiers served as their porters.[44] They protected officials when they traveled the roads.[45] They assisted officials in moving their belongings to a new appointment.[46] Prefectural soldiers also escorted the coffins of officials' relatives.[47] Even though the households of officials were not limited to soldier-servants, in more remote places officials could find themselves far more dependent on imported labor of men sentenced to exile and military service.[48]

The making of soldiers into servants turned them into a form of human capital available to officials. Officials made use of these men, often

(942–1014) selected two thousand men of the prefectural troops and repelled the enemy (*Chang bian*, 27.5.626). In 1041, when the imperial armies proved to be insufficient, Zhang Kang (994–1056) used the soldiers who had been doing corvée to fight. According to the given account, the bravery of these soldiers inspired the imperial armies to go back into battle (*Chang bian*, 133.3.3172). In 1042 the Purifying the Borders Army (Qingbian jun) was formed by enlisting over three thousand of the men who had been tattooed and assigned to the prefectural army. They successfully repelled the Xi Xia assault (*Chang bian*, 136.3.3246). In 1043 Fan Zhongyan used both imperial and prefectural soldiers for defense (*Chang bian*, 141.10.3390); in 1072 an edict placed defense responsibilities in the Xihe circuit (in modern Gansu) on the shoulders of prefectural soldiers (*Chang bian*, 239.38.5821). Prefectural troops participated in local defense in other parts of the empire, such as the city of Hangzhou (Su Song, *Suweigong wenji*, 19.3a–4a.266), and they participated in the first Song-Jin war (Xu Mengxin, *Sanchao beimeng huibian*, 69.1.81). Huang Gan (1152–1221) explained that the imperial soldiers and the prefectural soldiers were used for both defense and offense (Huang Gan, *Mianzhai ji*, 24.15a.266); Wang Shipeng (*jinshi* 1157) mentioned the use of prefectural troops in border defense (Wang Shipeng, *Wang Shipeng quanji*, 4.637–638). The prefectural troops played a part in the suppression of the Chen Tong uprising in 1179 (Lu You, *Weinan wenji*, 34.6b–7a.571), and when the Southern Song empire reached its final days, prefectural troops joined imperial troops in the defense of the Gongdi emperor (r. 1274–1276) (*Song shi*, 47.926)

44. Xie Shenfu, *Qingyuan tiaofa shilei*, 5.4b, 5.10a-b, 5.15b–16a.

45. Xie Shenfu, *Qingyuan tiaofa shilei*, 10.11a.

46. Xie Shenfu, *Qingyuan tiaofa shilei*, 10.7a.

47. Xie Shenfu, *Qingyuan tiaofa shilei*, 77.23b. After Sima Kang (1050–1090), the son of Sima Guang, had died, Fan Zuyu (1041–1098) asked that an escort of prefectural troops be provided for the coffin (Fan Zuyu, *Fantaishi ji*, 19.14a.249).

48. Qi Yi, prefect of Jiyang (in Hainan Island), wrote upon his arrival there, "all around among the servants there is not one who is not a tattooed soldier" (Zhou Hui, *Qingbo zazhi*, 7.17.302).

to a degree that their colleagues found to be excessive. Such transgressions were becoming common by the middle of the eleventh century, and this trend continued into the Southern Song.[49] The Song world was commercializing, and labor was one of the main commodities bought and sold. Officials used more and more of the soldiers under their authority as servants, keeping them for themselves as a trapping of power and comfort or renting out the soldiers' labor outside of the camp as a side source of income.[50] Soldiers with artisanal skills put those in the service of their superiors, providing them with another source of revenue.[51] This practice was common enough that a legal code promulgated during the Qingyuan reign period (1195–1200) had to include regulations for the number of soldier-servants allocated to officials according to their rank.[52]

The founding of the Song state and its new military system involved the creation of a new social hierarchy that lasted up until the final days of the Song period. By the end of the tenth century, beneath the "honorable commoners," a new category of "soldier" came into being. This new group did not hold a mean or dishonorable (*jian*) status in the juridical sense, but it did have a lower social status compared with regular commoners, and soldiers were often contrasted with "respectable commoners" (*liang min*). Commoners were to be spared warfare and conscripted labor (as much as possible), but only so long as they behaved. Through the creation of the penal-military complex, the status of commoner was redefined and even elevated.[53] For the rest of the Song period, the soldier remained a figure of low status, a provider of labor, and, by extension, even a commodity.

49. Han Qi (1008–1075) complained of powerful people and their families who appropriated soldiers for their own ends, thereby exacerbating the burden on public funds while interfering in soldiers' labor and military functions (*Chang bian*, 123.15.2908). For Southern Song examples see Xu Mengxin, *Sanchao beimeng huibian* 174:1.311; Chen Fuliang, *Zhizhai ji*, 19.13b–14a.

50. Wang Yunchang, *Songdai jundui jingying wenti*, 275–86.

51. *Song huiyao*, 48.114, Xuanhe, 2nd year, 4th month, 4th day.

52. Xie Shenfu, *Qingyuan tiaofa shilei*, 11.1a–16b.

53. Wang Ying and Chen Feng explain that a growing gulf separated soldiers from commoners, and that soldiers were less likely to gain assistance from commoners ("Beisong jiceng shizu bianluan zhenglun").

CHAPTER 2

Dawn of the Age of Tattooing

In the middle of the ninth century, in the grand city of Chang'an, the capital of the Tang empire, there lived Zhang Gan, the strongman of Daning Ward. Zhang Gan was an imposing man with tattoos running along both his arms. The tattoo on his left arm read, "Alive I do not fear the Metropolitan Administrator," and the tattoo on his right arm read, "Dead I do not dread the King of Hell."[1] The ninth century was a golden age for men like Zhang Gan, the thugs, the soldiers, and the bandits of the aging Tang empire. Those men populated the social spaces that stretched from powerful military garrisons in the border regions to the inns and shops of the capital city's small alleys, marginal spaces where one could rule an alley, a gambling den, or a table at an inn.

The century that followed saw tattooed men reach the height of their political power. It also saw the breaking of that power when the newly risen Sinitic-script states of the early tenth century, competing over the remnants of the Tang empire, put in place a series of policies aimed at breaking the standing and spirit of the rank and file. Tattooing played a central role in this process that culminated with the founding of the Song dynasty, as the tattooing needle became one of the Song state's most important tools in its grand project of social engineering. But to tell that story, one must first go back to the middle of the ninth century, to the dawn of the penal-military complex.

1. Reed, "Tattoos in Early China," 371–372; Duan Chengshi, *Youyang zazu*, 8.279.76.

Tattoos in the Late Tang Period (Ninth Century)

The rare available glimpses into tattooing culture during the ninth century reveal that tattooed men became a social problem in the capital of the Tang empire. In the streets of ninth-century Chang'an, groups of young toughs, with shaved heads and bodies covered with colorful and elaborate tattoos, drank heavily, brawled, and stole. Some of these men were soldiers, and some engaged in other less-than-respectable trades, such as dog butchers. Officials attempted to control these men with beatings and executions, not always successfully.[2]

Soldiers and thugs were not the only tattooed people in the ninth-century Tang empire, and tattooing already had a long history in the Sinitic-script world. Since the early days of the Sinitic-script world, tattooing was a form of punishment for criminals as well as a tradition of body decoration among groups outside of Sinitic-script civilizations.[3] By the eighth century, tattooing had evolved in range and complexity.[4] By that time, Sinitic-script states had long stopped the practice of penal tattoos, using them only sporadically. Instead, the tattooing of slaves and servants had become common practice in wealthy households.[5] In some cases, elite women tattooed their maids' faces out of anger or jealousy.[6] Tattooing also made an impact beyond the ranks of slaves and convicts and became a source of inspiration for makeup trends among both elites and commoners, the ninth-century equivalent of "heroin-chic."[7] Even though tattoos fascinated men and women of many walks of life, one of their main function was to create and mark power: power of civilization over the uncivilized, of the state over its subjects, and of master over servant.

2. Duan Chengshi, *Youyang zazu*, 8.279.76, 8.289.78; Wang Pu, *Tang hui yao*, 607.67.33a.17.

3. Sima Qian, *Shi ji*, 68.2231–2232; Zhuang Zhou, *Zhuangzi jinzhu jinshe*, 25; *Li chi: Book of Rites*, vol. 1, 229; Fu Changze, *"Qingxing sankao,"* 97.

4. Much of the evidence for late Tang tattooing comes from the late Tang miscellany, the *Youyang zazu*. For more on this text, see Chen Yuanpeng, "Shenti yu huawen"; Reed, "Tattoos in Early China," "Early Chinese Tattoo."

5. Duan Chengshi, *Youyang zazu*, 8.286.77, 8.300.79.

6. Duan Chengshi, *Youyang zazu*, 8.288.78, 8.293.79.

7. Duan Chengshi, *Youyang zazu*, 8.292.78–79, 8.293–294.79.

The tattoos of soldiers and thugs of the ninth-century Tang empire turned the meaning of tattoos on its head. For them, tattoos symbolized pride, masculinity, and defiance.[8] Resistance to official authority, as in Zhang Gan's arm tattoos, was an important theme. In one ninth-century anecdote, a military camp jailer in Shu (Chengdu) tattooed the words "kill Yin" (*sha Yin*) on his arm after the general Yin Yan had had the jailer's brother savagely beaten for raising his voice at him while drunk.[9] Some used tattoos to subvert authority instead of confronting it directly. In one such case that took place during the late Yuanhe reign period (806–820), a man fond of brawling tried to escape flogging by having the image of a religious deity tattooed on his back.[10]

These soldiers and thugs used tattoos not only as an oppositional tool but also for decorative purposes. At the same point in history that elite men began collecting art as part of their social and cultural identity, the "thugs" or "loafers" of the ninth century collected tattoos.[11] Tattooed men used tattoos as cultural and social capital that allowed them to bond with and elevate each other. These tattoos could be inspired by the cultural world of the elite, quoting famous paintings and poems. Other tattoos echoed a different element of elite cultural life, the production of private histories. Lower-class men tattooed their individual histories: various adventures of drinking and gambling or the details of their romantic partners. These tattoos were referred to as "needle histories," a textual genre now completely lost.[12] Although no records survived of these individual histories written on skin, their existence reveals that people of a lower social standing documented their own lives even if their social betters did not deem their thoughts and actions worthy of preserving.

8. Scholars pointed out tattooing and a culture of resistance as features of the urbanizing world of the late Tang (Chen Yuenpeng, "Shenti yu huawen," 35–37; Reed, "Tattoos in Early China," 375; Reed, "Early Chinese Tattoo," 50–52.)

9. Duan Chengshi, *Youyang zazu*, 8.287.78.

10. He tattooed the image of the Heavenly King Vaisravana (*pishamen tianwang*) (Duan Chengshi, *Youyang zazu*, 8.280.76).

11. For more on the changing elite culture of the Middle Period, see Egan, *Problem of Beauty*.

12. Duan Chengshi, *Youyang zazu*, 8.281.76–77, 8.282.77, 8.283.77; Tao Gu, *Qingyi lu*, 1047.67.2b.889.

The popularity of tattooing spread far beyond the walls of the Tang capital, with Sichuan being a center for tattooing.[13] Late eighth-century Jingzhou (in modern Hubei) had an active local tattooing scene with specialists who quickly completed elaborate tattoos by using prepared stamps with multiple needles.[14] Most of the evidence for late Tang tattoos dates to the ninth century. However, the geographic extent of tattoos, the technological mastery needed to produce elaborate designs in a timely manner, and the diverse range of symbols and meanings suggest that Middle Period tattoos developed over a significant time preceding the ninth century.

In 881 the entry of Huang Chao's rebel army into the capital city of Chang'an and the carnage that followed marked the ending point of the old Tang elite, not just by the destruction of the political institutions it relied on to monopolize its power but also through the physical destruction of elite families.[15] The forces of the rebel Huang Chao who reached Chang'an in 881 included men who spoke a language foreign to the capital dwellers, their faces tattooed with characters boasting of their past achievements (probably a form of "needle histories").[16] Close to a century later, when large parts of the Sinitic-script world were once again consolidated under the Song dynasty, the destruction of the Tang elite and state was a lesson well learned. Tattooed men were a danger to elites, not just because of small acts of violence in the marketplace. Left unchecked, these men posed a threat to the elites' way of life, even a threat to life itself.

The Dawn of Coercive Military Tattoos: Late Tang and Five Dynasties

In the year 888 the entire town of Suzhou was tattooed. It happened during a siege, after many people had taken refuge within city walls. According to one account, a military force conscripted all people within the walls

13. Duan Chengshi, *Youyang zazu*, 8.290.78.

14. Duan Chengshi, *Youyang zazu*, 8.291.78. The bundling together of tattoo needles might have been the source of the tools and methods in traditional Japanese tattooing.

15. See Tackett, *Destruction of the Medieval Chinese Aristocracy*.

16. Wei Zhuang, *Wei Zhuang ji*, 105–9.

(most likely the males) and had their faces tattooed with the characters for "Willing-to-fight-for-the-south Battalion" (Yuan zhan nan du).[17] This is one of the earliest records of a mass tattooing in a military context. There was a stark difference between those facial tattoos and the ones in Huang Chao's army. Instead of the decorative, individualistic tattoos that boasted of violent masculinity, these tattoos shared a standard form, implying a top-down decision rather than a voluntary one. Their content was grounded in the locality or tied to a specific military unit, and the courage they called for was in the service of a regional political entity. The mass tattooing in the siege of Suzhou was a sign of things to come. As the ninth century drew to a close, the collapse of the Tang empire became a free-for-all. Competition over the collapsing Tang empire required that the contestants build up their armies, but the general population was often reluctant to join. To survive and expand, warlords needed to acquire and retain soldiers, and for that purpose they turned to tattooing.[18]

Zhu Wen (852–912), a pioneer of coercive military tattoos, was the greatest warlord of the closing years of the Tang, and it was he who had finally put an end to the Tang dynasty and founded its successor, the short-lived Later Liang dynasty (907–923). The records explain Zhu Wen's decision to tattoo soldiers' faces as a measure against desertion, a common problem in his armies.[19] Because Zhu Wen served under the rebel Huang Chao, he must have been no stranger to the sight of tattooed soldiers. Zhu Wen's important innovation was tattooing soldiers with the name of their unit, binding them in the process to their commander.[20] This new practice of tattooing soldiers' faces transformed the meaning of military service and contributed to the decreasing status of soldiers.[21] If the men with facial tattoos in Huang Chao's rebel army terrified the residents of Chang'an, Zhu Wen's policy of facial tattoos served as an instrument of terror and control applied against his own soldiers.

17. Qian Yan, *Wuyue beishi*, 464.1.14b–15a.1.

18. For more on tattooing soldiers during the Five Dynasties period, see Huang Qinglian, "Tangmo wudai qingzu."

19. Tao Yue, *Wudai shibu*, "Taizu wen jian'er mian," 1.326; *Song shi*, 193.4799.

20. Huang Qinglian, "Tangmo wudai qingzu," 112–13, 137.

21. Tsuji, "Sō-hatsu no hairu to hai-gun," 333–34.

Zhu Wen's adversaries also turned to tattooing to form and mark military units. In 888 the warlords Zhu Jin and Zhu Xuan formed a unit of crack troops, several hundred men strong, their faces tattooed with a pair of wild geese on their foreheads, naming the unit the Wild Geese Battalion (Yanzi du). This must have made some impression on Zhu Wen, who, having heard of the new unit, also picked several hundred men and formed a unit named Crashing Wild Geese Battalion (Luoyan du).[22] The men who ruled that world were military men who led the transformation of soldiers into expressions of their leader's power, a canvas that could be written on, named, and renamed, in conversations with other powerful military men.

During the early tenth century, the rising demand for military manpower made the world a dangerous place for males fit for military service, regardless of social background. Zhu Wen's adversaries, father and son Liu Rengong (d. 914) and Liu Shouguang (d. 914), went on large conscription campaigns that included facial tattoos for new recruits.[23] They did not limit their conscription campaigns to a particular segment in society, conscripting and tattooing groups not yet incorporated into the Sinitic-script states.[24] Others, like the warlord An Congjin, conscripted refugees and scoured the roads for traveling merchants they could capture and tattoo into their armies.[25]

Elite men also found themselves tattooed and forced into military service. In 906, after several failed military campaigns, Liu Rengong conscripted all the men between the ages of fifteen and seventy in the territory he controlled (around two hundred thousand men) and tattooed them. However, Liu Rengong made a concession to elite men. Whereas the rank and file were tattooed on their faces with the inscription "Deciding

22. Xue Juzheng, *Jiu wudai shi*, 64.856; Ouyang Xiu, *Xin wudai shi*, 45.496; Li Shangjiao, *Jinshi huiyuan*, 850.3.2a.273. "Crashing wild geese" suggests that the Wild Geese Battalion will collapse before them like wild geese flying in fright. It remains unclear if Zhu Wen also tattooed those troops accordingly.

23. Xue Juzheng, *Jiu wudai shi*, 67.889; Ouyang Xiu, *Xin wudai shi*, 28.308.

24. Liu Rengong and Liu Shouguang also had the non-Han groups of Xi and Xi[1] tattooed on their faces and conscripted (*Chang bian*, 27.2.604).

25. An Congjin began increasing his forces in preparation for a confrontation with the Emperor Gaozu (892–942) of the Later Jin (Ouyang Xiu, *Xin wudai shi*, 51.586).

Hegemony Battalion" (Dingba du), men of higher social standing were tattooed on the arm with the inscription "Serving the ruler with all my heart" (*yixin shizhu*).[26] This concession sheltered elite men from some of the social-leveling effects of indiscriminate mass-tattooing campaigns. Still, men who had been protected by their property, family ties, education, and reputation found many of these qualifications erased. Instead, they became males at the age of military service, subject to capture, tattooing, control, and the dangers that came with military service.

During the first half of the tenth century, tattoos were both instruments of control and symbols of martial pride and camaraderie. When the general Wang Jingchong (d. 949) suspected that the men of his subordinate Zhao Siguan (d. 949) might not be loyal to him, he wished to have them tattooed. Zhao Siguan volunteered to have himself tattooed first.[27] Tattoos were a deed of ownership, tying the soldiers to their commander, but they also stood for the bonds shared between fighting men.

Camaraderie could be fake as well. The Wuyue general Gao Li (d. 918) conscripted villagers and had their faces tattooed. Later, he ordered all men in the area tattooed within three days on pain of death. In the course of the conscription campaign, Gao Li had his own face painted in solidarity, but once all the local people had their faces tattooed, he washed his face clean, winning him the nickname "clear-faced demon" (*baimian yecha*).[28] This fake act of solidarity finely captured the spirit of the time: a world of warfare, opportunity, and camaraderie across the military ranks, but also the decreasing appeal of military service and the decline in the status of low-ranking military men.

In the commercializing world of the tenth century, the use of military tattoos to bind soldiers to a specific leader supported the growing commodification of soldiers and their transformation into a form of capital. The Wuyue kingdom used the character *yuan* to mark military uniforms and various vessels and objects that belonged to the state. The kingdom also tattooed the same character on the shoulders of its soldiers.

26. Xue Juzheng, *Jiu wudai shi*, 135.1801–02; Ouyang Xiu, *Xin wudai shi*, 39.424.

27. Ouyang Xiu, *Xin wudai shi*, 53.605. It is unclear whether the troops were all tattooed following that exchange.

28. Qian Yan, *Wuyue beishi*, 464.2.8a–9b.528.

This character stood for the Wuyue ruling house, the Qian family, and it signaled that both the soldiers and the material objects belong to the Qian house.[29] If in the ninth century tattoos expressed a soldier's individual qualities, past, and aspirations, by the tenth century, some rulers used tattoos to turn soldiers into chattel.

In addition to the symbol of the thug and of human property, the Five Dynasties period saw tattoos become the mark of the convict. The use of convicts for war and labor, coupled with mutilating punishments, appeared (in various combinations) in the ancient Sinitic-script world. During the Han period (202 BC–AD 220), the state used convicts as an important source of labor and military manpower in border outposts, eliminating disruptive social elements in the process.[30] However, early in the Han period, in 167 BCE, Emperor Wen (r. 180–157) abolished mutilating punishments.[31] Over the centuries following the fall of the Han, penal tattooing made sporadic appearances. At one point at the turn of the seventh century, a female official with a penal tattoo on her face became a dominant figure in the Tang court.[32] During the early tenth century, the Later Jin dynasty (936–947) brought back the punishment of banishment combined with penal tattooing. The banishment often involved military assignment, stigmatizing both tattoos and military service.[33] The following dynasties, the Later Han (947–951) and the Later Zhou (951–960), continued to use penal tattoos.[34]

The end of the ninth century and the first decades of the tenth century saw the transformation of facial military tattoos into a coercive device, the resumption of penal facial tattoos, and rising social mobility

29. Qian Yan, *Wuyue beishi*, 464.1.27a–27b.

30. Lewis, *The Early Chinese Empires: Qin and Han*, 248–52.

31. Sima Qian, *Shi ji*, 10.427–428.

32. Shangguan Wan'er (664–710) was a powerful and famous female official who had been tattooed on her face as punishment by Empress Wu Zetian (624–705) (Liu Xu, *Jiu tang shu*, 51.2175–2176; Ouyang Xiu, *Xin tang shu*, 76.3488–3489).

33. Ma Duanlin, *Wenxian tongkao*, 613.168.14b.732; Wang Pu, *Wudai huiyao*, 607.9.16a; Gao Cheng, *Shiwu jiyuan*, 920.10.16b.275; Dutton, *Policing and Punishment in China*, 130–34.

34. Liu Xu, *Jiu wudai shi*, 107.1407; Sima Guang, *Zizhi tongjian*, 310.208.24b.632; Wang Pu, *Wudai huiyao*, 607.25.11b–12b.667–68.

for fighting men. These trends criminalized fighting men yet at the same time also offered them new opportunities. The arrival of tattooed men at the centers of political power created some tense situations. Men who would otherwise be designated the "losers" of the social order were sometimes catapulted from the far margins of society to one of the many emerging political centers. The entourage of Wang Jian (847–918), the founder of the Former Shu state (907–925), included men with shaved heads and tattooed faces and bodies, both marks of convicts. Officials mocked their appearance, calling Wang Jian's men "demons"; his lieutenant Xu Yao was referred to as the "demon chief." The tattooed entourage struck back. They recorded the officials' names and later had them all killed.[35] Later on, the eleventh-century Song scholar Ouyang Xiu described the Five Dynasties as a time when tattooed and shaved-headed people and smugglers filled the rulers' courts.[36] For scholar-officials like Ouyang Xiu, this recent chapter in history served as an important historical lesson: tattooed men needed to be disciplined and controlled.

In the first half of the tenth century, despite the rise of coercive military facial tattoos, the colorful thug tattoos of the late Tang did not disappear, and a culture of underclass tattooing continued to exist (figs. 1 and 2). A Song dynasty anecdote tells of two men of humble beginnings, both young and cunning and of a violent disposition. One day they had themselves tattooed by a man described as a traveling practitioner of the esoteric arts (probably referring to skills ranging from magic to healing and tattooing). The practitioner tattooed a sparrow on the right side of one man's neck, and on the left side a mulberry tree and grain. For his friend, he tattooed a jar with wild geese in it. Later, the man with the tattooed neck became Guo Wei, the founder of the Later Zhou dynasty, and the man with the jar and geese tattoo was Feng Hui, his famous official. The tattoo gained the future emperor the nickname Guo "Sparrow" (*que'er*).[37] Guo Wei's tattooed body was evidence to the social mobility of

35. Ouyang Xiu, *Xin tang shu*, 186.5432; Zhang Tangying, *Shu tao wu*, 9b–10a, 226–67.

36. Ouyang Xiu, *Xin wudai shi*, 61.747.

37. Zhang Shunmin, *Huaman lu*, 197.

FIG. 1. Tattooed laborer carrying a basket of grain. Detail of Wei Xian, *Sluice Gate (Zhakou panche tu)*. Five Dynasties—Early Song. Scroll, ink and color on silk, ht. 53.3 cm, w. 119.2 cm. Courtesy of Shanghai Museum.

fighting men in the middle of the tenth century. However, after he ascended the imperial throne, Guo Wei became one of the architects of the military policies that brought soldiers back under the control of a centralized government and in the process diminished greatly the status of fighting men. Yet this man was himself a tattooed thug, the first and last of his kind to occupy an imperial throne.

FIG. 2. Tattooed laborer standing in front two baskets of grain. Detail of Wei Xian, *Sluice Gate* (*Zhakou panche tu*). Five Dynasties–Early Song. Scroll, ink and color on silk, ht. 53.3 cm, w. 119.2 cm. Courtesy of Shanghai Museum.

The Standardization and Expansion of Military Tattoos under the Song

In 963 the Song military official Li Chuyun (920–966) caught many bandits, and he had his troops eat the fatter men among the captives. He then had the younger bandits tattooed on their faces and sent them to

Langzhou (in modern Hunan) with the purpose of striking fear into the hearts of the bandits there.[38] This took place only a couple of years after the official date of the Song's founding, and the incident recalls the world of the Five Dynasties: strong generals who used tattoos freely as an instrument of terror. Yet the days of such men and such actions were numbered.

With the founding of the Song dynasty, generals lost their power to author their troops' tattoos. The military tattoo system was standardized and unified on an empire-wide level. The new military tattoos contained the name of the soldiers' battalion, the basic operational unit in the Song military, containing about 250–500 men.[39] Military tattoos no longer signaled ownership by a specific general but instead located the soldier in a specific battalion within the Song military.

Military tattoos often began as relatively short inscriptions, amounting to about six characters ("battalion name" + "battalion number" + "battalion," i.e., "Unrivaled Second Battalion"), but they often grew in length over time since soldiers' military assignments were not permanent. Soldiers could be transferred due to punishment, merit, disease, or need. Following a transfer, a soldier's tattoo was altered accordingly. Such a process was called "altering the tattoo" (*gaici*).[40] This could mean adding lines to existing tattooed characters. More likely, it meant adding new tattoos, as was certainly the case with penal tattoos. The tattoos on a soldier's face told the story of his service record: the various battalions he had served in or crimes he had committed, a new kind of "needle history" authored by the state.

Military tattoos empowered the centralized state at the expense of both soldiers and military officials. By standardizing the format, content, and circumstances surrounding tattooing, the Song founders took away a commander's privilege of authoring his own tattoos on the bodies of his soldiers. Tattoos became a reminder of the power of the state, and officials could partake in that power, but only as agents of the state. Laws and regulations governed the process of tattooing in the Song's penal-

38. *Chang bian*, 4.1.86–87.
39. *Song shi*, 193.4780.
40. *Song shi*, 193.4819.

military complex, and the hand that wielded the tattooing needle was that of the centralized state.

Not all the soldiers were tattooed, but evidence points to tattooing as the prevailing custom in the Song military. The *Song shi* describes tattooing as one of the prominent features of the Song military system, a legacy of one of its recent predecessors, the Later Liang dynasty.[41] One Song source describes the standard process of recruiting soldiers as "conscripting, tattooing, and giving tips."[42] According to the *Wujing zongyao*, a mid-eleventh-century source, tattooing was a regular feature of the imperial armies.[43] One anecdote mentions a "tattooist" (*ciziren*) within the military camp, implying that this was a specialized role within the Song armies.[44] Tattooed adult males were a minority in Song society as a whole, albeit a significant one.[45] Military tattoos were common enough among adult males to make them a well-known feature of Song civilization. When a Koryŏ emissary came to pay tribute to the Song court in 1015, he described his own country as a place where (in contrast to the Song), "The people and the army are mixed together, and when assigning to the military [we] do not tattoo the face."[46]

PENAL TATTOOS

The mid-to-late tenth century was a transitionary period in the Song empire, situated between the reign of military men in the early tenth century and the rise of the scholar-officials to prominence in the early eleventh century.[47] An important transition took place within the military as well, as tenth-century emperors (Five Dynasties and early Song) revived the punishment of tattooing and combined it with flogging, banishment, and

41. *Song shi*, 193.4799.
42. Shi Su, *Jiatai kuaiji zhi*, 4.1–2, 6775.
43. Zeng Gongliang, *Wujing zongyao*, 1.16b.245.
44. Shao Bowen, *Shaoshi wenjian lu*, 18.203.
45. McKnight, *Law and Order in Sung China*, 348–49.
46. *Chang bian*, 85.12.1957. Koryŏ was a kingdom in the Korean Peninsula.
47. For more on this periodization, see Deng Xiaonan. "Tan songchu zhi 'yu wuchen dushu'"; Chen Feng, *Beisong wujiang qunti*, 348–352; Lorge, *Reunification of China*, 278–86; Fang Cheng-hua, "Yangbing weimin," 72–78.

military labor.[48] The tattooing of convicts with ugly, degrading, and utilitarian tattoos and their assignment to military units, often to do hard labor, became defining traits of the Song state's penal-military complex in the centuries to come.

In 1003, when most of the soldiers who fought in the Song's founding wars had already died, the Song state made an important change to its penal code. Masters were no longer allowed to punish their servants with tattoos. Instead, only the state had the authority to tattoo.[49] Just as the state claimed the power of generals by standardizing military tattoos, it promulgated tattooing laws that allowed the state to intervene in local society at the expense of elite households. Wealthy households continued to have their servants tattooed, but they had to do so through the mediation of the state, by filing complaints and having them punished by the authorities. The state successfully claimed the tattooing needle from elite households but, in the process, made its own hands that much bloodier.

Although penal tattoos were diverse and varied across time, they all functioned as the convict's mark, punishment, and criminal record, a living warning to all observers. Penal tattoos were designed to be highly visible and painful by making them larger than military tattoos and by their prominent location, always on the face except special cases.[50] The tattoo could include the name of the punishment itself, *cipei*, which meant "to tattoo and assign."[51] Other penal tattoos came in the form of shapes that marked the severity and type of the crime (perhaps to facilitate recognition by the illiterate population or to simplify the tattooing procedure): a tattoo behind the ear for a bandit; a square for

48. Dai Jianguo, *Tang song biange shiqi,* 240–41.

49. *Chang bian*, 54.9.1189. The *Song shi* attributes this decision to Zhenzong's father, Emperor Taizong (*Song shi*, 201.5016).

50. *Song huiyao, xingfa*, 4.7 (Dazhongxiangfu 7th year, 2nd month, 1st day); in 1024 a decree ordered that severe offenders should have one of the sides of their faces tattooed with large characters (*Song huiyao, xingfa*, 4.11, Tiansheng 2nd year, 2nd month). An example of a special case occurred in 1071, when family members of mutinous soldiers in Qingzhou were enslaved and tattooed on their hands (*Chang bian*, 221.49.5383).

51. In 1116 the Ministry of Punishments requested that convicts' faces be tattooed with these characters (*Song huiyao, fangyu*, 15.27, Zhenghe 6th year).

penal servitude; a circle for a beating. Repeat offenders were tattooed in more prominent locations on their head and face.[52] Because the criminal record was documented on the face, repeat offenders had highly tattooed faces.[53]

The military crime of desertion had its own unique tattoos, probably containing the word "deserter" (*taozou*).[54] Desertion was extremely common in the Song armies, not just among convicts but among all troops. Some men had started their military careers with standard military tattoos, but after they had deserted from their units they were punished with "deserter" tattoos. The penal-military complex turned convicts into soldiers, but also soldiers into convicts.

Officials were granted some protections from the penal code. After 1033, death sentences for officials were usually commuted to flogging, tattooing, and banishment.[55] About forty years later the Song state stopped the flogging and tattooing of officials.[56] Tattoos, however, continued to cast a shadow within official circles. After the grand councilor Cai Jing (1047–1126) fell out with Li Miao, he was reported to have said: "Li Miao has such a face, it needs a tattooing," terrifying Li in the process.[57] Yue Ke (1183–1234) related an incident where a slip of the tongue by Chao Zhongshi brought about the end of Chao's career. Yue Ke wrote that "a disre-

52. This is according to an edict promulgated in 1085. The edict also ordered that those punished with beating for the third time would have the tattoo moved to the face, its diameter not longer than half an inch (*Chang bian*, 362.25.8667).

53. Hong Mai tells of a man named Xie Si who was caught stealing three times but was not executed. His face was covered in tattoos, a sign of a rich criminal record (Hong Mai, *Yijian zhi, fuzhou xiesi*, 1534).

54. *Chang bian*, 467.30.11154.

55. Additionally, officials still had the possibility of a pardon and release from the military register (*Song shi*, 201.5017).

56. During the Xining reign period (1068–1078) the official Zhang Zhongxuan was sentenced to death, but his sentence was commuted to flogging, tattooing, and banishment. The official Su Song argued that the ancient custom was not to punish high officials like this and that it might create a disturbance among officialdom. Zhang was spared the flogging and tattooing and was merely banished. From then on officials were no longer flogged or tattooed as a punishment (*Song shi*, 201.5018).

57. Wang Mingqing, *Huizhu lu, yuhua,* 2.401.302.

spectful word was uttered, and he took on himself the shame of a tattooed man."[58]

TATTOO REMOVAL

Middle Period sources contain some references to tattoo removal. One anecdote tells that when an official in ninth-century Chang'an executed a group of tattooed men, the tattooed people of the marketplace all hastened to remove their tattoos with moxibustion.[59] In 1052, during the campaign against the Nong Zhigao Rebellion, Emperor Renzong (r. 1022–1063) ordered his general Di Qing (1008–1057) that men who had been tattooed on the face by the rebels were to have their tattoos removed, be given documents, and released.[60] Di Qing himself started out as a low-ranking soldier and had a facial tattoo. When offered the opportunity to have his facial tattoo removed, he declined out of a sense of solidarity with his own troops.[61] In the 1160s Miao Xi refused to have his tattoos removed after he was summoned back from exile, and as a result he won the pity and respect of the emperor.[62] These accounts of tattoo removal make it clear that at least in some cases, tattoo removal was an option, even if its level of efficacy remains unclear.

The painting *Moxibustion* (*Zhi'ai tu*) (fig. 3) by Li Tang (1070–ca. 1150) shows an itinerant doctor conducting a painful procedure on another man's back. The itinerant doctor's shabby appearance gives away his low social station. Moxibustion, a well-known medicinal method, was also a tattoo-removal technique. Very likely, the same people offered both tattooing and tattoo-removal services.

After their removal, tattoos left both physical and social scars. When Emperor Song Taizong (r. 976–997) rewarded a sailor with the removal of his tattoos, he was still reluctant to award him an official position, saying: "This man's face still has scars [from the tattoos]. Is this someone who could be called an official?"[63] Zhang Yan was an official who had been tattooed for a crime. During the Zhenghe reign

58. Yue Ke, *Tingshi*, 12.141–42.
59. Reed, "Tattoos in Early China," 371–72; *Youyang zazu*, 8.279.76.
60. *Chang bian*, 173.7.4175.
61. Fang Shao, *Bozhai bian* (short version), 1.74. More on Di Qing in chapter 7.
62. Ye Shaoweng, *Sichao wenjian lu*, 1.34.
63. *Chang bian*, 24.15.559–60.

FIG. 3. Countryside tattooing was probably very similar to this scene of moxibustion. Li Tang, *Moxibustion* (*Zhi'ai tu*). Song Period. Hanging scroll, ht. 72.4 cm, w. 264 cm. Courtesy of the National Palace Museum, Taipei.

period (1111–1118), he was transferred to a new position. When someone urged him to use medicine to remove the tattooed characters, Yan said: "My face has already been tattooed. I will always be despised among the officials."[64] The moment of tattooing signaled a physical, legal, and

64. Zeng Zao, *Gaozhai manlu*, 107.

social transition. Even though an individual's legal status could be changed back to what it had been, the body and the reputation could not be recovered in the same manner. The scars would always remain.

MILITARY TATTOOS OUTSIDE OF THE REGULAR ARMIES

The Northern Song state organized the population of the border zones into local militias managed by officials. The process of registering men for the local militias sometimes included a tattoo, most often on the back of the hand.[65] Militia tattooing practices varied among the different regions, and not all militias were tattooed. The Shaanxi militias, for example, were tattooed on the back of the hand. In 1064 the official Han Qi sought to expand this practice to the militias in Hedong and Hebei (facing the Liao state), suggesting they were not tattooed at the time.[66] Officials carried out initiatives to tattoo local militias on an ad hoc basis, in part due to high levels of resistance by local people to militia registration and tattooing.[67] In the circuits close to the threatened borders, tattoos were both a physical manifestation and a barometer of state power. The more threatened a region, the greater the state's drive to tattoo the local people. The more tattooed a region, the stronger the presence of the centralized state.

Some groups that lived within the Song empire were more loosely incorporated into the Sinitic-script state. Song officials tended to treat them as less civilized, and their allegiance to the Song state needed to be secured. As a solution to concerns of loyalty and imperial security, the Song state initiated tattooing campaigns. Tattooing of those groups was done on a relatively small scale, due in part to their smaller numbers but also because it reflected locally negotiated agreements between the state and groups living in border areas, each agreement with its own tattooing scheme. In 1042, five thousand Frontier Tribal Troops were tattooed with the characters "loyal and brave" (*zhongyong*).[68] In 1081 Zhong E reported

65. Lü Gongbi (1007–1073) had local militias tattooed with the characters "first class" (*shang deng*) on the backs of their hands (*Song Shi*, 191.4734).

66. *Chang bian*, 203.2.4914–15.

67. See the discussion of resistance to tattooing of local militias in chapter 6.

68. In 1042 the court approved the request by Qingjian fort prefect Zhong Shiheng, who asked to recruit five thousand soldiers and tattoo the characters "loyal and brave" on the backs of their left hands (*Chang bian*, 135.17.3229; *Song shi*, 191.4751–52).

that the soldiers of the Exerting Obedience (Xiaoshun) Battalion (made up of surrendered soldiers) were tattooed with the two characters "returning to Han" (*gui han*).[69] Despite the superficial display of loyalty and submission, the act of tattooing Sinitic characters on reluctant people considered external to Sinitic-script civilization speaks volumes to the true nature of that relationship or alliance.

Because groups that were more loosely incorporated into the Sinitic-script world often made unenthusiastic partners to the Song state's project of tattooing and military registration, the state was willing to pay for their cooperation, and it used the allocation of lands in the border areas in order to pressure those groups to accept military tattoos.[70] The official Zhao Xie reported non-Han tactics of resistance to military registration: using false documents, sending the old and the weak to military service, and sending the same person a number of times under different identities. In 1072 Zhao Xie used the promise of gifts of land at a time of famine to pressure non-Han groups into accepting Song military tattoos.[71] The exchange of grain for tattoos facilitated the state's penetration into non-Han areas, and the state used such opportunities to rank the male members of those communities and record their names.[72]

When groups considered outside of Sinitic-script civilization were brought into the fold of the Song state, tattooing them became an important part of their transformation into allies. Surrendered groups presented themselves for tattooing of the hands and shaving of the heads and received gifts from the Song state.[73] Non-Han groups who allied themselves

69. *Chang bian*, 318.65.7694.

70. When the Fuyan circuit military commissioner's office asked in 1072 to seek empty lands and lands encroached on in the border zone, these lands were to be used to conscript and tattoo archers. It was decreed to first select lands to give to surrendered Qiang groups without land (*Chang bian*, 237.15.5763).

71. *Chang bian*, 238.42.5802–03.

72. In 1075 the court approved a request by the Huanqing circuit military commissioner's office that in the non-Han areas that had asked for support in grain, they should tattoo the outpost's name on the back of their hands, divide them into three ranks, and write down their surnames and names (*Chang bian*, 262.26.6400–01).

73. During the Song's disastrous campaign in the 1081 war with the Xi Xia, Li Xian reported that following a victory in the Nüzhe Valley, twenty-two leaders of the Kanpojijia tribes surrendered, altogether nine thousand households. The Song shaved

with the Song state received lands together with their tattoos.[74] This was not unique to the north, as the process of registering and tattooing non-Han groups took place also in the south of the Song empire.[75] From the perspective of non-Han people, military registration and tattooing were hallmarks of the Song state. When the Song military incorporated non-Han people closer and closer into its military institutions, Sinitic characters appeared on their bodies, and their names appeared in the Song state's military registers. In the process, the non-Han population was made legible to the state, while the state made itself present in the border areas as both state and civilization, inserted itself into non-Han communities, declared ownership of non-Han people, and, by modifying the bodies of non-Han men, it made the Song state ever present in their social and cultural lives.

The Song policy of rewarding soldiers according to the number of enemy heads they caught turned tattoos into an important marker of identity, not just among non-Han groups but among all those who lived in the border regions. Before their battalion was transferred to a new assignment, both Han and non-Han soldiers sometimes took the heads of local women, children, and old people and presented them for rewards.[76] Some Han soldiers killed non-Han troops and then presented their heads as enemy heads. To protect themselves, non-Han soldiers agreed to have the words "Frontier Tribal Troops" tattooed by their left ears.[77] Men on corvée duty in non-Han areas had their foreheads tat-

---

their heads, tattooed their hands, and gave them surrender flags, brocade robes, and silver belts (*Chang bian*, 316.24.7640–41).

74. In 1099 the Qinfeng circuit military commissioner's office reported on non-Han leaders who switched their allegiance to the Song and requested that they be given lands and be conscripted and tattooed as archers (*Chang bian*, 505.42.12041–42).

75. In 1084 the government approved a request by the Lunan border military commissioner's office to tattoo and give payment to a newly submitted "raw" non-Han clan that was willing to organize as a militia (*Chang bian*, 350.33.8396).

76. In 1097 an edict warned the Shaanxi and Hedong military commissioner's office of Han and non-Han soldiers who engaged in this practice when transferred (*Chang bian*, 493.46.11721–22).

77. The court authorized this policy in 1073, following many instances of Han soldiers who had robbed and killed soldiers of the non-Han Frontier Tribal Troops and presented their heads as enemy heads to gain military merit (*Chang bian*, 251.75.6133; *Song shi*, 190.4714).

tooed to avoid having their heads taken by non-Han soldiers.[78] While the local people agreed to be tattooed out of fear, the Song state was mapping the human geography of its physical and social peripheries, both Han and non-Han. The border between the Song and the Xia was marked on human skin.

78. In 1081, Mai Wenbing of the fiscal commission requested that in the Zi and Kui circuits, men on corvée duty who entered the non-Han areas should have their foreheads tattooed. When military officers captured heads, the guard officers were to inspect them (*Chang bian*, 314.15.7602).

CHAPTER 3

A Motley Crew

Sources for Military Manpower

People are the raw material fed into the military machine. The choice of manpower determines many of the qualities of the final product, the soldier. In the case of the Song state, military manpower demands reached very high levels, with the army reaching the size of a million men by the early eleventh century.[1] The Song state chose a few groups to bear the brunt of military service. These various groups were the building blocks that the Song state used to construct a military underclass with tattooed soldiers at its core, a social group unique to the Middle Period.

The army of the early Song state was a patchwork institution. When Zhao Kuangyin overthrew the Later Zhou through a military coup and founded his own dynasty, the Song, the soldiers who had originally served under the Later Zhou continued to serve the new Song state. Professional salaried troops formed the core of the Later Zhou–Early Song military, and their loyalties tended to lie not with the state but with the military superiors who paid their salaries. Together with those professional troops served soldiers who had come from a wide range of sources: surrendered

1. The Song armies grew from 370,000 late in Taizu's reign (960–976) to 650,000 at the end of Taizong's reign (976–997), to almost one million (of whom 820,000 belonged to the greatly enlarged imperial guard forces) by the end of Zhenzong's reign (997–1022). By Zhenzong's time the military consumed three-quarters of the state's annual income (Mote, *Imperial China*, 114–15).

troops of collapsed states, as well as volunteers seeking pay or opportunity, conscripts, and convicts.[2] The composition of the early Song military serves as a snapshot of a world at the twilight of one age of war and the dawn of another as a lasting and stable empire was becoming a reality.

Following the destruction and annexation of the other Sinitic-script states, the Song state still clung to its huge standing army; made it an important part of its economic, legal, and social system; and spent much of its resources on procuring and keeping soldiers. However, the world had changed following imperial consolidation. The professional soldiers of the old Later Zhou army would grow old and die. There were no more surrendered troops in great numbers, nor could generals be allowed to press the male population of entire regions into military service. A stable and lasting state demanded a stable and predictable system for military manpower. For this purpose, the Song state turned to several groups: soldiers' families, the poor and the idle, local militias, non-Han groups, convicts, and refugees.

Conscripting the Families of Soldiers

The families of soldiers provided the Song state with its most important and most easily available pool of military manpower. Wives, children, and siblings of soldiers resided in the military camps. When the need arose, the government could call on the male family members of soldiers to become full-time soldiers themselves.[3] From its early days, the Song state used families of soldiers. It could be temporary service for a labor project, but very often conscription meant lifelong military service.[4]

2. McGrath, *Military and Regional Administration in Northern Sung China*, 144–45.

3. *Song shi*, 193.4799.

4. In 965 a few thousand family members of soldiers were conscripted for work on the river (*Song huiyao, fangyu*, 1.11, 16.2); After 976, family members of the soldiers of the imperial Cloud Cavalry (Yunqi) were conscripted to the same battalion, with those of lesser quality assigned to the imperial Martial Cavalry (Wuqi) Battalion together with other cavalry soldiers of lesser quality (*Song shi*, 187.4591). In 999, the imperial Soaring Vicious (Feimeng) Battalion was created by conscripting the strong and brave

Sudden manpower shortages, such as those caused by disease, could lead to the conscription of families.[5] A military crisis, a common occurrence in the Song period, also led to the conscription of military families. When the Song-Xia wars of the second half of the eleventh century led to the militarization of the northwest, the Song military used the families of soldiers to reinforce its armies in the border regions.[6]

Even without explicit laws forcing them into service, family members of soldiers were locked into military service by circumstance. Family members of soldiers numbered in the millions. The military family, relatively impoverished and landless, faced diminishing possibilities outside of the army. Not all soldiers had the skills and knowledge needed for agriculture. Many were too poor to buy land or start afresh somewhere else. Yet there were still strong coercive elements in the assignment of soldiers' relatives to the military. They were often ordered to do so, and they could not leave the military once their economic conditions had changed.[7]

---

family members of soldiers of the imperial Dragon Vicious (Longmeng) and Valiant Cavalry (Xiaoqi) Battalions (*Song shi*, 187.4586). In 1000, the imperial Valiant Victory (Xiaosheng) Battalions were formed using family members of the soldiers of imperial Instructed Steed (Jiaojun) and Valiant Cavalry Battalions (*Song shi*, 187.4586). In 1065 the military conscripted the local people of Shaanxi together with family members of soldiers who resided in the military camps (*Song shi*, 193.4801).

5. This was the case in 1080 when Jingnan imperial troops of the Mighty Strategy (Xionglüe) and other battalions suffered great losses due to malaria during their transfer to Shunzhou. To make up for the losses in manpower it was decided to tattoo and conscript male members of soldiers' families (*Chang bian*, 301.14.7327).

6. During the 1040s war with the Xia, clerks conscripted family members of soldiers in all the armies in the attempt to meet the state's manpower goals (*Song shi*, 187.4574). In 1082 the court authorized the request by the Hedong military commissioner's office to tattoo and recruit the sons and brothers of soldiers in the imperial Linzhou Flying Cavalry (Linzhou feiqi) and imperial Fuzhou Revered Afar Battalions even if they fell slightly below the required height standard for these units (*Chang bian*, 325.43.7823).

7. While modern states often let social and economic forces push the lower classes into their assigned positions, they too have proven themselves willing to use violence to keep them at work. It was often with beatings and machine guns that the miners were kept in the mines, the workers in the factories, and the plantation workers in the fields.

Conscripting Local Militias during the Northern Song

Although professional lifelong soldiers came to dominate the military sphere after the mid-eighth century, the Tang state and its successor regimes of the Five Dynasties period continued to employ militias.[8] During the Song period too, militias remained an important element of the state's military system. Males served in the militias for most of the productive part of their lives. Broadly speaking, militia service lasted between the ages of eighteen to fifty-eight during the Northern Song, and twenty to fifty-eight during the Southern Song.[9] The conditions and terms of service varied widely between regions: the number of males recruited from each household, their duties, to what degree they were tattooed, the amount of taxes paid, whether they worked their own fields or government fields, and so on.[10] The government formed different contracts with commoners who lived in different regions of the empire. Even though they lived in a single empire, the experience of the imperial subjects was highly fragmented, depending on their status and location.

The Northern Song maintained large numbers of militias along the northern borders of the empire, and it made them into an integral part of its overall defense strategy. The state summoned militia members for drilling several times a year, and they provided much of the manpower necessary for supplying the regular armies in the northwest.[11] In the process of militia registration, the state expanded and updated its population registers. This had advantages for the state for tax reasons but also because the militias served as a recruitment pool for the regular armies. Though they were not professional troops who lived on the state's pay, the local militias served as an extension of the Song state's regular forces.

The militia system put great strain on commoners who lived in the border regions or in the circuits surrounding the capital. Sometimes a single household had to supply as many as two or three men. They still had

8. Graff, *Medieval Chinese Warfare*, 189–90, 209, 212, 216.
9. Wang Zengyu, "A History of the Sung Military," 218.
10. Wang Zengyu, *Songchao junzhi chutan*, 87–90.
11. *Song shi*, 175.4216.

to work the land and pay taxes. Furthermore, the registration to the militias put the names of family members in the military register, turning them into candidates for full-time service. Whenever the need arose, the state transferred militia members into the regular armies.[12] When a militia member fled, grew old, or died, the state used their household members as hostages and replacements.[13] It took a special sacrifice, like the death of a militia member in battle, to provide a family with an exemption from militia service.[14]

In theory, the poorest of households were not supposed to serve in local militias, but the reality was that rich men were far less likely to serve in militias than poor men.[15] When the state turned to the militias to reinforce its regular armies, men of means used their resources to pay other men to take their place. They hired their servants or local loafers and troublemakers, and sometimes those also assumed the names of the men they replaced.[16] In some cases, tenants were allowed to stand in for their landlords in militia service.[17] When the state demanded men for

12. In 1002 Associate Censor Tian Xi argued these were the issues facing commoners in the capital area due to service in local militias. The militias were used for defense against the Liao in the north, but they could be transferred to the regular armies in the western border in a time of military need (*Chang bian*, 52.24.1134).

13. In 1029 a decree ordered that Shaanxi archers who were tattooed on the hand and escaped were to be replaced by a younger brother, and if they did not report within three months, their relative would replace them permanently (*Chang bian*, 108.10.2528). In 1042 Jia Changchao described the poor condition of local militias in the north: Indomitables (Qiangzhuang) in Hebei and Hedong, Bow and Arrow Men (Gongjianshou) in Shaanxi. He offered that the strongest of each family would replace the old and weak. He also suggested that those exceptional in their ability could be used to fill the missing quotas of the regular armies (*Chang bian*, 138.28.3317–18). In 1064 Sima Guang explained that the Warriors for Righteousness militiamen in Shaanxi were tied to the register until they died or were too old and sick and were then replaced by their sons (*Chang bian*, 203.2.4914–18); this practice was already in place during the Later Zhou's Guangshun reign period (951–954) (*Song shi*, 190.4709).

14. A 1070 decree exempted households from service in the Warriors for Righteousness militia if they had lost a member in battle. Instead, men from other households were to be conscripted and tattooed to make up the quota (*Chang bian*, 215.51.5248).

15. Zhang Fangping, *Lequan ji*, 22.1b–2a.207, 22.7a–8a.210; Liu Chang, *Gong shi ji*, 18.13b–14a.552–3.

16. *Chang bian*, 138.11.3312, 159.9.3849.

17. An edict of 1082 decreed that the shortages in the quotas for the Shaanxi Bow and Arrow Men should be filled by strong and young members of the household. If

the local militias, a process of negotiation and evasion began at the local level. Those who could hire replacements did so, whether legally or illegally. The service in the local militias helped create and reinforce a local social hierarchy, and it pushed the most marginal elements of each locality toward the state's military register.

The Northern Song's conflicts with its northern neighbors exacted a horrible price on the local militias. Following the conflagration of the first Song-Xia war in 1038, much of the burden of the war rested on the shoulders of the border-zone population. In addition to taxation and natural disasters, commoners faced high conscription rates that sometimes even led to the loss of most of the local workforce.[18] As military tensions between the two states continued to flare in the decades to come, households in Shaanxi supplied both the militias and the regular armies with men. This led some to sell their lands, and it severely undermined the agriculture in the area.[19] The creeping militarization of the northwestern border continued, not just in times of active warfare but throughout the second half of the eleventh century. In one major conscription effort that took place in 1064, the official Han Qi expanded the Shaanxi Warriors for Righteousness (Yiyong) militias by a hundred and fifty thousand men. These recruits were tattooed on the back of the hand, drilled, and sent to transport grain. At that point, about a third of the adult males in Shaanxi were soldiers or militia men.[20]

Just a few years after Han Qi's conscription campaign, the Song state embarked on its most ambitious expansion of the militias under the leadership of the official Wang Anshi. Wang's comprehensive system of reforms, the New Policies, included organizing the entire population of the empire into mutual-surveillance units, or *baojia*. The *baojia* took charge of local policing, but those of the border regions were to be trained for combat so that they could ultimately replace the regular armies.[21] The *baojia* system was not completely new but rather an extension of an important principle of the military manpower system into greater society: that mili-

---

there were none, tenants should be picked to be tattooed and recruited (*Chang bian*, 323.54.7787).

18. See the poem *Tian jia yu*, "The Peasant's Words," by poet Mei Yaochen (1002–1060) (in *Ideology, Power, Text*, 22–23).

19. *Song shi*, 190.4709.

20. *Chang bian*, 203.2.4916–22; *Song shi*, 192.4772.

21. *Song shi*, 192.4767.

tary household units and their individual members were interchangeable parts that could be shuffled and transferred according to need.

The Song state never fully achieved the ambitious goals it set for the *baojia* reform. Instead, there were reports of understaffed units, out-of-date registers, abandoned fields, and people who had used the confusion to take over these newly vacated plots.[22] The Song state dismantled the *baojia* system less than twenty years after having put it in place, and many *baojia* members found themselves transferred to the regular armies rather than released. This did not cure the Song military of its chronic ailments. In the last decades of the Northern Song, both regular troops and local militias fell short of their assigned quotas.[23] When the Jurchen onslaught of 1126 began, both the regular armies and the local militias of the Northern Song proved to be an empty shell.

Although the ambitions of the Song government's military policies tended to exceed their means, they had a tremendous effect on local society. The Northern Song's local militias were a two-way portal. They brought government presence and power into the local level, but they also drew commoners into the orbit of the penal-military complex as militia men and soldiers. In the process, the state conducted a much deeper investigation and analysis of local society in the militarized border zones: the number and age of males, the property they owned, and their physical and medical condition. Even if its reach was limited by the technological constraints of the time, there is no mistaking the Song state's desire to investigate, measure, register, and control the population of border zones.

Non-Han Units during the Northern Song

The Song period saw the rise of a shared cultural and social identity that scholars today view as "proto-national." Yet this largely concerns elite culture, elite society, and elite identity. Far less is known about the culture

22. This according to a report the official Lü Wenqing submitted in 1083 on the poor state of registering troops and fields in the border circuit of Qinzhou (*Chang bian*, 340.58.8188–89).

23. Wang Zengyu, *Songchao junzhi chutan*, 157.

and identity of nonelite subjects of the Song empire, the overwhelming majority of the population. Modern scholarship treats most of these people as "Chinese," contrasted with smaller groups considered different or peripheral.[24] Drawing the line that separated these groups from most of the population in the Song empire is hard if not impossible, considering the human diversity of the empire: people who lived in different regions, spoke different languages, had a different appearance, and had different customs and local social and political organizations. However, differences between those groups emerge if one sets aside the question of culture and identity to focus instead on how the Song state "saw" and organized these groups through its military institutions.

The border regions of the Northern Song were home to groups more loosely tied to the Song state. The state categorized those groups on a spectrum running from "raw" (*sheng*) to "cooked" (*shu*[1]). The categories of "raw" and "cooked" were administrative, reflecting the degree of those groups' incorporation into the Song state's military system. These categories also suggest a process of "cooking," a transformation into a different state. One cannot call this a cultural and ethnic transformation ("sinification"). Rather, the categories reflected the degree of the group's incorporation into the Song state's military organizations. I use the term "non-Han" to refer to these groups more loosely tied to the Sinitic-script state.

The most important non-Han military units of the Northern Song, the Frontier Tribal Troops (Fan bing) of the northwest border regions, were located closer to the "cooked" side of the spectrum. However, they did not begin as such but gradually transitioned into a "cooked" status over the course of centuries. Both the Tang state and the early Song state used the "loose-rein policy" (*jimi*), where these groups were free to run their own affairs in times of peace and the central government called on them in times of military need.[25] This system went through significant changes during the first century of Song rule for a number of reasons: the decline in the relative numbers of groups considered non-Han, the exacerbating military conflict, and the growth in the Song state's re-

24. Kim refers to them as "different ethnic groups" whereas An's study treats them as "peripheral ethnic groups"; Kim, *Sōdai no seihoku mondai to iminzoku seisaku*; An Guolou, *Songchao zhoubian mingzu*).

25. Kim, *Sōdai no seihoku mondai to iminzoku seisaku*, 314.

sources, bureaucratic capability, and drive to register the population of the border regions.[26] By the time the Song state went to war with the Tanguts in 1042, the Frontier Tribal Troops became forces that could be mobilized by the central government as part of the larger war effort.

During the late eleventh century, under Emperor Shenzong's reforms and the establishment of the Area-Generals System, the Song state made a strong push to integrate non-Han units with the regular military units.[27] During the reform effort, the official Wang Anshi promoted a policy of military integration and standardization toward the Frontier Tribal Troops, attempting to organize them along similar lines as those of the regular armies.[28] Non-Han leaders became Song officials, and the non-Han households were recorded in the Song state's military registers.[29] The militarization of the northwest's non-Han population in the course of the late eleventh century was reflected in the heavy burden of military registration among families serving in the Frontier Tribal Troops. In some cases, over half of the males in a single household could be called in for militia service.[30] In other regions where the non-Han groups were not as closely integrated, the Song state still used its military apparatus to incorporate them more closely.[31] The Xihe region (in modern Gansu), a strategic area on the Song-Xia border, had a large non-Han population as well as a large number of regular troops. During the reform period, the state pushed the units in the region toward the "cooked" end of the spectrum, placing military units with a mix of Han and non-Han troops under the command of state officials.[32]

The Dongding of Guangxi and the southwest fell under the "raw" category. Considered of lesser military value, the Song state used them

26. An Guolou, *Songchao zhoubian mingzu*, 2–3.

27. Kim, *Sōdai no seihoku mondai to iminzoku seisaku*, 314–16.

28. An Guolou, *Songchao zhoubian mingzu*, 67–69, 71–73.

29. An Guolou, *Songchao zhoubian mingzu*, 73–74, 221–25.

30. In 1075 the court decreed to organize units of Frontier Tribal Troops in the border areas of all Shaanxi circuits and pick the men twenty years old and over, with each household supplying men according to the following ratio: five out of nine, four out of six, three out of four, two out of three, and one out of two, up to a maximum of five. They were then to be tattooed on the backs of their hands (*Chang bian*, 270.44.6626).

31. An Guolou, *Songchao zhoubian mingzu*, 221–25.

32. An Guolou, *Songchao zhoubian mingzu*, 74–75.

mostly for local defense, whereas the regular troops in the region carried out the more important military missions. The *dongding* were active in other regions in the wars of the mid-twelfth century, a testament to the Song state's need to draw on all hands in that severe military crisis, but those units were never as big or as well organized as the Frontier Tribal Troops of the northwest.[33] Some military units composed of non-Han people (sometimes referred to as *yijun*) were given fields and expected to feed and clothe themselves. Such groups were active in the first great Song-Jin war, but their power decreased with the loss of the north.[34]

Within the large military organization of the Northern Song, the various military units formed a hierarchy of value, trust, training, and pay. Non-Han units were arranged according to a spectrum marking their degree of incorporation into the Sinitic-script state. The passage of a group from "raw" status to "cooked" status was not a process that happened naturally due to demographic trends or the awe and majesty of Song civilization. The Song state took active measures to "cook" those tribes by incorporating them into its military structure. "Sinification" did not mean "Confucianization" of those groups. Rather, it meant militarization.

The Criminal Element: Convicts in the Song Military

The foundations for the Song state's penal-military policies were laid during the Five Dynasties period. The Song practice of assignment of convicts to the military can be traced back to the Tianfu reign period (936–944) of the Later Jin dynasty.[35] The Later Zhou, continuing the trend, allowed convicts to volunteer for the army, and in the process also have their punishment commuted.[36] The Later Zhou's Emperor Shizong

33. An Guolou, *Songchao zhoubian mingzu*, 79–85.
34. An Guolou, *Songchao zhoubian mingzu*, 85–88.
35. McKnight, *Law and Order in Sung China*, 390.
36. Xue Juzheng, *Jiu wudai shi*, 114.1511.

(r. 954–959) formed a military unit composed solely of convicts.[37] Political consolidation under the Song state brought with it a time of relative peace and the resumption of the rule of law in the empire. As is often the case with the rule of law, it ensured a steady supply of convicts. The Song state channeled convicts into the ranks of the army where the punishment of military service usually included tattooing the face, a flogging, and assignment to the prefectural armies to perform labor.[38]

The Song state's benevolent reputation stems, in part, from its legal policies. In 974 Emperor Taizu declared an important change to the penal code. He raised the threshold for executing thieves from five strings of cash worth of stolen goods to ten strings.[39] However, in this case, what appears as a relatively soft approach to crime and punishment might be better described as utilitarian. Although the Song state commuted death sentences, it brought back mutilating punishments on an unprecedented scale. It drove great numbers of people into its penal system, and many of the lives spared from the death penalty came to an end doing hard labor in the penal-military complex.

In the Song state's penal policies, practical manpower concerns played an important part—just as important as ideas about justice and social rehabilitation. When the military needed men, it took them regardless of a criminal background.[40] The strong resemblance between penal and military tattoos proved helpful in this regard. Penal tattoos, like military tattoos, were located prominently on the face. They included the names of the units the convict had been assigned to as well as his place of banishment.[41] The similar format facilitated the integration of ex-convicts into regular military

37. McKnight, *Law and Order in Sung China*, 391.

38. For more on the punishment of tattooing and military registration, see Sogabe, "Sōdai no shi-hai ni tsuite."

39. *Chang bian*, 16.8.338–39.

40. In 1112 the chief command bureau of Guangxi reported that the military unit fell 60 percent short of its assigned quota of manpower and requested to supplement the existing soldiers by tattooing and conscripting all but the worst offenders (*Song shi*, 193.4805–06); a similar decision was reached in 1116 after a request by the Ministry of Works, when the official Zhang Kemao reported that 4,770 soldiers were missing from thirty-four dams under his command (*Song huiyao*, *fangyu*, 15.27).

41. A 1013 edict declared that in addition to the tattoo of their military battalions, convicts should have the name of their place of banishment tattooed on their faces (*Song huiyao*, *xingfa*, 4.7, Dazhongxiangfu 6th year, 2nd month, 1st day).

units once they completed the term of their punishment or simply when the state needed more fighting troops.[42]

The Northern Song's combat troops, the imperial armies, also resorted to conscripting convicts. The Song state incorporated bandits and convicts into the imperial armies from its early days. Imperial battalions composed of bandits included the Dragon Vicious Cavalry Battalion, Returning from Afar (Guiyuan) Infantry Battalion, and the Duangong Recruits (Zhaoshou duangong) Infantry Battalion.[43] According to need, the military transferred convicts from maximum-security labor camps, such as Shamen Island, or from other prefectural battalions into the imperial armies, although the severity of the criminal record sometimes determined the location.[44] As war made way for peace, the type of convicts changed. The Strong and Brave (Zhuangyong) Infantry Battalion originally enlisted bandits who had been put to labor in the capital. In 997 the military reinforced the unit with pirates, and in 1006 it added soldiers who had committed crimes.[45]

The number of convicts in the Song military was significant, even if no exact figures are available. One Southern Song estimate puts the number at a hundred thousand.[46] Convict-soldiers, however, made an impact that went far beyond their relative numbers. There were some regulations that separated convicts from other soldiers, but in reality convicts served side by side with other soldiers, and they performed labor together with other commoners.[47] Placing convicts in the army contributed significantly

42. McKnight, *Law and Order in Sung China,* 348–49.

43. The Dragon Vicious Cavalry Battalion was established in the Taipingxingguo reign period (976–984) using bandits for troops (*Song shi,* 187.4586). The Returning from Afar infantry battalion was established in 986 using surrendered soldiers. In 999 it was reinforced with soldiers who committed various offenses (*Song shi,* 187.4597). The Duangong Recruits Infantry Battalion was founded during the Duangong reign period (988–9) from captured bandits and was reinforced with pirates and captured deserters. In the early Qingli reign period (1041–1049) it was promoted to the rank of an imperial army (*Song shi,* 187.4598).

44. See these cases from 1042 and 1060: *Chang bian*, 135.8.3228, *Song shi,* 194.4829.

45. *Song shi,* 187.4598.

46. Hong Mai, *Rongzhai suibi*, part 2, 5.418, "*Tang wu xiang.*"

47. A 1091 report by the Jinghu Southern Circuit mentioned artisans who were performing corvée in the coin mints together with tattooed convicts assigned to military service, as well as with men who had been requisitioned from the prefectural armies (*Chang bian*, 464.40.11079).

to the decline of soldiers' status and the criminalization of military service.[48] The mixing of soldiers with other marginal groups within the military extended the criminal label to an entire host of other social groups, and tattooing made them physically similar.

The Song state's penal code supported both its social and official hierarchies. It provided protections to men of property or high office and instead targeted the lower levels of its society and bureaucracy. Wealthy people enjoyed protections from a penal code that gave preferential treatment to master over servant and landlord over tenant.[49] High officials came to enjoy protections from the penal code, whereas officials of relatively low positions and clerks convicted of crimes were still brought into the ranks of the armies. There was even a special infantry battalion named Staff Reserves (Yuanliao shengyuanzhi), composed entirely of bureaucrats who had been demoted and exiled for crimes.[50] The benevolence of the state varied according to one's position.

There were voices in court that warned the Song state went too far in its penal policies. In the late twelfth century, an official told of a trend that ran through the entire reign of the Song dynasty: as laws became more complex, the number of crimes increased, and growing numbers of people were assigned to the penal system. In the beginning of the thirteenth century, the court authorized creating two separate tracks: keeping hardened convicts and serial offenders in the regular armies while leaving a path to rehabilitation for men who merely stumbled.[51] The court made this decision in 1204, 244 years after the founding of the Song state and only about thirty years before the outbreak of the Song's great wars with the Mongols.

The assignment of convicts to the military created a direct link between criminal justice, economic production, and imperial defense. The Song state's soldiers became the biggest group of salaried producers and

48. Tsuji, "Sō-hatsu no hairu to hai-gun," 351.

49. A 1090 report by the Ministry of Justice called for harsher punishments for tenants who committed crimes against their landlords and more lenient punishments for landlords who committed crimes against their tenants (*Chang bian*, 445.25.10716–17); see also McKnight, *Law and Order in Sung China*, 491–98.

50. The battalion was established during the Xining reign period (1068–1078) (*Song shi*, 188.4619).

51. *Song shi*, 201.5020–21.

consumers in the Song economy. The military's central position in the Song's economic system meant that its manpower had a huge labor value.[52] The army itself produced and consumed iron in great quantities, and the state closely monitored military production.[53] By the Song's founding in the mid-tenth century, tea had become another commodity of great importance for the Song state, both for reasons of revenue and as a commodity that could be traded for horses for the military.[54] The state's monopolies extended to other areas, such as bronze and wine.[55]

The Song state's relatively frequent use of amnesties bolstered its benevolent image. The Song, like other dynastic regimes, declared imperial amnesties periodically. On such an occasion, the sentences of convicts were reduced, death sentences commuted, and some convicts gained freedom or were allowed to come out of hiding and become respectable commoners once more.[56] The Song dynasty, however, declared amnesties at a higher frequency than any other dynasty.[57] Amnesties were a manifestation of imperial grace that allowed for the rehabilitation of convicts. Whereas local officials took charge of the stick (punishments, taxes, labor), the emperor's mercy extended throughout the empire. Amnesties also eased some of the pressure on the judicial system by clearing the courts and prisons.[58] The lives that were spared were not necessarily granted freedom. Rather, they continued to work for the state in the Song's vast labor system.[59]

52. McKnight, *Law and Order in Sung China*, 333.

53. For growth in the iron industry, see Hartwell, "Revolution in the Chinese Iron."

54. For the tea monopoly, see Smith, *Taxing Heaven's Storehouse.*

55. *Chang bian*, 94.1.2170.

56. In 1077 an amnesty commuted death penalties to exile. This was followed by a gradual reduction in penalties for less severe crimes. Those who committed crimes deserving of exile and below were to have their punishment decreased by one degree. Those who committed a crime deserving of a beating or a lighter punishment were to be released (*Chang bian*, 281.26.6886). Other amnesties were more specific about the cases they covered. An amnesty from 1086, for example, commuted the death sentence of those who had killed in a brawl under mitigating circumstance (*Chang bian*, 387.5.9418).

57. McKnight, *Quality of Mercy*, 73–93.

58. McKnight, *Law and Order in Sung China*, 472–506.

59. In 1018 Zhenzong decided not to execute commoners from Shaozhou who had stolen livestock and sold it across the border. Instead, he had them tattooed on the face, flogged, and taken to a prison citadel (*Chang bian*, 91.3.2103). In 1018 an amnesty reduced death penalties to penal servitude and exile (*Chang bian*, 91.8.2111); in the same year, Zhenzong decreed that (except for the most severe of criminals who conspired to

Many of the Song's amnesties were directed at soldiers who deserted. Desertion, one of the most common crimes committed by soldiers throughout history, took on massive proportions during the Song period. In theory, deserters were executed. Reality was different. The state declared amnesties on a routine basis, leaving deserters a path to return to the fold. Amnesties allowed a certain amount of time for deserters to return. The Song emperors often eased the restrictions and reduced punishments for deserters.[60] In the process, they received valuable manpower, decreased banditry, and bolstered the image of the court at society's lowest levels at the expense of local officials. The laws demanded bloody outcomes, leaving the Song's subjects always dependent on their emperors' whims of mercy.

The Marginal Element: Unsavory Types

Stories of some of the Five Dynasties' dynastic founders paint them as young men who joined the army in dubious circumstances. Liu Zhiyuan (r. 947–948), founder of the Later Han (947–951), nearly joined the army after a bad streak in gambling.[61] The first Later Zhou emperor and his

murder, those who committed premeditated murder, and those who committed robbery deserving of a death sentence), convicts would all be tattooed and sent to prison citadel in their areas in line with the precedent set for robbers (*Chang bian*, 94.13.2165). A 1038 edict commuted death sentences and replaced them with exile, tattooing, and labor (*Chang bian*, 122.2.2872–2873).

60. In 1005 Emperor Zhenzong reduced the punishments for deserters who were captured, and he spared from execution deserters who were captured within the limits of an amnesty (*Chang bian*, 61.20.1359). In 1036 an amnesty promised that deserters would be exempted from tattooing of the face (*Chang bian*, 118.17.2786). In 1072 Emperor Shenzong agreed to a reduction in the penalties for deserters from the imperial armies: those caught within seven days would have the punishment reduced by one degree to tattooing and conscription to a prison citadel in Guangnan. Those who turned themselves in would be flogged a hundred times. This replaced the policy of executing deserters once three days had passed (*Chang bian*, 235.16.5704–05).

61. Reed, "Early Chinese Tattoo," 25–26. Though this Yuan dynasty tale might not be a reliable source for Liu Zhiyuan's life, it still is illustrative of Five Dynasties practices.

top official began as a couple of misbehaving tattooed young men.[62] The Song period continued to see the military as a space suitable for unruly men with violent inclinations. Criminals were only one element in a larger social circle of dubious, unsavory, or dangerous characters that served in the Song military. The Song state made the army into a space for controlling men from a bad social background by turning them into guards, not just of their own prison but of the entire empire.[63]

When the Song went on the war path, the size of the armies increased, and the level of the manpower dropped. In 1040, during the first Song-Xia war, many of the soldiers in a newly formed army were the "weak and cowardly of the marketplace."[64] In 1125, during the first Song-Jin war, the Song state opened up its purse and conscripted whoever it could. In Hebei and Hedong they used money to seduce the loafers and misfits from Shaanxi to come and join the army.[65] In Fujian they conscripted hunters from "raw" non-Han groups, *baojia* militias, local law enforcement (archers), commoners, traveling monks, and soldiers who committed crimes.[66] When the Jurchen troops reached the Song capital Kaifeng, many of the soldiers manning the walls were beggars who had been conscripted at the last minute.[67] The worse the military crisis, the greater the need of the army for manpower; the greater the social scope of conscription, the deeper the draft officers' foray into the spatial and social margins of the Song world.

The military became the suitable space for dubious social types, regardless of a military crisis. The Southern Song scholar Hong Kuo (1117–1184) once voiced his concern regarding the presence of beggars in Hangzhou, the capital of the Southern Song. He argued that they were casing out the richest houses with the intent of robbing them. Hong petitioned

62. Zhang Shunmin, *Huaman lu*, 197. This anecdote was mentioned in the previous chapter. For a discussion of the social background and character of Five Dynasties rulers, see Clark, "Scoundrels, Rogues, and Refugees."

63. Ma Duanlin, *Wenxian tongkao*, 152.14a.419; *Chang bian*, 327.68.7883.

64. *Song shi*, 187.4574.

65. *Song shi*, 193.4808.

66. The Bureau of Military Affairs memorialized about this in the fall of 1126 (*Song shi*, 193.4810).

67. The conscripted beggars rioted and killed a few dozen officers. When they were deployed in battle they collapsed before the Jurchen cavalry, who proceeded to slaughter the beggar-soldiers (*Song shi*, 193.4810).

to take the big and strong among the beggars and tattoo and conscript them into the prefectural army. Even though Hong remarked that the beggars would also gain food and shelter that way, the role of the military as a space for controlling dangerous social types is clear.[68]

Refugees

An agrarian empire with a large population, the Song (just as other agrarian empires) often experienced great disruptions of the agricultural cycle due to natural disasters. Floods, droughts, locusts, earthquakes, and other disasters created large numbers of refugees in a short span of time. Homeless and starving commoners could turn into great bands of bandits and rebels. The Song state used some of the traditional solutions for natural disasters by maintaining the dykes and dams, and by maintaining granaries that provided food in times of crisis and lessened the evil of speculation on food. The Song state also added to those a new measure: the conscription and tattooing of refugees and victims of natural disasters.

Natural disasters were often followed by instances of local unrest such as the stealing of food. Those who stole or robbed in the aftermath of a natural disaster were punished by military law.[69] The government would arrest the ringleaders and punish them with standard Song methods: executions for some, flogging, tattooing, and assignment to labor in the military for others.[70] When great numbers of people might have been involved

68. Hong Kuo, *Panzhou wenji*, 43.534b–535a.

69. Zhang Ming, *Songdai junfa yanjiu*, 5–73.

70. In 1008 Shouzhou prefect Chen Yaozuo reported the capture of more than seventy people who tried to steal food from a granary during a famine. The emperor ordered that instead of execution they should be tattooed on the face and banished to a prison citadel, the leader to a distance of 500 *li* and the others within the prefecture. Afterward, Chen Yaozuo and his clerks gave rice to the hungry in the prefecture, allegedly saving tens of thousands (*Chang bian*, 57.7.1252). In 1025 it was decreed that in the Shaanxi prefectures hit by a natural disaster, those who took up weapons and robbed the granaries but did not hurt their superiors would not be executed but would be tattooed and sent to a prison citadel in a neighboring prefecture (*Chang bian*, 103.2.2378). In 1034 in prefectures and military prefectures in Huainan that suffered a natural disaster, those who became bandits but did not kill and turned themselves in within two months

in criminal activities, focusing on the ringleaders helped the state make a point while not incurring the wrath of the entire population. In other cases, though, the Song state did not stop with the ringleaders, nor did it stop with those who committed a crime. It went as far as tattooing great numbers of refugees and conscripting them into the army. The conscription of refugees did not necessarily result in local assignments. Refugees could be drawn from various parts of the empire or recruited in one place and employed in another.[71] The historical records show that the Song state conscripted refugees on numerous occasions. The numbers of refugees conscripted in a single effort could be in the tens of thousands.[72]

Areas more prone to natural disasters experienced a higher frequency of conscription campaigns. The Northern Song state conducted numerous large conscription campaigns of refugees in the Hebei region. This happened after the Yellow River changed its course in 1048, so that it flowed to the sea north of the Shandong Peninsula rather than south, passing through the Hebei region. This change in the river's course created a

---

would have their record cleared, and then were to be tattooed and registered to a base citadel. The brave fighters among them would be assigned to the imperial troops in the capital (*Chang bian*, 115.2.2688). In 1039, famine victims in eastern Chuan and western Chuan who robbed a granary but did not kill anyone in the process were to be tattooed and sent to a prison citadel 500 *li* away. The leaders and repeat offenders were to be sent to the border area of Chuan and wait for the end of their sentence according to the regular system (*Chang bian*, 124.8.2924–25). In 1071 in the Hebei prefectures hit by a natural disaster, bandits who should have been executed were to have their punishment reduced to tattooing and conscription to a Guangnan prison citadel. The edict stated that once the plentiful days returned, the policies should return to normal (*Chang bian*, 224.5.5440). In 1074 it was decreed that in the areas hit by natural disasters—Hebei, Hedong, Jingdongxi, Jinghu, Huainan, Jiangnan, Fujian, Liangzhe, Yongxing, Qinfeng, and Zizhou—death sentences would be commuted and punishments would be reduced. Only leaders were to be punished according to regular law. The edict was to be expanded to men of all prefectures who turned to banditry out of hunger (*Chang bian*, 251.85.6139).

71. In 1068, starving people from all circuits were recruited to the prefectural armies (*Song shi*, 193.4801); in 1079, starving commoners from Yan, Yun, Qi, Ji, Bin, Di, De, and Bo, all prefectures in the Shandong area, were conscripted to fill the missing quotas of soldiers in the borders of the Kaifeng metropolitan area, as well as in Jingdong and Jingxi (*Song shi*, 193.4802).

72. During the Qingli reign period (1041–1049) over thirty thousand refugees entered Jingdong after a flood in Hebei. The official Fu Bi enlisted them and used them to form an army. Fu Bi had them trained as soldiers, and even though they were paid as a prefectural army, their duties were those of imperial armies (*Song shi*, 189.4642–43).

huge flood, with a million people losing their homes. During the decades that followed, a series of floods ravaged the Hebei region, with especially severe flooding in the years 1056, 1068, 1081, 1099, and 1108. The Hebei circuits—an important strategic region bordering the Khitan Liao Empire—relatively densely populated and an important source of grain, suffered greatly. As a result of the recurrent floods and famines, the number of households shrank significantly between 1048 and 1128. Following big floods, the dead, the injured, and the homeless numbered in the many hundreds of thousands.[73] The environmental disasters played an important role in the militarization of the Hebei border region. During those eighty years of great floods, faced with famine, homelessness, and banditry in the floods' aftermath, the government repeatedly turned to tattooing and conscription in the Hebei region.[74]

Because natural disasters posed a major threat to the material welfare of the Song's subjects and, as a result, to the social and political stability of the empire, social control played an important part in the Song state's disaster-relief system. The Song's scholar-officials were well aware of the role popular rebellions played in the fall of the Tang dynasty.[75] However, the Song's methods of postdisaster conscription reveal that the state's interest went beyond disaster relief as the military incorporated natural disasters into its cycles of conscription. The military wanted strong men, and the size and strength of individual refugees were taken into consideration.[76] Officials were awarded according to the number of soldiers

73. Zhang, "Changing with the Yellow River," 1–3.

74. In 1080 a flood in Hebei left many without food; Emperor Shenzong ordered that they be enlisted (*Song shi,* 193.4802–03). In 1098 a big flood in Hebei brought about the drafting and tattooing of refugees into the imperial armies (*Song shi,* 187.4580). In 1099, after floods in Hebei gave rise to famine and banditry, it was decreed that in the twenty-two prefectures of Hebei circuit, Daming Superior Prefecture, and other areas, they were to conscript and tattoo the refugees and create twenty-seven imperial Vast Might (Guangwei) Cavalry Battalions, each three hundred men strong, and twenty-nine imperial Defending Victory (Baojie) Infantry Battalions, each four hundred men strong. The total number of men recruited here would have been 19,700 (*Chang bian*, 517.25.12300).

75. In 1046 Zhang Fangping explained that big rebellions, such as the Huang Chao Rebellion (874–884), were instigated by negative elements in the countryside in times of bad harvests (*Chang bian*, 159.9.3848–50).

76. In 1023 Emperor Renzong ordered: "In Yi, Li, Zi, and Kui circuits they should recruit commoners into the army. When they reach the allotted number of troops, they

they conscripted and therefore had their own vested interest in conscripting large numbers.[77] Moreover, once the disaster came to an end, the refugees were not necessarily released back to their homes. Instead, many of them spent the rest of their productive lives in the army.[78]

The Song state's provision of help to the homeless and the starving fits well within a Confucian worldview, but it had very practical reasons to do so. In its handling of natural disasters, the Song state allowed nature's cycle of order and chaos to pump new workers into its elaborate system of military barracks and prison citadels. The ever-undermanned units of the Song military received men, the officials in charge of those units were rewarded, and the state deepened its grasp on the populace as its register contained more and more names of commoner men.

Press Gangs, Late Northern Song and Southern Song

By the early twelfth century, the Song military found a new solution to the lack of military manpower: press gangs. This phenomenon became great enough in scale that in 1106 Emperor Huizong issued an order allowing soldiers illegally pressed into service to bypass the regular hierarchy

---

should hand them over, and assign them to [the imperial battalions] of the Emissaries (Fengjie), the Exerting Loyalty of Chuan (Chuan xiaozhong), and the Loyal and Virtuous of Chuan (Chuan zhongjie). Therefore, the strong and brave commoners who lost their livelihood will all have a place to turn to" (*Song shi,* 193.4800).

77. In 1023 "Emperor Renzong sent out an edict ordering to recruit soldiers from Jingdong, Jingxi, Hebei, Hedong, Huainan, and Shaanxi circuits. Those turning the troops over should have them tattooed with the two characters 'battalion' and provide grain rations to their families. When the military officials return, they should be rewarded or punished according to the number of soldiers they recruit" (*Song shi,* 193.4800).

78. Sima Guang argued that rather than merely helping refugees in times of crisis, the state tattooed and conscripted them, forever trapping them in the military register (*Chang bian*, 204.6.4941–43). In 1093, a report by the Bureau of Military Affairs argued that the starving commoners who were conscripted lacked proper training. The report advised training the refugees for half a year before sending them to battle (*Song shi,* 193.4804).

and file a suit for release.[79] Yet the problem persisted, and press gangs remained an important, albeit illegal, track for military service. Press gangs grew in scale and became more frequent during the late years of the Northern Song and throughout the Southern Song.

In the early twelfth century, traveling in some places became more dangerous for lone travelers—especially around the capital, where the demand for military manpower was extremely high. In one instance, when the Bureau of Military Affairs set sudden deadlines for the military to meet manpower quotas, imperial armies went into a frenzy of conscription and tattooing. Soldiers patrolled the roads, seeking men they could press into the army. Traveling monks, for example, were an easy target. When the press gangs spotted a candidate, they gave him a beating and dragged him off to the army. Press gangs used all sorts of ruses to trap entire groups of men. In one case, a group of commoners who gathered in a building suddenly found the door blocked. The tallest and strongest among them were dragged off to the army.[80]

The beginning of the hostilities between the Song state and the Jurchens exacerbated the Song's need for soldiers. In 1126, due to the deteriorating military situation, panic spread in the capital and its vicinity. When no men responded to the call to join the army, military units kidnapped villagers and travelers.[81] Song armies, shaken by defeat, employed a cruel practice that the Mongols later became infamous for: using prisoners as human shields. The men pressed into the Song military had to walk in the front line of the army so that they could absorb the brunt of the enemy's offensive.[82]

The government's own policies of setting manpower quotas and attaching monetary value to soldiers contributed to making press gangs such an intractable problem. Within the military, the victims of press gangs could find this crime hard to report because the perpetrators were often the soldiers' new superiors. Neighbors of the kidnapped men could also make a profit by taking over their lands. Some officials called for

79. Those who had already been tattooed were to have their tattoos corrected (*Song shi*, 193.4805).

80. *Song shi*, 193.4806–07.

81. *Song shi*, 193.4809.

82. *Song shi*, 193.4818; Allsen, *Rise of the Mongolian Empire*, 356.

reform that would clarify the laws governing conscription and replace coercion with monetary gifts, but the incentive for kidnapping soldiers (their monetary worth) remained in place.[83]

After the capital city of Kaifeng fell to the Jurchens in 1127, the war raged on for fifteen more years. In the beginning of the war, large parts of the Song military collapsed. New forms of local armies rose, based on local leadership.[84] New regular armies gradually came into being under the command of strong generals. These armies likely contained a meaningful component of volunteers. At the same time, within the regular armies, press gangs became standard practice despite the court's protests. In 1134, in response to reports of press gangs, the court once more issued an edict forbidding the practice and ordering release and compensation for press victims.[85] The prohibitions did not stop the phenomenon. One official even suggested a compromise, alternating voluntary enlistment with press gangs.[86] Such was the extent to which press gangs had become an intrinsic part of the Song military system.

In the first Song-Jin war of the early twelfth century, generals paid little heed to the warnings of the court and continued to press men into their armies. Some of these generals were characterized as criminals, like one general who was said to be a weak and opportunistic man and who set his troops loose, capturing and tattooing commoners, pillaging, killing, and injuring in great numbers.[87] Far more powerful military figures also engaged in this practice. The famous general Zhang Jun, one of the four great generals who saved the Song state from destruction, pressed ten thousand surrendered soldiers into his army and had them tattooed accordingly rather than release them as the emperor ordered.[88] Even the Palace Command (Dianqian si) pressed commoners

83. This according to an official's warning in 1122 (*Song shi,* 193.4807).

84. See Huang Kuan-chong's study of local military forces during the Southern Song, *Nansong difang wuli.*

85. *Yaolu*, 77.1466, 79.1491.

86. *Yaolu*, 85.1622.

87. *Yaolu*, 87.1657.

88. This according to the account by Zhou Bi in 1137. Zhang Jun had them tattooed and assigned as loyalist soldiers (*yibing*). Zhang Jun's actions demonstrate why the titles of "loyalist armies" or "volunteer armies" should be treated carefully (*Yaolu*, 114.2125). More on this army in chapter 7.

into the army, leading the emperor to call for restraint in conscription once again.[89]

The conclusion of the first Song-Jin war in 1142 did not put an end to press gangs. In the years following the Shaoxing peace treaty, reports of press gangs came in from all over the empire, and Emperor Gaozong issued a number of edicts forbidding the practice, to no avail.[90] In 1156 press gangs were common enough that when the emperor allowed the Palace Command to conscript commoners, he had to add a caveat that forbade pressing men by force.[91] In the same year, the Bureau of Military Affairs once again reported units pressing commoners to cover manpower shortages, and once again the emperor forbade the practice.[92] The following year, reports of press gangs continued.[93]

Despite the court's displeasure with press gangs, the Song state designed its military system with almost an obsession for great numbers of men. In 1158, while the court was still issuing decrees forbidding press gangs, the Bureau of Military Affairs rewarded the official Shen Diao, who recruited soldiers for the Three Commands (*san ya*), the administrative units that managed the imperial armies, and took in more soldiers than the quota demanded. The official Yang Chun warned that such a promotion would provide an incentive for officials to forcefully tattoo and conscript people out of a desire for promotion.[94]

89. According to the report by Liao Gang in 1139 (*Yaolu*, 129.2432). The Palace Command was one of the main administrative headquarters of the imperial armies.

90. In 1145 Liu Bao was demoted for appropriating private forests and for tattooing and conscripting people against their will (*Yaolu*, 154.2907); In 1146 Vice Censor-in-Chief He Ruo reported that commoners everywhere were kidnapped, tattooed, and conscripted. The emperor again forbade the practice (*Yaolu*, 155.2933). In 1150, the *jinshi* Deng Jie reported that commoners everywhere were tattooed and conscripted against their will (*Yaolu*, 161.3052).That same year the emperor forbade the practice again, and in 1151 he ordered that armies should not go about recruiting and instead should report manpower shortages to the Bureau of Military Affairs (*Yaolu*, 161.3052, 162.3070).

91. *Yaolu*, 172.3296.

92. *Yaolu*, 173.3307.

93. In 1157 the official Wang Gui, an opponent of press gangs, accused Feng Shixing of tattooing and conscripting commoners during his tenure as an official in Wanzhou, causing a great disturbance to the people and almost bringing them to the point of rebellion (*Yaolu*, 178.3418).

94. *Yaolu*, 180.3466.

Because conscription involved payment to the new conscripts, it offered opportunities for pilfering and skimming for the soldiers who carried it out. In 1158, when the battalions of the Palace Command fell short of the manpower quota by a few thousand men, they went about conscripting. The soldiers in charge of conscription kept the joining bonus for themselves, and instead they went to the marketplace and kidnapped woodcutters and peddlers, leading to a state of panic in the area. The emperor merely repeated his admonishment to the military.[95] However, in 1160 reports of Three Commands press gangs continued to come in.[96]

Officials voiced concerns regarding press gangs and offered solutions. In 1160 one official suggested giving money to local officials instead of the regular armies. He explained that local officials could use the money to recruit from among refugees in their areas, and the refugees would also be more willing to serve.[97] In 1162 another official suggested a closer supervision on recruitment, as well as publicly tattooing the recruits with their new military unit, proving that they volunteered in earnest.[98] Such a suggestion reveals a great level of distrust among the general population toward the military's conscription tactics.

During the last decade of Song rule (1270s), the military crisis with the Mongols reached a climax, and press gangs reached new levels of ingenuity. Military units disguised conscription ships as merchant ships or transport ships, and the unfortunate men who went on board to trade or travel found themselves shipped to the army. Military units even used soldiers' wives as bait, having them seduce travelers by the side of the road. The situation deteriorated to the degree that commoners preferred to travel in large groups when going to places such as the marketplace, where press gangs tended to be more active.[99]

Cycles of stability and chaos featured different methods of conscription. In times of military crisis, press gangs became more prominent. When the state emerged from a military crisis and went back to a "law-and-order"

95. *Yaolu*, 179.3421.
96. *Yaolu*, 184.3550, 187.3632, 187.3635.
97. *Yaolu*, 179.3421.
98. *Yaolu*, 199.3923.
99. *Song shi*, 193.4822.

mode, the press gang was replaced with the convict's march. The biggest crime press gangs committed was not pressing men into service but, rather, doing so without the central government's approval while ignoring the state's criteria for assessing military manpower. Both the extralegal press gang and the extremely legal assignment of convicts to military service demonstrate the strong coercive aspect of the military manpower system, a system designed for taking in men against their will, keeping them, and using them.

Conclusion

At the time of the founding of the Song, the status of soldiers was already in decline. The Song state contributed to this trend by channeling the most marginal sectors of Song society into the military: convicts, refugees, the poor, loafers and thugs, non-Han groups, and the families of soldiers who came to be trapped in military service over generations.[100] As a result, the tattooed soldiers of the Song took on the labels of savage, criminal, indolent, and poor. By the end of the tenth century, the tattooed soldier became the symbol of the Middle Period's new underclass.

The state's motivations for conscripting marginal populations extended beyond the role of a benevolent and strict father who feeds his children but does not spare the rod of justice. The state made use of soldiers for labor and war, but it also used the military register to supervise and control groups at the social and spatial margins of the Song world: the border zones, the alleys and marketplaces, and the military camps. These pockets of unruly populations were rationalized and standardized, made to look like soldiers, and made to work for the state.

When the state assigned to military service the worst that society had to offer, it had already determined what it expected of such an army. It was not that military victories were not desired; they were. Yet the social

100. Moyar reviews trends in military history and argues that "some of the most sophisticated recent histories have shown how military power has facilitated the extension of a government's influence into its outer territorial reaches or the fringes of another country" (Moyer, "The Current State of Military History," 234–35). In the Song case, the state used the military to penetrate its social margins as well.

order of the Song world was founded on the marginality of the groups that served in the army. At least to a certain degree, they were designed to fail. Despite all this, the fact that there were still valor, sacrifice, and camaraderie in the ranks of the Song military stands as a testament to the foolhardiness and greatness of these forgotten men.

CHAPTER 4

The Human Disassembly Line

The Cycle of Service in the Song Military

In the military camps of the Song empire stood a wooden stick. Candidates for military service presented themselves before it: a hungry peasant who came to the army seeking food; the convict sentenced to military service; the son of a soldier, ordered to present himself for conscription; the weathered soldier whose days in the army were numbered.[1] The stick was well known among the Song's subjects who saw officials and clerks carry this stick with them when they went to the villages to register men for the army.[2] This stick was not meant for flogging. Rather, it was used to measure a man's height. Following this examination, a lifetime of military service awaited the new soldiers, years spent in the shadow of the wooden stick. In the Song's penal-military complex, soldiers' bodies determined their assignment, their terms of service, and their career trajectory, from recruitment and until discharge, from youth to old age, from the prison citadels through the regular armies and to the ranks of beggars in the big cities.

1. *Song shi*, 193.4799.
2. *Chang bian*, 136.15.3255–56.

The Birth of the Wooden Standard

Zhao Kuangyin, the founder of the Song dynasty, had a clear vision in his mind for the kind of soldiers he needed: tall men with "legs as thick as a pipa, a body as stout as an axletree."[3] His standards were rooted in his early life and military experience. He and his brother Zhao Kuangyi (who replaced him as emperor) came from a military family, part of the group of professional military men that became prominent in the latter half of the Tang dynasty and during the Five Dynasties period that followed it (eighth century to tenth century).[4] Zhao Kuangyin spent much of his life in the military camp and on the battlefield, and he became a capable and seasoned general.[5] The standards he set for soldiers reflected the needs of the time: a strong mobile army that was suitable for territorial expansion. In this, the Song founders resembled other dynastic founders: military leaders who led a military enterprise.[6]

During the early Song, to satisfy the emperor's standards, local military units from around the empire sent new recruits as well as their own best soldiers up the military hierarchy and into the political and military heart of the empire, the capital Kaifeng. The top new recruits, already having passed one inspection, arrived in the capital, where the Office of Military Commanders (Juntousi) inspected them. The emperor then personally inspected the recruits and the promoted soldiers, after which the military assigned the recruits to their units. The top military commands of the Northern Song (the Palace Command, the Metropolitan Cavalry Command, and the Metropolitan Infantry Command) received the strongest and biggest men. At the same time, weaker and older soldiers were demoted into units lower down the military ladder or into the reserves.[7]

3. Zhang Shunmin, *Huaman lu*, 208.

4. For more on the military history of the Tang dynasty, see David Graff, *Medieval Chinese Warfare.*

5. *Song shi*, 1.1.

6. Lorge explains that during the tenth century, military men dominated the political realm (Lorge, *The Reunification of China*, 1–4; Lorge, *War, Politics and Society in Early Modern China*, 17–38).

7. *Song shi*, 194.4825; Ma Duanlin, *Wenxian tongkao*, 613.152.7b–8a.416. More about the reserves later in this chapter.

Because the selection of candidates for the army was carried out across the empire, a unified standard had to be found for translating the emperor's vision into a clear code for conscription that could be used at the local level. At first, the capital sent big and strong soldiers around the empire to serve as a model for recruitment. The military later replaced these men with a wooden stick used to measure the height of candidates for military service, and top candidates were sent for inspection in the capital.[8] The use of a standardized stick for measuring height transformed the emperor's vision into objectively measurable criteria that could be replicated. The Wooden Standard was born.

Following the measuring of height, the candidate went through a series of tests that determined his suitability for military service. The recruiters tested his riding skills, including jumping, and his eyesight by asking the candidate to identify how many fingers the tester help up. (Later, instead of raising fingers, the testers used a hand-shaped wooden board daubed with white mud.) Following the tests, the candidate's face was tattooed with the two characters "battalion" (*zhihui*), and he was escorted to his new assignment.[9] The new soldier was also given his payment: clothes, straw sandals, and strings of cash. In some cases, the authorities gave the payment to the soldier's family. This process was referred to as "conscripting, tattooing, and giving tips." A thirteenth-century gazetteer describes this as the standard practice since the founding of the Song.[10]

The assessments of soldiers or candidates for military service relied on observable and measurable criteria. The measuring of height could be considered perhaps the most objective and simple test to conduct, but age and strength, like height, could also be expressed in numbers. The military measured a soldier's strength by having him stretch a bow or load a crossbow, with the result equivalent to a certain weight. Eyesight and riding skills were harder to assess, but they could still be measured with standardized and relatively simple tests.[11] The establishment of de-

8. *Song shi,* 187.4571. Also see *Chang bian,* 6.1.156; *Song shi* 193.4799–4800.

9. The logic here is that soldiers first received a generic "battalion" tattoo, and later when they arrived at their battalion, the name and number of the battalion would be added to create the full name of the unit.

10. *Song shi,* 193.4780; Shi Su, *Jiatai kuaiji zhi,* 4.1b–2a.6775.

11. The *Song shi* has a description of the selection process for promoting officers to fill vacant positions. The test demonstrates the procedure for measuring strength:

tailed procedures for testing whose results could be expressed in standardized numerical terms gave the higher administrative levels more power to intervene in and supervise military manpower administration at the lowest levels. This impersonal system reduced individuals to measurable parts, but the creation of an impersonal, technical language for assessing humans also made the officials in charge of the inspection more expendable and replaceable. Officials too found themselves becoming cogs in a machine.

Evolution of the Wooden Standard

The Wooden Standard did not remain fixed. With time, the Song armies grew. When the demand for soldiers outstripped the supply, the military abandoned the original criteria set by the founding emperor, and the original standard declined. Around fifty years after the founding of the Song, the Wooden Standard became a ranking system, composed of five ranks ranging from 5 feet 5 inches to 5 feet 8 inches. Soldiers were assigned to their units according to their height.[12] At this point, the Wooden Standard no longer reflected the founding emperor's vision of a strong soldier. It became the reflection of negotiations and debates by a faceless bureaucracy. Instead of the ideal of a big and strong soldier rose the idea that soldiers could be represented and managed through numerical formulas.

Beyond deciding the fate of new soldiers, the military used the Wooden Standard to manage transfers of soldiers between the different units. When the state ordered officials to send the "big and brave" among their men for promotion to a better unit, it did not allow the officials to

---

"Whenever the various camps would go about transferring and reinforcing, the authorities inspected jumping, and getting on and off horses; they would hold fingers twenty feet away [from the candidate] and have one of his eyes covered so they could test his eyesight in the right and left [eyes], each one five times. In [the test of] military arts, [the recruits had] to stretch the bow with the force of 5 *dou* [approx. 60 lb.], load the crossbow with the force of one *shi* and five *dou* [approx. 180 lb.], and have some training with spear and sword." (*Song shi*, 196.4878).

12. This took place in the Dazhongxiangfu reign period (1008–1017) (*Song shi*, 193.4800).

choose those soldiers themselves.[13] Instead, the state provided them with numeric criteria for size and strength. This left the officials in charge of the troops with diminished authority, no longer allowing them to choose soldiers but merely to measure soldiers and transfer accordingly.[14] The use of a standardized stick, at least in theory, robbed officials of their discretion in deciding which men to keep, and it provided the centralized state with a tool for measuring officials' performance.

The Wooden Standard became a prism through which the state and its representatives could see and measure the subjects of the Song empire—and especially the residents of the northern border zones, where conscription campaigns to local militias and to the regular armies took place on a regular basis. The scholar-official Ouyang Xiu recounts:

> Whenever [the people] go through a bad year, then the local clerks go and measure the people's size and test the strong ones among them and send them to the imperial armies. Slightly smaller [men] who do not reach the standard and slightly weaker [men] are assigned to the prefectural armies. The clerks who recruit many men get a reward. When the people are in dire straits, they fight over joining [the army]. Therefore, following a bad harvest, only the old and the infirm stay in the fields. Officials say that those who do not become soldiers will become bandits.[15]

Because the Wooden Standard was a physical object, one way out of military service was "cheating the standard." The official Li Zhaoliang (993–1063) argued that sixty thousand soldiers succeeded in gaining discharge by bending down their necks and knees to appear shorter during the height exam.[16] The Wooden Standard became a vehicle for expressing the state's standards and demands, but it also represented the future

13. In 1002 in Huan (in modern Gansu), Qing (in modern Gansu), and other (probably northwestern) prefectures, out of over six thousand men of the prefectural cavalry and infantry armies, they selected four and a half thousand men and assigned them for defensive duty in the forts to replace the imperial armies. The criteria for selection were "big and brave" (*Song shi*, 194.4825).

14. In 1047 prefectural soldiers who measured above five feet seven inches were to be tested for transfer to the imperial armies (*Song shi*, 193.4800).

15. *Chang bian*, 136.15.3255–56.

16. Sima Guang, *Sushui jiwen*, 5.63.

that awaited the candidates for recruit or transfer. By manipulating their own bodies to achieve discharge, soldiers attempted to gain a measure of control over their own future.[17]

With time, the original height standard declined. This led the official Tang Jie (1010–1069) to protest, in 1062, that because of the decline of the standard, the Song's imperial troops became too small and weak to carry out their duties. Emperor Renzong approved Tang's suggestion to reestablish the original height standard within some of the imperial battalions.[18] Yet just a few years earlier, during Emperor Renzong's Huangyou reign period (1049–1054), the Song armies reached their peak number, around 1.4 million soldiers.[19] Such a sizable number makes it doubtful that the armies were fully staffed using the original height standard.

The military used the Wooden Standard as part of a larger formula where height perhaps occupied the central position, but it also included the assessments of a man's strength, age, health, skills, social background, and merit. A high score in one field could compensate for a low score on a different one. A young age, for example, could compensate for short stature.[20] The government continually changed the formula and adapted it to the specific needs and circumstances of a battalion or a region.

When the Song acquired great numbers of men, the assignment formula allowed their orderly absorption into the military. During the reform period that began in the 1070s, with the goal of building an alternative to the Song's professional military, the state organized the commoners into local militias and mutual-surveillance units known as

17. More on soldiers' strategies of resistance in chapter 6.

18. *Song shi*, 193.4801.

19. Cheng Minsheng, *Songdai renkou wenti kaocha*, 99.

20. In 1082 the court approved a request by the Hedong military commissioner's office to tattoo and recruit the sons and brothers of the imperial Linzhou Flying Cavalry and Fuzhou Revered Afar Battalions. They allowed those battalions to conscript men slightly shorter than the standard: men twenty-five years and younger who were shorter than the standard by up to two inches, or men twenty years and younger who were shorter than the standard by up to three inches (*Chang bian*, 325.43.7823). In 1086, following a request by the Bureau of Military Affairs, a decree allowed the imperial armies to conscript and tattoo men under the age of twenty-five if they were shorter than the standard by one inch (*Chang bian*, 381.18.9278).

baojia. Following the death of Emperor Shenzong in 1085, the new antireform government rolled back the sweeping reforms, including the *baojia* system. Once the state disbanded the militias, it found itself in a situation much like the aftermath of a great war. In both cases, the Song government had at its disposal large numbers of men from a military organization that had just been disbanded (disbanded militias, surrendered enemy troops), and it absorbed them into its regular armies.

The criteria for assignment of *baojia* militia men to the regular armies show a degree of flexibility. Within a certain height category, the younger the militia member, the higher his assignment could be.[21] Military skills, such as archery, could be calculated together with age when making an assignment. When the state suddenly increased the size of the military (this could happen due to both high demand and high supply), the standards for age and skill could be lowered or set aside completely.[22] Such adaptations reveal that the basic criteria for measuring men were perhaps too rigid. A more nuanced formula was necessary to assure that the end result would be a soldier capable of executing his duties.

The decline of the standard attests to the difficulty of gaining both quality and quantity. Each unit had to meet certain manpower quotas, but the military also had standards for the physical condition of each soldier. The Song military used a wide variety of ad hoc solutions. In one case, an edict allowed a cavalry battalion to take in soldiers beyond its assigned quota if the recruits were tall-enough men who brought their

21. "A decree already ordered that the *baojia* of the Hebei circuit would be conscripted to fill the missing quotas of the imperial armies in the capital. As for men under twenty who join the Spirit Dragon Guard [Shenlongwei] or men under twenty-five who join the Middle [imperial] armies, if they fall short [of the required height] by one inch, it should be allowed to conscript and tattoo them" (*Chang bian*, 373.36.9042).

22. In 1086 a decree allowed for the conscription and tattooing in the Kaifeng Superior Prefecture of archers of the first rank of the *baojia* combat-ready units who were willing to join the army. A joining bonus was to be given to them and their families. Archers of the middle rank under the age of twenty-six could be conscripted and tattooed if they were shorter than the height requirement by no more than an inch. Men under the age of twenty-five could be conscripted without regard to skill or height (*Chang bian*, 383.12.9326).

own horses.[23] At other times, the court allowed for some units to conscript regardless of the physical standard.[24]

The military manpower policies of the late Northern Song government contributed to its military decline. In 1105 Emperor Huizong decreed that the prefectural armies should enlist and tattoo strong young men while disregarding the Wooden Standard.[25] Unsurprisingly, about fifteen years later, in 1120, the same Emperor Huizong discovered to his great dismay that the ranks of the prefectural armies were filled with cowardly, young, and small men who fell short of the physical standards and could not even carry out their duties.[26] Yet beyond the poor decisions attributed to Emperor Huizong, the military decline of the late Northern Song also resulted from a deep contradiction within the Song's military manpower policies: the drive to fill the military quotas clashed with the attempt to standardize the quality of the soldiers and with the declining status of military service.

The Wooden Standard was an object with many layers of meaning to it. It began as a physical manifestation of the will of the Song's first emperor. It gradually became the opposite, a tool representative of the faceless administration of the army's manpower. For officials it represented a standard they needed to adhere to and would be used for the assessment of their performance. For the commoners and soldiers, the Wooden Standard stood as a symbol of the state's requirements on their bodies and lives, a fine companion to the whip, the club, and the tattoo needle.

23. In 1072 a decree ordered that even though the cavalry quota of the Hebei West circuit was already full, men who satisfied the size requirement and agreed to bring a horse and join the army should be especially recruited and tattooed, await an opening, and be dispatched accordingly (*Chang bian*, 235.3.5696).

24. A decree from 1082 allowed corvée-managing prefectural armies of all circuits to temporarily conscript and tattoo with no consideration of the soldiers' size (*Chang bian*, 324.44.7807).

25. *Song shi*, 189.4645.

26. *Song shi*, 193.4806.

Demotions and Promotions

The official Tian Kuang gave voice to some of his reservations concerning the Song military of the mid-eleventh century. The military had close to a million soldiers, he explained in 1043, a threefold increase since the previous reign. Tian worried about the quality of those troops, the tall among them not strong enough to fight, the smaller ones not even fit for labor.[27] Tian's complaint touched on two major concerns for Song officials: the military grew too big and costly, but it also showed itself incapable of fighting effectively. The Song military had an elaborate system of transfer and discharge, aimed at addressing these two main concerns: maintaining the quality of the military and cutting down on military expenses.[28]

The Wooden Standard and the assessment system it stood for offered a possible solution to the problems of redundant and ineffective military manpower. Soldiers were measured and assessed not only at their point of entry into the military but throughout their military career. For the rank and file of the Song military, promotions and demotions meant a change of assignment, not a change of individual rank. Assessment could lead to a transfer to a different battalion farther up or down the military hierarchy, and such a transfer meant a great change in pay, duties, living conditions, and location. Soldiers who grew too old or sick to carry out their duties could be demoted to a reserve unit, where they received half pay and carried out less-demanding tasks. Soldiers unable to do any kind of work were discharged.[29] Because size mattered in the Song military,

27. *Song shi*, 194.4829.

28. Koiwai, "Sōdai no rōei ni tsuite," 85.

29. In 1034 a decree ordered that when choosing from among the imperial Instructed Steed Battalion and transferring to the imperial Saluting Sages (Gongsheng) Battalion, they should demote the old and sick into the reserves and discharge to commoner status the men who could not carry out labor (*Song shi*, 194.4828). In 1049 the state reviewed the imperial armies and prefectural armies of Hebei, Hedong, Shaanxi, Jingdong, and Jingxi, and it put the old and sick on half salary. The state also provided the hard cases with food and sent them back to their villages. Convicts assigned to military service in remote areas who had earned merit in war were granted a transfer to the reserves (*Song shi*, 194.4829).

the height hierarchy scaled to the military hierarchy. The higher-ranked units had higher height and strength standards. Soldiers' bodies could also be ranked within units, implying certain privileges and duties varied within units as well.[30]

At the same time, each tier served as a recruitment pool for the tiers above it.[31] The military was supposed to carry out inspections of troops for promotions routinely every three years.[32] Promotions took place when a large number of men became available, as could happen at the end of a large labor project.[33] When an imperial unit's manpower fell below its designated quota, it compensated by promoting able-bodied men from the prefectural army.[34] In some cases, entire battalions could be promoted. In response to manpower shortages during the military crisis with the Liao, the military promoted entire prefectural battalions to imperial army status.[35] During the Southern Song, the state restructured the military system, but the same principle remained. The military continued to reinforce its fighting units with soldiers from weaker or nonfighting units.[36]

30. In 1057 the state recalibrated the Wooden Standard in a wide range of units, from the imperial Four Superior Armies to the prefectural Martial Reverence (Wusu) and Exerting Loyalty (Zhongjing) Battalions. The soldiers in those units were measured and ranked according to height groups. Some battalions were ordered to recruit men according to skill alone; in other battalions, such as the Storehouses Battalion, the height standard was not to be employed at all (*Song shi*,193.4800–01).

31. In 1027 emissaries measured strong prefectural soldiers, granting promotion to the Superior Armies to those among them who met the Wooden Standard (*Song shi*, 194.4827).

32. In 1064 an edict ordered holding inspections for transfer in base citadels and prison citadels once every three years (*Song shi*, 194.4829–30).

33. In 1027, at the end of a labor project on a river, the state conscripted the young and strong among the laborers who showed willingness to join the imperial armies (*Chang bian*, 105.11.2452).

34. In 1080 the court approved the promotion of able-bodied soldiers who committed light offenses from prison citadels into the imperial army units (*Song shi*, 194.4831).

35. *Song shi*, 187.4572–3; *Chang bian*, 52.21.1133–4.

36. Li Xinchuan, *Jianyan yilai xinian yaolu*, 190.3688; Cai Kan, *Dingzhai ji*, 1.22b–23a.577; *Song shi*, 42.826.

SKILLS

In addition to a periodic assessment of the soldiers' bodies, the military considered other aspects of a soldier's record, including his military skills. One imperial decree made deteriorating skills the equivalent of being overweight or having medical issues in the limbs.[37] The military examined the soldiers' martial skills, allowing those who failed some time to improve and retake the tests. Imperial soldiers who failed to maintain their military skills could find themselves demoted to the prefectural armies.[38] Units within the regular armies were also arranged in a hierarchy, and demotions could take place between different sub-tiers of the same army. Imperial cavalry soldiers who failed to pass their tests within a given time were demoted to the imperial infantry; underperforming imperial infantry soldiers were demoted to the prefectural armies.[39]

Besides martial skills, the state also put a high premium on artisanal skills. Men who possessed those could be assigned to artisanal work regardless of their physical condition.[40] A considerable part of the Song

37. In 1083 cavalry soldiers under the age of fifty who had grown lax in the military arts and in training, were overweight, or had diseases in their limbs and fingers were to be taught the military arts of infantry, have their tattoos altered, and demoted to infantry (*Chang bian*, 341.13.8206).

38. When the Bureau of Military Affairs went about training the cavalry in Hebei in 1068, it faced criticism that the soldiers of Heshuo (an area north of the Yellow River) were soldiers by name only. The bureau authorized a suggestion to train the armies and demote to the prefectural armies the soldiers who failed to reach the desired level after a period of training (*Song shi*, 195.4855).

39. In 1078 Emperor Shenzong ordered that this be the practice in Jingdong, Jingxi, and the Kaifeng area (*Chang bian*, 294.58.7173); in 1085 a similar edict issued to the Palace Cavalry and Infantry Armies office stated: "All the soldiers recently chosen for the imperial armies should first be instructed in the camp for a hundred days. Those who do not reach the second rank should be given another two months. If they fail again after the time limit passed, they should be instructed in the training arena for another two months. After waiting for the time limit, the cavalry who fail the test should be transferred to the infantry. The infantry should be transferred to the prefectural armies" (*Chang bian*, 354.42.8477).

40. In 1091 the court approved a plan by the Bureau of Military Affairs regarding inspections of the armies: "[Soldiers of] the imperial armies in the capital who do not meet the original size requirement should have their tattoos altered and be assigned to the next lower military level. Those not strong enough to wear armor will be assigned to the prefectural armies. Those who have artisanal skills will be tested, have their tattoos

military manpower specialized in production, and, in some situations, production could be rated as more important than warfare. Military spaces became more and more commercialized, and many officials rented out soldiers' labor as a source of revenue.[41] The sale of soldiers' labor to offset officials' expenses resulted from the creation of a huge state-run market for men's bodies and labor, a worthy competitor to the Song empire's markets of female bodies that boomed in response to a rising demand for concubines and courtesans. Yet in contrast to the mostly private trade in female bodies (excluding government courtesans and other forms of female servant/slave labor for the state), the market of male bodies remained mostly state-run. Both markets served the same social order, giving powerful, elite men access to the male and female bodies of the lower classes.

MOTIVATION

Demotions and promotions served as a tool for increasing the motivation of troops to train and behave properly. Motivation occupied a higher position in the imperial battalions, where soldiers had to be strong, willing to carry out drilling and exercising, and potentially also go to war. In 1048 Zhang Fangping called for the demotion of soldiers from the imperial armies to the prefectural armies. The transferred soldiers should have been "the weak and frail, who shrink from drilling, and willing to transfer to the prefectural army."[42] The motivation of soldiers continued to serve as part of the transfer criteria well into the Southern Song. An early thirteenth-century gazetteer explains: "The imperial armies dismissed men for laziness and demoted them to the prefectural armies. They call this 'to fall into the prefecturals.'"[43]

The fact that consent served as a criterion speaks much to the unwillingness of the soldiers to transfer to the prefectural armies. Soldiers had good reasons to oppose a demotion into the prefecturals: it dramatically

altered, and be assigned to work as artisans without receiving a joining bonus. Those who cannot fight or do labor, whether in the prefectural or imperial armies, should be given their papers and discharged" (*Chang bian*, 467.30.11154).

41. Wang Yunchang, *Songdai jundui jingying wenti yanjiu*, 38–52.

42. *Chang bian*, 163.6.3924.

43. Shi Su, *Jiatai kuaiji zhi*, 4.1b.6775.

altered the soldier's life, decreased his income, worsened his duties, and lowered his status. It tore him away from his unit and could also lead to his transfer to a different location, cutting him off completely from most of his support network. Pushing the soldiers too far could prove to be a dangerous move. When the government determined military manpower policies, it had to continually gauge the mood within the army and avoid provoking the soldiers too much, perhaps for fear of a violent response. As ambitious as the Song military manpower policies were, the power of the state had its limits.

MERIT

Soldiers who proved themselves in battle or in other extraordinary circumstances could climb up the ranks. When a deserter attacked an official with a drawn blade, the imperial soldier Li Qian shielded the official with his own body and sustained sixteen stab wounds in the process. In 1018 the court awarded him the rank of an officer.[44] Li Qian achieved the rare accomplishment of a promotion from the rank and file, but cases like Li Qian's serve as the exception rather than the rule.

It was usually during times of war and crisis that fighting men had their chance to shine and climb through the ranks. The Song dynasty's most famous generals, Di Qing and Yue Fei, began their careers as low-ranking fighting men.[45] Di Qing and Yue Fei succeeded in climbing to the highest positions of power based on their skills as fighters, leaders, and strategists. Their success took place within the army, but it launched them out of the "soldier" class and into the "official" class. Di Qing's sons did not have to climb through the ranks like their father but instead began their careers as officials.

Prominent scholar-officials recognized the value of promoting men from lower down the military ladder. Fan Zhongyan argued for the need to recognize men of talent within the army.[46] Ouyang Xiu called for the expansion of the group of candidates for generalships to include men of a lower standing, and to rely on talent in appointments of generals.[47]

44. *Chang bian*, 95.14.2199.
45. More on the obstacles Di Qing and Yue Fei faced in their careers in chapter 6.
46. Zhao Ruyu, *Song mingchen zouyi*, 64.9b–10a.784–85.
47. *Chang bian*, 136.15.3255–6.

Some soldiers won promotions, but the state usually reserved promotions in rank to those who had already been officials. The state rewarded the soldiers of the rank and file (*shibing*) and their officers (*junyuan*) with gifts of money or other material rewards.[48] Merit in war could also provide a convict-soldier serving in a remote area with a transfer to the reserves and a lighter workload.[49] Relatively few men broke through the status of "soldier" to attain an official position, and their achievements tended to be exceptional. As for the soldiers who climbed through the ranks to become generals, at that point they found themselves surrounded by imperial retainers and affines who tended to monopolize most of the top military positions.[50] The world of the top military leadership was both martial and elite, and most of the men who occupied the top ranks of the Song military had close ties to the Imperial Palace.

CRIMINAL RECORD

Because the state assigned convicts to military service, the Song's penal-military complex also served as a correctional space. This contributed to the perception that the design of the military system contained a moral rehabilitative component.[51] Some of the laws for transfer support this notion. Height and strength could gain a man a promotion to the imperial armies, but a record of banditry and a penal facial tattoo could mean a more dangerous assignment to an army in the border area.[52] In other cases, promotions were given to soldiers with no serious criminal record.[53]

48. Zhao Dongmei, *Wenwu zhi jian*, 201–2.

49. *Song shi*, 194.4829.

50. See Chen Feng's study of the social composition of Northern Song generals: *Beisong wujiang qunti*.

51. Brian McKnight argues that the Song penal system had a strong rehabilitative aspect. McKnight, *Law and Order in Sung China*, 67–116.

52. In 1060 soldiers assigned to the imperial armies were selected from among Jingdong, Jingxi, Shaanxi, Hebei, and Hedong base citadels, prison citadels, river dredging units, transport units, and postal stations. The soldiers had to be at least five feet three inches tall and strong enough to wear armor. Those among them who had once been bandits and had facial tattoos were to be assigned to the Returning from Afar and Strong and Brave Battalions in the external prefectures (*Song shi*, 194.4829).

53. In 1080 young and big soldiers, strong enough to wear armor, who served in prison citadels for committing less serious crimes, were to be selected for the imperial armies (*Song shi*, 194.4831).

More serious offenders could be denied promotion and a joining bonus, whereas convicts who had demonstrated good behavior were moved to the regular promotion track.[54]

It was still often the case, however, that the Song military considered a criminal record in relation to an individual's height and strength criteria. The size and strength of a soldier could make up for light offenses, and promotions of convicts were reserved for the big and strong. Convicts who were weak and small could be blocked from assignment to relatively high-paying labor units.[55] Life in the Song military offered certain advantages to strong and healthy men, including convicts, but they denied them to law-abiding individuals judged as small, weak, or simply lazy.

A criminal record could block a soldier's promotion, but usefulness to the state or to one's superiors could also deny a soldier a promotion. In one case, in the year 1091, severe criminals and deserters were blocked from promotions together with artisans and soldiers in charge of transport.[56] Yet these other groups were simply those who had been too useful within their original battalions. In the Song's penal-military complex, it appears that usefulness often trumped rehabilitation as a guiding principle for manpower management.

54. An imperial decision from 1045 limited promotions to convicts who did not have tattooed faces (usually meaning a lighter crime) and denied them a joining bonus. The decision further stipulated that if they did not commit more crimes as soldiers, they should be transferred to the regular promotion track (*Song huiyao, xingfa*, 4.21, Qingli, 5th year, 11th month, 12th day).

55. The official Qian Weiji complained that weak convicts gained transfers to the Yongning base-citadel battalion, where young and strong soldiers earned a relatively high salary. He asked that they stop assigning weak convicts to this unit. In 1017 Emperor Zhenzong ordered that weak convicts who committed severe crimes should be assigned to a prison citadel instead of a base citadel (*Song huiyao, xingfa*, 4.8, Tianxi 1st year, 8th month, 5th day).

56. "From the prefectural armies [they] will choose [soldiers] forty years old or younger and assign them according to their size. [They] should still select and order [them] at the end of the year. Excluded from selection should be those of them who have committed a crime punishable by exile or who have been tattooed as deserters, or certain artisans who have been attached to an official of the degree of squad leader or above, or those who have been attached to civil or military officials or to non-Han areas in the north or east to supply transport services, and those who have committed crimes of witchcraft, or bandits" (*Chang bian*, 467.30.11154).

The military realm served as the space for disciplining criminals, but soldiers also served as the disciplining arm of the state. Scattered around the empire, local military forces (*tubing*) oversaw law enforcement in their areas. Yet the watchmen of the state were also being watched by it. In 1083 the court approved an official's request to weed out old and weak men from among the local soldiers, alter their tattoos, and send them to the prefectural armies.[57] The local soldiers, in charge of local law enforcement, were paid less than prefectural soldiers, many of whom were convicts.[58] They could still be transferred to the prefectural armies where convicts did hard labor. In the penal-military complex, a fine line separated those who enforced the law from those sentenced to labor. In this case, the line was simply that of performance.

Discharge

At the very end of the process of transfer and demotion came the moment of discharge. Soldiers worked for salaries, and once their military service came to an end, so did the state's financial support. Discharge of weak and underperforming soldiers had clear military and fiscal advantages for the state. It allowed the Song military to keep up its strength by replacing old soldiers with young soldiers, and it saved money. Yet the military served as both the hand that punished and restrained the wicked and the hand that fed the hungry. What was to become of soldiers and their families following discharge? What was to become of the world once soldiers were released back into it?

57. Acting Jingxi circuit fiscal commission assistant Sun Lan (1043–1101) complained of the bad state of the conscription system: "Examining the intent behind the law that soldiers [serve as] the patrolling inspectors of all circuits, it was that local people know the conditions among the people of the area and the roads coming in and out, and it would be easy for them to catch bandits. I recently inspected the various circuits and saw many old and weak [men] among the soldiers recruited. [Men] capable of wearing armor and catching bandits barely number three or four out of ten, and they are not necessarily local people" (*Chang bian*, 340.30.8183).

58. Zhao Dongmei, *Wen wu zhi jian*, 234.

The official Fan Zhongyan voiced his reservations regarding the thorny issue of discharge. In 1033 Fan explained that once a soldier reached the age of seventy, after decades of service, he could no longer fit into the world outside. The home that he knew no longer existed, his relatives had already died, and there were no people he could rely on for assistance.[59] Fan recognized that military service transformed an individual's life to such a degree that he could no longer simply go back to wherever it was he had come from. At least in this case, the emperor ordered that some of the imperial soldiers in the capital be transferred to serve closer to their home areas, but the problem of discharge continued to grow.

Discharge became a particularly severe problem in the aftermath of a great war. A few years after voicing his concerns regarding discharge, Fan Zhongyan, together with the official Han Qi, took charge of the Song's war with the Xi Xia state. The war caused a huge increase in the size of the Song military. In 1044 Fan and Han called for discharge, arguing that the conscription campaign had acquired weak men, added to the fiscal burden of the state, and damaged the region's agriculture.[60] Discharging mass numbers of soldiers in a short span of time, though, came with its own host of dangers. In the aftermath of the military campaigns of the Kaixi reign period (1205–1208), discharged soldiers who had nowhere to return to scattered and became bandits.[61]

The negative social background of soldiers, coupled with concerns that soldiers had become "institutionalized," no longer able to fend for themselves outside of the army, led officials to believe discharged soldiers would turn to crime. High rates of desertion and a high frequency of am-

59. As a solution, Fan Zhongyan suggested that they choose men unfit for duty from among the Palace Army, cavalry, and other imperial units and transfer them to imperial army units that would be set up in their home areas. That way, they would have family networks to fall back on in their old age. According to the account, the emperor gladly adopted Fan's plan (*Chang bian*, 112.11.2624–25).

60. This concerned the great numbers of local militias who had been transferred to the imperial Defending Victory Battalions during the first Song-Xia war (*Chang bian*, 149.1.3599, 150.2.3623).

61. *Song shi*, 192.4791–92. This refers to local soldiers from the Huai and Xiang (in modern Hubei) regions. In 1206 the Song launched an invasion of the Jin empire known as the Kaixi Northern Expedition (Kaixi beifa). The invasion failed, and the Song found itself forced to sign another peace treaty with the Jin in 1208.

nesties for deserters also meant that soldiers moved back and forth across the lines, from convicts to soldiers to bandits and back to soldiers again.[62] Officials voiced concerns that discharged soldiers, scattered back in their home villages but with no source of income, would also turn to banditry.[63] The fact that this group possessed military skills only added to officials' concerns.[64] The official He Tan (1004–1072), worried about the exhausted and unmotivated troops in Shaanxi, called for their discharge in 1049, but he still argued that discharged soldiers should be kept under supervision with the option of summoning them back to service should the need arise.[65] The social, professional, and physical transformation of men who became soldiers could not be simply reversed through discharge.

Discharge reversed the understanding and treatment of soldiers' bodies. Within the military, strong bodies were sought for and rewarded, whereas discharged soldiers with strong bodies were a cause for concern. In 1105 Hong Zhongfu argued that the soldiers who were not attending to their duties properly would not resume their position as farmers peacefully. The strong ones would become bandits, and the weak ones would become

62. Sima Guang wrote of the imperial Dragon Vicious Battalion that had conscripted bandits into its ranks in the late tenth century. Some of the soldiers of that battalion later scattered and became bandits. These brave and fierce bandits pillaged and terrorized the people of Shu (*Sushui jiwen*, 7.84). For more on amnesties during the Song, see McKnight. *The Quality of Mercy*. 73–93.

63. In 1050 the official Fu Qiu had commented on an imperial edict ordering the release of soldiers in Shaanxi over the age of fifty and short of the height requirements by as much as four inches. Fu Qiu expressed his fear that suddenly depriving soldiers of their income would lead them to form gangs of bandits in their home villages. That year, the Shaanxi armies released thirty-five thousand men from their ranks. Despite early concerns, the release succeeded, leading to a decrease in border expenses and allowing the people of Shaanxi some respite. However, the soldiers who failed to gain a discharge became extremely resentful (*Sushui jiwen*, 4.47–48).

64. In the attempt to cut expenses, the government discharged sixty thousand soldiers back into regular commoner status, and it cut by half the material support for twenty thousand others. Shi Changyan and Li Zhaoliang warned that those who had relied on government support for a long time would not be willing to turn to agriculture. They explained that since all the soldiers received training in using bows and swords, they would all surely become bandits upon being suddenly scattered in the villages (Sima Guang, *Sushui jiwen*, 5.63; Wei Tai, *Dongxuan bilu*, 178–79).

65. *Chang bian*, 167.10.4020.

a burden on the court again.[66] There was no need to discharge disciplined and strong soldiers, but both weak soldiers and unruly strong soldiers would make for poor commoners. Therefore, when was it a fitting time for a soldier to leave the army?

The Song state addressed the problem of discharge by creating institutions that softened the transition out of the army and into commoner life. The reserve units, first of those institutions, served as a stepping-stone toward discharge. The use of reserves goes back to the early days of the Song state, when the Song military had in its ranks soldiers from foreign countries: *Bohai,* Khitans, and Japanese. Because they could not be sent home following discharge, they were assigned to reserve units attached to their own units.[67] The Song military continued to use reserves as a solution for soldiers who resisted discharge or had no means of supporting themselves outside the army. Soldiers in the reserves received lower pay and therefore were a lesser burden on the state.[68]

Starting in the late Northern Song, the Song state began to build institutions for assisting veterans.[69] Some of the state's efforts were aimed specifically at veterans and their families, such as assisting them in becoming farmers and making a living in agriculture.[70] Veterans were also an important component of urban poverty, and the state assisted discharged soldiers as part of a bigger group of urban poor.[71]

Military tattoos complicated the problem of discharge. Once the army discharged a soldier, it provided him with his discharge papers, but his skin still marked him as a soldier. This meant that the discharge papers were all that shielded the veteran from a charge of desertion. One account displays the almost mystic power of the discharge papers in an

66. *Song shi,* 193.4805.

67. This took place in 1012 (*Song shi,* 189.4640–42).

68. In 1008, when discharging soldiers from the imperial armies, they had men with no homes to return to as assigned to reserves in various prefectures (*Song shi,* 187.4573).

69. For more on veterans and welfare institutions, see Koiwai, *Sōdai heiseishi no kenkyū*; Saitō, *Sōdai boheisei no kenkyū.*

70. In 1157 the emperor approved a plan to help soldiers become farmers after discharge to protect their families from poverty (*Song huiyao, shihuo,* 1.39, *nongtian zulu er,* Shaoxing 27th year, 5th month, 11th day).

71. Wu Zimu (1161–1237) described the various welfare mechanism in Hangzhou as targeting both commoners and soldiers (Wu Zimu, *Mengliang lu,* 18.21b–23b.153–54).

anecdote about a deserter who gained his discharge papers at the ripe old age of 108.[72] Soldiers who had been properly discharged were in a vulnerable position, and the loss of their papers could lead to their return to the military.[73]

One anecdote about discharge captures the acrimonious relationship between soldiers and their civil superiors in an account of one unlucky soldier and one ruthless official. Li Fugui (*jinshi* 1041), an official reputed to be talented in military matters, was appointed prefect of Guanghua Military Prefecture, where he ran into a problem with a military veteran:

> A discharged soldier asked to pay a higher rent on a government land and drive the current tenant-farmer off the land. Li Fugui said, "You are a discharged soldier. How could you work government fields?" The soldier replied: "My strength has not declined." Fugui replied, "You were discharged on account of your declining strength, but since your strength has not declined, you should rejoin the army." He called the tattooer to tattoo his original military position. Everybody praised him for it.[74]

The story of Li Fugui and the soldier illustrates some of the contradictions in the Song military demotion and discharge policies. If a soldier were strong, he would not be discharged. If a discharged soldier were weak, he would not be able to fend for himself and would thereby become a social liability. Although it labeled the release of the old and the sick as a "return to farming" (*guinong*), the state had no intention of letting go of manpower that could still wage war or do labor. The discharge of useful soldiers posed a clear and present danger to the social order, but it also wasted the labor of men who still had some productive value left over.

One cannot help but detect another far more sinister element in the anecdote about Li Fugui and the discharged soldier. Debates about social stability and the need to allow for the discharge of soldiers so that they could "return to farming" touched on crucial issues in the Song state's military administration: state finances and military readiness. However,

72. *Yijian zhi, zhiding, Zhao Sanweng*, 8.1027–28.
73. *Yijian zhi, yizhi, Jiang jiaoshou*, 2.195–97.
74. Shao Bowen, *Shaoshi wenjian lu*, 18.203.

the official faced the individual soldier from another, more personal perspective. For him the discharge of a physically able soldier, beyond the loss of potential labor, meant something else. Letting the soldier go would allow him "to get away with it" or to "have it easy." The soldier with his own case based on precedent and justice faced an official with the great power accorded him by both his official position and social status. The soldier could argue the details all he wanted. The official kept the soldier in the army because he could. That is how power works and is maintained. That is why one cannot understand systems, organizations, laws, and policies without contemplating the social attitudes and tensions within human society.

Old Soldiers

Once a soldier reached a certain age, somewhere between fifty and seventy, or once he could no longer execute his duties due to disease or injury, his time in the army came to an end, and he became a veteran, referred to in Song sources as an "old soldier."[75] His years of service left visible scars on his body: the tattoos on his face telling his service history, the signs of wear and old age, and the scars of discipline, training, warfare, and labor. Perhaps he had some cash, a farewell gift from the military. At this point, he had to reinvent himself and find a way to make a living in the world that sprawled outside of the army.

Soldiers' families served as the most important institution for the support of discharged soldiers. Sons of soldiers often joined the military, thereby keeping a military salary within the household.[76] Hence the predicament of Xiong Ming, an old military veteran, whose son Xiong Er refused to take care of him.[77] Old soldiers with no families could end up like Du De, who was buried by the side of the road, his corpse exposed by the rain.[78]

75. For a study of old soldiers during the Song period, see Koiwai, "Sōdai no rōei ni tsuite."

76. As in the case of a son who took his dead father's place as a boat captain in the military in 1161 (*Yijian zhi, yizhi*, juan 3, *zhouren wang gui*, 203).

77. *Yijian zhi, zhijia, xiong'er buxiao*, 3.732–33.

78. Peng Cheng, *Moke huixi*, 8.372.

Veterans, like soldiers, tended to concentrate in urban areas, where they often made a living as servants. An old soldier testifies in a Southern Song anecdote about his position in a rich family's house: "I am a discharged soldier, and I often do labor in his house."[79] Old soldiers served as doormen.[80] They watched over houses.[81] They served as night watchmen.[82] They did various chores around the house, such as serving food.[83] Others labored outside, like the old soldier Liu Wen who worked in construction in Wuxi.[84]

Song texts tell us that some old soldiers labored in the houses of officials.[85] The texts do not always state clearly whether these were discharged soldiers or simply soldiers who were advanced in years. This ambiguity results, at least in part, from the drift of soldiers toward servitude. In such an environment, officials who appropriated soldiers as their personal servants became a common phenomenon.[86] The social status of soldiers, their social trajectory, the relationships between them and officials—all of those extended beyond the military. This ambiguity of the term "old soldier" reflects the many meanings and functions of "soldier": warrior, laborer, servant, convict.

Song anecdotes often depict old soldiers as incompetent servants. Wang Anshi fired an old soldier who started a fire.[87] When Su Shi's concubine sent an old soldier to the market, he got her a snake, confusing it for seafood. As a result, she grew sick and died a few days later.[88] Su Shi

79. Wang Zhi, *Mo ji*, 2.29–31.

80. *Yijian zhi, jiazhi, shengpingfang guanshe*, 16.142.

81. In Suzhou, following the first Song-Jin war, a brave old soldier from Shaanxi worked as a house guard (*Yijian zhi, yizhi, canglang ting*, 17.331). In an anecdote taking place in 1150, an old soldier guarded a storehouse (*Yijian zhi, zhigeng, Maoshan daoren*, 8.1197).

82. *Yijian zhi, yizhi, Luzhou laobing*, 4.216.

83. The wife of an official fell ill, and old soldiers brought her meat (*Yijian zhi, zhiyi, Zhao Buyi qi*, 5.833).

84. *Yijian zhi, bingzhi, bingjia xiaohong*, 19.522–23.

85. The official Huang Minzhan had an old soldier as a servant (*Yijian zhi, zhiwu, Huang Huizhou*, 2.1067–8), as did the official Wang Zhongheng (*Yijian zhi, zhigeng, Wushan xinzhai*, 4.1165–6).

86. The Southern Song legal compendium *Qingyuan tiaofa shilei* contains regulations for the number of servants allowed for an official according to his position.

87. Chen Shidao, *Houshan tancong*, 3.46 (101).

88. Zhu Yu, *Pingzhou ketan*, 2.137–38 (84).

grew angry at an old soldier who poured water into his ink stone.[89] A soldier cook purchased frogs instead of chickens because he did not know frogs were also called "paddy chickens."[90]

Not only incompetent, old soldiers were also morally questionable. An old soldier selling Sima Guang's horse did not understand why he needed to let potential buyers know that the horse had lung disease.[91] In one instance an old soldier smuggled items into the palace at the request of a palace lady.[92] Cai Tao (active 11th century–12th century) wrote of a smart parrot that caught an old soldier stealing rice.[93]

The old age of discharged soldiers who worked as servants did not protect them from the wrath of their masters. One old soldier in Hangzhou, over seventy years old, angered a retired official, who took him to the local court and had him flogged despite the pleas of his family members. He died as a result.[94] Another soldier in the service of the Zizhou[1] (in modern Sichuan) prefect was flogged after his master's son in-law falsely accused him of stealing a silver utensil. Unable to pay for the missing item, the soldier hung himself.[95] Received wisdom tells us people in imperial China venerated old age, but, at least regarding the Song period, such veneration only existed so far as it supported the Song's social hierarchy.

The struggle of discharged soldiers for survival took place within a growing economy and an urbanizing society, and some of them built small businesses in the Song empire's cities and towns. One soldier, upon reaching the appropriate age, was discharged from the Palace Maintenance Office in the Southern Song capital of Hangzhou. The discharged soldier married late in life a Madam Tang,[1] who used to serve the palace women. He supported himself by selling fruit.[96] The discharged soldier Zhao Xiaoge made a name for himself as a healer.[97] A tattooed soldier

89. Ye Shaoweng, *Sichao wenjian lu*, 3.118–19.
90. Ye Shaoweng, *Sichao wenjian lu*, 3.98–99.
91. Zhu Yu, *Pingzhou ketan*, 3.154 (136).
92. Wen Ying, *Xiangshan yelu*, *xulu*, 1.68–69.
93. Cai Tao, *Tie wei shan congtan*, 6.111–12.
94. *Yijian zhi*, *dingzhi*, *Chen yuanyu*, 6.584.
95. *Yijian zhi*, *zhiding*, *Feng Zizhou xu*, 7.1024–25.
96. *Yijian zhi*, *yizhi*, *mi zhangjia*, 11.275–76.
97. *Yijian zhi*, *yizhi*, *zhao xiaoge*, 18.339–40.

from Jinling (in modern Jiangsu area) set up a fortune-telling shop.[98] At least some discharged soldiers could avail themselves of the new possibilities created by economic growth.

Soldiers who had been injured in the course of their service sometimes became beggars in the towns. The soldier Zhan Zhiyong from Xinzhou (in modern Jiangxi) suffered an injury at the age of twenty-two while practicing riding and archery. His injury did not fully heal, and he had to use crutches to walk. As a result, the army discharged him, and he became a beggar.[99] The beggar Li Quan received his discharge from the army after having suffered injuries to his eyes and legs during the Shaoxing war of 1161. He became a blind beggar in the marketplace, stumbling along on a pair of crutches.[100]

Hangzhou, the capital of the Southern Song, became home to many discharged soldiers turned beggars. Its beauty and its size, with a population of over a million, made Hangzhou into a magnificent city. Yet as many as a quarter of a million of its residents were beggars, many of them discharged soldiers.[101] The official Zhou Bida (1126–1204) reported that in Hangzhou and its vicinity were sick discharged soldiers and their families, all in a state of great poverty. They held their military documents while begging in the marketplace.[102] This was part of the penal-military complex's unique contribution to Song urbanization: supplying the towns with servants, but also with beggars and thugs.

Old soldiers were characterized by an old, dirty, and sickly appearance. Du De, the old postal-station soldier, was called "pock-marked bearded Du" (*ma hu Du*).[103] The discharged soldier Zhao Xiaoge had a short and stocky figure, as well as cloudy eyes, probably some form of cataracts.[104] A deity impersonating as a soldier wore tattered clothes made of green fabric, old hemp shoes, and carrying two bamboo baskets. It barged into a religious gathering and asked for food and wine, very likely

98. *Yijian zhi, zhigeng, xinling qingzu*, 4.1164–65.
99. *Yijian zhi, zaibu, Zhu daoren zhi jiaoluan*, 1796.
100. *Yijian zhi, dingzhi, Lijia yuxian dan*, 2.551–52.
101. Takahashi, "Nansō Rin'an no kasō-min to toshi gyōsei," 123–24.
102. Zhou Bida, *Wenzhong ji*, 140.11a-b.548.
103. Peng Cheng, *Moke huixi*, 8.372.
104. *Yijian zhi, yizhi, zhao xiaoge*, 18.339–40.

behaving in the fashion of other beggar-veterans.[105] Soldiers became so closely associated with a miserable appearance that when the scholar-official Wang Anshi, infamous for his bad hygiene, was mourning his mother, a man delivering a letter saw his emaciated face and mistook him for an old soldier.[106]

The *biji Sichao wenjian lu* contains a more detailed description of a discharged soldier:

> I do not know where he came from, nor do I know his surname or given name. He spoke with a Hangzhou accent, and on the side of his forehead he had a tattooed character. He must have been a discharged soldier. His head was a mess and his face was dirty. Sometimes he would not eat for days. None knew where he stayed. Bao Daocheng once shared a quilt with him and said his body burned hot as if he had a fever. Daocheng became sweaty and moved to cover himself with a separate quilt. Whenever [San Wangde] arrived, he would spit and curse aggressively, even holding broken roof tiles and scolding the children. I once called him over, but he would only stare straight at me without speaking. When Guangzong (r. 1189–1194) started attending the imperial temple, he held the third place in line for the succession. Nobody knew yet who would be heir-apparent to Emperor Xiaozong (r. 1162–1189). One day, he intercepted the prince's (later Emperor Guangzong) carriage on the road, and the guards dragged him away. The prince asked him for his name, but he merely kept on saying "*san wang de, san wang de*" (literally: "the third prince attains"). The prince understood the omen and let him go. When the prince ascended the throne, he ordered the man to appear before him, but [the man] did not bow and simply departed. When people would run into him on the road and give him money, he would say no word to thank them.[107]

The story of the discharged soldier resembles many other descriptions of old soldiers: nameless, homeless, of an unknown birthplace, facial tattoos, dirty, with a touch of the supernatural. His features made him into an object of curiosity but also of ridicule and contempt. If soldiers posed a threat to society while they still had strength in them, these old dregs

105. *Yijian zhi, zhijia, Yuan'an laobing*, 6.755–56.
106. Wang Zhi, *Moji*, 3.48.
107. Ye Shaoweng, *Sichao wenjian lu*, 2.53–54.

of people personified the success of the Song military machine in neutralizing that threat. A man such as the discharged soldier in the story was the end result of the Song's manpower policies.

Conclusion

Social standing, moral character, skill, merit, and criminal record were all factors that were taken into consideration while assigning and transferring men within the army. However, physical features, much more than any moral factor, were the most important factors for assessment of manpower in the army. Criminals could rise through this system, whereas men of clean record could be demoted for declining health, laziness, lack of military skill, or simply for aging. The supreme reign of physical criteria clearly demonstrates that despite the close links between the military and the penal system, justice and morality were secondary considerations in the handling of military manpower.

The Wooden Standard at first represented the will of the first emperor, but it became an end unto itself, a representation of an impersonal system governed by numbers. At the same time, this system, took away much of the military officials' discretion regarding the management of military manpower. Assignments and transfers were determined by empire-wide policies, and the state set clear criteria for assessing their performance. The standardizing of soldiers' bodies through the measuring of size and strength and the tattooing of faces and hands turned them, at least in principle, into interchangeable parts that could be shuffled around. The attempt to eliminate the personal relationships between officials and soldiers reduced the soldiers to their functional value to the unit. This was no moralistic hierarchy but rather a machine.

The repeated complaints of Song officials attest to the Song state's failure to strictly enforce the size requirements for military manpower. Part of this resulted from contradictions within Song military policies and goals. The state rewarded soldiers according to their bodies, but it rewarded officials according to the numbers of soldiers they had. From the perspective of military officials, quantity often made more sense than quality. The conflict between the military's various functions (imperial security, social order, labor, production) further complicated the task of administering military manpower. The technological limitations of premodern record keeping placed another constraint on the system. High rates of desertion and fraud in the management of the Song's military manpower added to the gargantuan task of monitoring and recording the physical condition of hundreds of thousands of men.[108]

Facial military tattoos provided the state with a tool for overcoming the technological constraints on their ambitions. Facial tattoos turned the soldier's face into a service dossier. Whatever details the military register contained about a soldier, many of them could be verified by examining his body and the marking on his face. In addition, the facial tattoos stayed on the skin regardless of a soldier's motivation to serve.

The absorption of lower-class males into the military and their subsequent journey through the military system reveal the gendered aspects of class in Song society. The Song period saw the rise of trade in women, especially as concubines and courtesans, and for some of those women, the trade opened opportunities for climbing the social ladder.[109] Whereas females of the lower classes had new opportunities of moving socially upward and spatially toward the commercial and economic centers as concubines and courtesans, lower-class males were pushed downward and outward, into the ranks of the army, stationed on the empire's borders. While female bodies became merchandise available to the rich, male bodies were measured, tattooed, and monetized as an expense item in the state's defense budget.

The Song system of military manpower assessment and management created a human disassembly line. Men went into the army at their prime. As old age and disease took their toll, the soldiers moved farther down the military hierarchy, from cavalry to infantry, from combat duty to labor, from full pay to reserves. Eventually, they were discharged and went through their final transition, from soldier to "old soldier," that group of degraded men who often sustained themselves by becoming servants at the houses of the wealthy. Those old tattooed men who scratched a living in the margins of society were the final product of life in the penal-military complex.

108. More about this in chapter 6.
109. Bossler, *Courtesans, Concubines, and the Cult of Female Fidelity*, 411.

CHAPTER 5

The Military Family

An anecdote in the *Dongxuan bilu* tells of a fortuitous encounter between long-lost siblings in the beginning of the eleventh century. When the empress Yang first entered the imperial palace as a palace woman, she left behind her younger brother, Yang Jingzong (b. 983). Later, she became an empress, but her brother did not fare as well and became a convict doing hard labor. One day, as she was riding her carriage on the way to the palace, she ran into her brother as he labored on the side of the road. After years of separation, she could barely recognize him, as his face was covered with penal tattoos. Their story has a happy ending. Following the reunion with his sister, Yang Jingzong received an official position and ultimately moved into the mansion he helped build as a soldier-convict.[1]

In this story of a family torn apart along gender lines, the brother and sister headed toward two different worlds: the brother entered the Song dynasty's penal-military complex, whereas the sister was sold in the growing market for women. For lower-class females, being sold as concubines and courtesans could mean a climb up the social ladder, into the households and social circles of elite men.[2] It was this transition that

1. Wei Tai, *Dongxuan bilu*, 2.22.

2. For more on courtesans of the Song period, see Bossler, "Shifting Identities"; Bossler, *Courtesans, Concubines, and the Cult of Female Fidelity*; Ebrey, "Women, Money, and Class."

rendered them interesting and meaningful to elite men, and, as a result, visible to us. Lower-class men often appear in the sources on the other side of the social spectrum, as soldiers and convicts in the Song state's penal-military complex, a vast system in charge of warfare, law enforcement, punishment, and labor. However, most lower-class women did not climb from lower-class society through the sex trade.[3] Many men did not serve in the military but had male relatives who did. Soldiers and their close male and female relatives, here referred to as military families, all lived in the social world of the penal-military complex. The members of military families of the Song period formed a sizable social group numbering in the millions, and their story forms an integral part of Song social history.[4]

Studies of the Song military (and many other military histories) tend to reflect the implicit or explicit assumption that the military was a masculine space, a realm of men. Modern-day scholars study the thought and actions of male generals, battles fought by males, military institutions staffed by male officials and officers, and, more and more often, the soldiers of the rank and file. Yet if one thinks of the military as a social-cultural-economic space, then the picture becomes more complex. These men had families: wives, parents, siblings, and children. These members of military families were tied into the military realm by law, by custom, by necessity, and by brute force. The story of the penal-military complex is also their story.

Middle Period sources tell us relatively little about soldiers, and even less about their families. Even so, the primary sources still allow for some general observations about the wives, parents, siblings, and children of soldiers: the composition of military families, their patterns of service, their urban setting, the functions of military families, the connections between the military and the rising sex trade, and the different responses of the state to the military family. This chapter draws much of its evidence from the *Yijian zhi*, a collection of strange tales by Hong Mai

3. The sex trade included the selling of women as concubines for the purpose of producing offspring.

4. For more on the families of Song generals, see Yang, "The Emperor's Generals"; Fang Cheng-hua, "Military Families and the Southern Song Court"; Ho Koon-wan, *Beisong wujiang yanjiu*; Chen Feng, *Songdai junzheng yanjiu*, 72–90.

(1123–1202). Hong Mai's text offers some of the most detailed descriptions of the characters who inhabited the military camps. Like many scholars of the Song period, Hong Mai's interests lay in the supernatural: ghosts and spirit possessions, miracles and demons, but Hong Mai's record of the supernatural is no mere tale of fiction. His stories open an important window into the spiritual and religious world of the Song period. In his quest for the bizarre and unique, Hong Mai collected stories about people from all walks of life. In the process, he reveals colorful details about ordinary people's lives during the twelfth century: where they lived, how they lived, whom they loved, their joys and sorrows. Although one may question the veracity of any specific story of spirit possession or love affair with the dead, the larger social picture reflected in Hong Mai's stories is true.[5]

Service over Generations

The families of soldiers served as an important recruitment pool for Song military manpower, and the conscription of soldiers' family members came to be one of the defining traits of the Song military. When the *Yuan shi*, the official political history of the Song dynasty written under the Mongols, recounts the Mongol conquest of the Song, it describes the Song military as having two unique traits: the soldiers had tattooed arms, and when a soldier died, a brother or a son served in his place.[6] When a soldier's wife gave birth to a female, her daughter joined the social world of the penal-military complex. It is reasonable to assume that a significant portion of the women in the military camps came from military families.

The Song military routinely conscripted the family members of soldiers throughout the Song period, but no formal contract commanded

5. Hymes explains that Hong Mai tried to separate facts from falsehoods in his accounts. Hong Mai's approach adds credence to the details of everyday life in the *Yijian zhi* (Hymes, "Truth, Falsity, and Pretense"). As for the veracity of supernatural encounters, that falls beyond the scope of this study.

6. Song Lian, *Yuan shi*, 13.269, 98.2519.

the state to carry it out. Rather, the military conscripted soldiers' relatives according to need, whenever it encountered manpower shortages. In some cases, the state promoted the conscription of family members, even allowing for the recruitment of men below the physical standard.[7] When the state needed more artisans due to high rates of desertion by artisan-soldiers, it conscripted men from the families of artisan-soldiers to supplement its skilled manpower.[8] The availability of this manpower made it very tempting for officials to turn to this group to fill up the ranks and maintain the funding of a fully staffed unit despite the fact that the soldiers' relatives often proved incapable of meeting their military duties.[9]

Though it did not become universal law, the channeling of soldiers' sons and brothers into the military became the norm. The scholar-official Wang Shipeng (1112–1171) wrote that "since young age soldiers are raised to be tattooed [soldiers] and gain their livelihood from the military."[10] Lü Zuqian (1137–1181) described the imperial and prefectural armies of the Southern Song as "entirely composed of sons and brothers."[11] Although most of the military families who appear in the sources had a single member serving as a soldier on active duty, the Southern Song scholar Yuan Xingzong reported that because of the state's haste to gain soldiers, a single household could end up with two or three soldiers.[12]

In theory, the law did not require the sons of military families to follow in their fathers' footsteps. Military life offered some opportunities for soldiers to accumulate some wealth: salaries, bonuses, and rewards from the state, but also other less official channels of income, such as the sale of labor or artisanal skills, as well as bribery and extortion. Military

7. *Chang bian*, 325.43.7823.

8. In two cases, from 1160 and 1165, when facing high rates of desertion, the state called for conscripting "sons and brothers of artisans who are capable of artisanal work" and "sons and brothers of soldier artisans from the East and West Palace Workshops" (*Song huiyao, zhiguan*, 16.13, Gaozong Shaoxing 30th year, 8th month, 12th day; *zhiguan*, 16.17, Xiaozong Qiandao 1st year, 8th month, 17th day).

9. In 1113 an imperial edict commented on understaffed military units that, wishing to maintain the funding of a fully staffed unit, conscripted and tattooed "the camp's young sons and brothers [of the soldiers] and other people unable to carry out labor" (*Song huiyao, fangyu*, 15.25, Huizong Zhenghe 3rd year, 1st month, 23rd day).

10. Wang Shipeng, *Mei xi ji*, 3.14a.95.

11. Anon., *Qunshu huiyuan jiejiang wang*, 13.18a.

12. Yuan Xingzong, *Jiu hua ji*, 1158.7.20b–21b.52–53.

families who had greater resources could use them to change the family's trajectory. Men like Qi Yanguang left the military profession and embarked on new paths. Qi Yanguang, a son of a fort soldier's family, had a basic reading ability and some legal knowledge. He left the profession that had been in his family for at least a couple of generations and turned to agriculture and trade.[13] His resources, however, were not available to all members of military families.

Military families could find chances for upward social mobility across generations within the military profession. Hong Mai tells of a soldier who rose through the ranks to become a commander due to merit in wars with the Xia. The soldier's two sons, Wu Jie and Wu Lin, became famous Southern Song generals.[14] Two of the Song's most famous generals, Di Qing (1008–1057) and Yue Fei (1103–1142), rose to the highest positions of power from a lower-class background. Their sons served in the military as well, but as military officials, no longer part of the rank and file.[15]

Most soldiers did not rise through the ranks, and military families tended to have male members serve as common soldiers across several generations.[16] The soldier's salary became the foundation for the family's survival strategy. In one of Hong Mai's stories, taking place in 1161, Wang Gui[1], a boat captain, died from sickness. His wife begged a eunuch to allow their son to take his place so that they could stay on the boat and the family could survive. The eunuch arranged for it, and the son was tattooed as a soldier the next day.[17] The Song state kept millions of people of the Song empire fed and clothed through the payment of military salaries, and it also granted them a measure of security by promising that the same path existed for their relatives as well.[18] The growing awareness that

13. *Yijian zhi*, *zhiding*, *juan* 9, *qi yanguang nü*, 1035.

14. *Yijian zhi*, *sanjian*, *xin juan*, part 4, *yi mingwen mingshu*, 1410.

15. For more on Yue Fei, see Deng Guangming's classic biography of Yue Fei, *Yue Fei zhuan*. For more recent studies on Yue Fei, see Wang Zengyu, *Jinzhong baoguo*; Wang Zengyu, *Yue Fei he nansong qianqi zhengzhi yu junshi yanjiu*; Gong Yanming, *Yue Fei pingzhuan*. More on Di Qing and Yue Fei in chapter 7.

16. The family of the soldier Gao Jun from the Formidables (Xiongwei) Battalion had served in the military for generations (*Yijian zhi*, *jiazhi*, *juan* 12, *gao jun ru ming*, 104–6).

17. *Yijian zhi*, *yizhi*, *juan* 3, *zhouren wang gui*, 203.

18. A local gazetteer explains that stopping the conscription of family members to save money would leave the sons and brothers of soldiers without a source of livelihood (Shi Su, *Jiatai kuaiji zhi*, vol. 7, 4.1b–2a.6775).

the military provided welfare for millions of people very likely had an important impact on the promulgation of regulations that made it easier for military families to stay on the payroll. Such regulations included lowering the physical criteria for conscription of soldiers' relatives and allowing older soldiers still capable of work to stay in the army past the age of discharge.[19] Even if not forced to do so by law, the need for an income pressured a male child to join the military for his family's sake. Their circumstances dictated this. For the same reason, the state shaped its policies to facilitate the entry of soldiers' relatives into the army and to allow for the presence of old soldiers within the military.

No clear line separated voluntary participation from coercion in the enlistment of soldiers' family members. The Song scholar-official Yang Wanli (1127–1206) describes the three main sources for Song military manpower: enlistment (*zhaomu*), relatives of soldiers (*zidi*), and criminals (*daozei*).[20] He separates the voluntary track for joining the army from that of sons and brothers of soldiers, implying there was a compulsory element in the conscription of soldiers' relatives. The behavior of the Song state and its agents reveals that it may be impossible to draw the line between voluntary service and coerced service among military families. The state gave orders to do so when it needed more soldiers. Families had a stake in having their sons join the army because they often had no other alternative for subsistence. Sometimes, local military officials decided to enlist soldiers' family members against the central government's judgment. If a woman of a military household gave birth to a male child, then military service most likely awaited him in the future.

Many of the women in military spaces came from military families, but not all women in the penal-military complex were born there. Accounts of the first two Song emperors mention women who ended up in the army through purchase and kidnapping. The first emperor furnished one of his generals with funds for purchasing wives for his soldiers. Soldiers

19. In 1064 the emperor allowed that in some battalions, children, grandchildren, brothers, and nephews under the age of thirty could replace soldier relatives over the age of fifty-five even if shorter than the height standard as long as they could carry out their duties. They allowed soldiers over the age of fifty-five to remain in the army if they were healthy, strong, and "happy to remain in the army" (*Chang bian*, 200.3.4852).

20. Yang Wanli, *Cheng zhai ji*, 88.25b.175.

also kidnapped women, sometimes already married.[21] Yet these events took place during the early years of the Song under the first two emperors, military men whose power base still lay with military. As the Song state matured, stories of women kidnapped by soldiers made way for a more orderly assignment of women into the military. Instead of random kidnappings, women who had committed crimes could be married to soldiers as punishment. In 1018 a maid named Chen was punished for starting a fire. Her punishment included a flogging and marriage to a soldier from the Kiln Office.[22] Marrying women to soldiers served as a punishment for their crimes—but also, because the military was an aggressive, masculine force that needed to be used, empowered, and contained, it served as an offering to a hungry and violent demon, a recognition of the military's need for women.

When males committed crimes and were sentenced to military service, their female relatives usually also became residents of the penal-military complex. In 1184 a man who worked in a storehouse was accused of stealing state rice. He was tattooed and assigned to penal registration. His family was also entered into the military register.[23] When the state sentenced their husbands and fathers to military service, the women of their households followed them into exile and labor. At that point, the convicts' social world also became their own.

21. Song Taizu gave his general Wang Jixun money to purchase wives for the soldiers. Yet Wang Jixun allowed his soldiers to kidnap women in broad daylight, taking wives and daughters from other families while the law enforcement authorities stood by helpless (*Song huiyao, xingfa* 7.1, *junzhi*, Qiande 3rd year, 11th month); *Song shi*, 187.4571. Song Taizong also confronted the problem of soldiers kidnapping women in Chengdu (*Song huiyao, bing*, 11.4, Zhidao 1st year, 2nd month, 20th day).

22. *Song huiyao, ruiyi*, 2.33, Tianxi 2nd year, 2nd month, 4th day. In 1023 an edict ordered the release of female artisans and wives of soldiers assigned to labor in the North and South Palace Workshops. The edict added that from then on, women's penal assignment should be marriage to soldiers from the Transport Service and Kiln Office who did not have families (*Chang bian*, 101.2.2336). In 1080, eight servant girls were flogged, then married to soldiers from the Kiln Office and the Wagon Camp (*Chang bian*, 304.41.7408).

23. *Yijian zhi, zhiding*, part 10, *zhongliweng shi*, 1043; A man tattooed for a crime and registered as a soldier in Jiankang moved his family with him to his place of banishment (*Yijian zhi, zhigui*, part 8, *yang daozhen yi*, 1280–81).

Striking the Right Balance

For the first century of its existence, with the purpose of restraining and controlling military power, the new Song state put in place a new military policy, the Rotation System. The state rotated military units between different locations and commanders in grueling and deadly marches to prevent the development of close ties between commanders and troops, and thereby greatly decrease the power of officials and generals over their troops. However, the Rotation System also had another consequence: it caused military families great pain and sorrow by separating the soldiers from their wives and children.[24] This was not merely a side effect, as the system had another goal: weakening the soldiers' ability to build households of their own. When soldiers spent long periods of time in rotation away from the families, they had fewer children, and small families meant less food and clothing expense.[25] Chen Fuliang (1141–1203) explains that the Rotation System intentionally made it harder for soldiers to plan building families.[26] He also notes that the hardships caused to soldiers by separating them from their wives and children would make them more pliable.[27]

The soldiers who married and had children of their own found their families to be just as important as their obligations to the Song military. Soldiers had built lives for themselves over the years: houses, trades, families. When the military prepared to send them away, angry soldiers might air their grievances and rise in mutiny.[28] Soldiers who longed for their families deserted so they could be with them.[29] Threats over families of soldiers who deserted sometimes backfired as deserters fled together

24. Wei Tai, *Dongxuan bilu*, 8.91–92; Cai Xiang, *Duanmingji*, 22.15a.514, 26.6b.545.

25. Shen Kuo, *Mengxi bitan*, 25.15b–16a.850–51.

26. Chen Fuliang, *Lidai bingzhi*, 8.2a.477.

27. Ma Duanlin, *Wenxian tongkao*, 156.8a–8b.485.

28. In 1137, "on the day of the order, the armies have long been stationed in Chuankou. Those among them who had houses, fields, trades, wives and families feared a distant campaign, and some of them spoke out in anger" (*Yaolu*, 130.2443).

29. In 1000 there were great numbers of captured deserters from the border regions. The deserters claimed they deserted because they missed their families (*Chang bian*, 46.9.1001); *Song shi*, 266.9169.

with their families.[30] In cases where the government grew concerned that military families would resist attempts to split them up, it allowed men to serve alongside their sons and brothers.[31]

The state displayed an ambivalent attitude to military families. When confronted with deserters who fled to be with their families, the state and its agents could show empathy and even mercy. In 1023 Emperor Renzong commuted the death sentence of the deserter Wang Mei on account of extenuating factors. Wang Mei, a fresh recruit who had not even received his first monthly salary, missed his mother and ran back home.[32] In 1052, when the Fuzhou[1] soldiers from the Vast Fighting Spirit and Rising Martiality Battalions heard their families had fallen victim to a flood, they asked for permission to return home. Upon being refused, they deserted and escaped back home. They did not find their families and ended up turning to banditry. The prefect recognized that breaking the law to save parents, wife, and children fell within the range of normal human emotions. He allowed the soldiers to gather their families' corpses and pardoned their desertion.[33] A case of a soldier who deserted following his mother's death led an official to request that they avoid sending soldiers with old and sick parents on faraway missions.[34] Soldiers' reluctance to part from their families very likely played a part in the government's decision to abolish the Rotation System as part of the large-scale reform effort of the New Policies, about a century after the founding of the Song.

30. In 1039 the official Song Qi reported that the prefectural soldiers, being unable to support their families on their low salaries, escaped together with their families and became bandits (*Chang bian*, 125.17.2942). In 1209, in response to an official who seized the army's grain supply and put the soldiers to labor, the soldiers took their families and escaped over the city walls (*Song huiyao, zhiguan*, 74.33, Ningzong, Jiading 2nd year, 6th month, 24th day). These cases also suggest the presence of women in another location, the bandits' lair.

31. In 1006 Emperor Zhenzong expressed concern that while sons and brothers of soldiers often wish to serve in the military, the fear of having to serve in different battalions deterred them from enlisting. Therefore, family members should be allowed to join the same battalion (*Chang bian*, 63.12.1411).

32. *Chang bian*, 100.11.2323.

33. *Chang bian*, 173.13.4167–68.

34. *Minggong shupan qingmingji*, 11.437.

The issue of soldiers who struggled to be with their families presented the Song state with a dilemma. State service often contradicted an individual's commitment to his family. When it came to officials, the state recognized the officials' duty to retire from office, at least temporarily, when they had to mourn the death of family members. The state did not show as much understanding when it came to common soldiers' need to mourn family members, but it could not deny the values underlying soldiers' actions when they chose to act against the state and be with their families. The state also recognized that going too far in breaking the integrity of soldiers' family units might undermine the state's military objectives. And although the military system put a heavy strain on the families of soldiers, on occasion the state agreed to show clemency and flexibility toward them. The military family was a fact of life that could neither be ignored nor simply trampled.

Composition of the Military Family

Military families tended to be small. In 989, just a few decades after the founding of the Song, the official Li Jue said: "The wife and children of a soldier do not [number] more than a few individuals."[35] In the twelfth century, almost two centuries later, small families continued to be typical among Song soldiers. Hong Mai's *Yijian zhi* contains numerous mentions of soldiers' nuclear families with a soldier, a spouse, and a small number of children, often one.[36] The soldiers sometimes lived in proximity to their

35. Ma Duanlin, *Wenxian tongkao*, 25.30a.564; *Chang bian*, 30.1.679.

36. The soldier Zheng Chao shared a house with a wife and a son (*Yijian zhi, zhiwu*, part 7, *xinzhou yingzu zhengchao*, 1104–05); a soldier who worked in the Xingguo prison had a wife who gave birth to a baby with no hands (*Yijian zhi, zhiding, juan* 2, *xingguo yuzu,* 552). The prison guard Kong Du had a wife (*Yijian zhi, zhiding, juan* 14, *kong du*, 656–57); prison guard Tang Sheng had a mother but no wife (*Yijian zhi, zhiding, juan* 19, *chenzu tang dian*, 698). A fortune teller read the fortunes of the two sons of a commander (*Yijian zhi, sanjian, xin juan,* part 4, *yi mingwen mingshu*, 1410); Liu Daochang was the idle son of a soldier from Yuzhang (in modern Jiangxi) (*Yijian zhi, zhiding, juan* 2, *liu daochang*, 551); the soldier Wen Di from the Military Inspectorate of Run Po in Yugan Prefecture (in modern Jiangxi) had a wife and a son (*Yijian zhi, zhijing, juan* 6, *wen di jia she,* 927); and Cui Zuwu from the Weisheng Military Prefecture in Hedong lived with his wife (*Yijian zhi, jiazhi, juan* 2, *Cui zuwu,* 19). The old postal sta-

parents, but they did not always share a house.[37] Some of the soldiers who had been assigned to the military as convicts also built families and raised children within the penal-military complex.[38]

When a soldier died, his family continued to reside within the same social space. Some of the families in the military camp were single-parent households, many of them with a single female parent.[39] Following a soldier's death, his wife and children continued to reside within the camp.[40] Military widows had to find new strategies for survival. One military widow made a living by setting up a small business for producing wine and smuggling it into the camp.[41]

Estranged families and tensions related to the military salary stand at the center of a few of Hong Mai's stories. The mother of the soldier Long Ze did not live with him but with her courtesan daughter. Long Ze's wife and son resented the fact that the mother would arrive to take part of his rice rations.[42] The son of the discharged soldier Xiong Er re-

---

tion soldier Rao Jun had a wife and a son (*Yijian zhi, yizhi, juan* 19, *wangxian yan*, 350), as did the soldier Mei Xian (*Yijian zhi, jiazhi, juan* 11, *mei xian yuren*, 91–92).

37. Long Ze, a soldier in the Palace Workshop of the Armaments Office, lived with his wife and son Guoseng. After his father's death, his mother lived with her daughter, the courtesan Tieshi (*Yijian zhi, zhiding, juan* 9, *long ze chen yongnian*, 613–14). The unfortunate soldier Wang Fu from Jianchang (in modern Jiangxi) had parents living nearby who tried to save him from a destructive relationship with a ghost (*Yijian zhi, zhijia, juan* 7, *jianchang wang fu*, 766).

38. Hong Mai tells of three boys who grew up in the military camp together, all of them sons to tattooed soldiers who had been banished there over thirty years before from other areas. One was a door guard in the censorate, another worked as a storehouse manager, and the third served as a minor officer (*Yijian zhi, zhigui, juan* 6, *chenghuang miao tan que*, 1268).

39. Hong Mai's *Yijian zhi* mentions one case of a male single parent. A discharged soldier from Xingguo military prefecture (in modern Hubei area) was a widower and had one son (*Yijian zhi, zhijia, juan* 3, *xiong er buxiao*, 732–33).

40. When the officer Li Jin from the Patrol (Youyi) Battalion in Jiankang (modern Nanjing) died of an illness, his wife and family took care of the funerary rituals (*Yijian zhi, zhijia, juan* 3, *zhang wenbao*, 733). The soldier Chen Fu from Mingzhou lost his father at the age of five or six and was raised by his mother (*Yijian zhi, jiazhi, juan* 14, *chao bu gui*, 125). Liu Sanniang was a crazy woman who ran around dirty in the marketplace and cursed at people, spending her nights sleeping in a temple. She had a soldier for a son but treated him with indifference (*Yijian zhi, zhiding, juan* 2, *liu sanniang*, 552).

41. *Yijian zhi, zhigui, juan* 3, *wu liu jingdu*, 1287–88.

42. *Yijian zhi, zhiding, juan* 9, *long ze chen yongnian*, 613–14.

fused to support his father.[43] There could be a monetary value to a soldier outside of his salary. When the soldier Zhou You fell ill, his wife ignored him. Instead of tending to him with food and medicine, she reported her husband dead and asked for burial money and permission to remarry, all while she was having an affair with another man from the camp. Her husband filed a complaint against her, leading to her execution.[44] The struggles over income in Hong Mai's descriptions demonstrate the limited resources at the disposal of military families. It appears that military families did not struggle over property they had but over money owed them by the state, whether as salary or as support for families of dead soldiers. The military salaries brought the state into the heart of family struggles, and they created a strong link between the existence of this social group and the state's military institutions.

The Urban Setting

Military camps were scattered around the empire, many of them in the cities and towns. In such cases, military camps developed into urban slums, poor neighborhoods where dilapidated buildings provided little cover or security. The decay of military camps brought with it another problem, the blurring lines between the urban military world and that of other poor commoners residing in the cities and towns. Due to lack of housing, soldiers moved out of the camps and into commoners' homes.[45] The state led projects of repair and renewal in military camps with the

43. *Yijian zhi, zhijia, juan* 3, *xiong er buxiao,* 732–33.

44. *Yijian zhi, bujian, juan* 2, *dingzhou bing qi,* 1564.

45. In 1186 the Bureau of Military Affairs reported on the housing crisis in Wenzhou (in modern-day Zhejiang): "Our prefecture lies in a remote and coastal area. The soldiers and the commoners live together, and this constantly causes trouble. The soldiers have no barracks to return to, and many of them rent lodgings outside. Hardly any available lodging places remain in all six camps including the [imperial] Mighty Victory [Weijie] Battalion, the [likely imperial] 33rd Formidable Integrity [Xiongweijie] Battalion, the [prefectural] 34th Revering Integrity [Chongjie] Battalion, and the prison citadels. I have already distributed money from the prefectural budget to gather timber for construction, so that the soldiers can all be brought into the camp for drilling" (*Song huiyao, bing,* 6.26 Chunxi 13th year, 1st month, 6th day).

purpose of drawing clear new lines between the soldiers and their commoner neighbors.[46]

Military families lived in close quarters. The plight of old and sick soldiers who had to share a single room with their families led Attendant Censor Li Hong (*jinshi* 1008) in 1032 to ask that in some cases women and children be allowed not to follow their husbands and fathers who had been sentenced to military service in the Chuan-Xia border region.[47] In Hong Mai's stories, military families struggled over sharing a single salary, but they did not always share a home. It was poverty, more than any Confucian values or practices, that dictated the form of the military family.

Soldiers lived close to other urban commoners and also intermarried with them. Some of the soldiers in Hong Mai's stories practiced uxorilocal marriage with local families, with the soldiers moving into the homes of their wives' families.[48] Affinal relations could also lead to military service, as in some cases male relatives of a different surname replaced a soldier.[49] This meant that the identity of a military family was also passed through the female members, not just the male soldiers. Affinal relations, an important trait of lower-class families in the Late Imperial period, were already important among military families of the Song period.[50]

Hong Mai's stories echo the perception of the military camps as spaces rife with violent and drunk individuals. Prison guard soldier Tang Sheng was a weird character, suffering from a speech impediment and

46. There are a few Southern Song examples of this, during the early twelfth century, in the Shaoxi reign period (1190–1195), and in 1223: Li Gang, *Liang xi ji*, 104.6a–6b.282; Zhang Hao, *Baoqing guiji xuzhi*, 1.4b–5a.7094; Zhou Yinghe, *Jingding jiankang zhi*, 23.29a.1700.

47. *Song huiyao, xingfa*, 4.18, Tiansheng 10th year, 10th month, 16th day.

48. The soldier Zhao Xing moved in with his wife's parents, but there was great animosity between him and his mother-in-law (*Yijian zhi, bujuan, juan* 5, *Zhao Xing su yuan*, 1588–89). The soldier Zhang the Fifth had an affair with a young daughter of the Liu family. When her mother and elder sister caught them in the act, Zhang killed all three. Zhang had an older brother who married into the Zhan family. They had an unmarried younger sister who also married a soldier later (*Yijian zhi, bujian, juan* 15, *chenghuang fu hui*, 1702).

49. *Chang bian*, 200.3.4852.

50. Bossler used literary sources to demonstrate the importance of affinal relations among the lower classes during the Late Imperial period (Bossler, "A Daughter Is a Daughter," 92–97).

mentally unstable. Tang Sheng loved drinking so much, one could mix dirt into his drink, and he would still drink it. He would take his clothes off and have people hit him so he could show off his allegedly rock-hard body.[51] Soldier's son Liu Daochang, barely literate, drank wine and lazed about. He used to harass the shops in the market, and he was once flogged in the local government building.[52] Like their ninth-century tattooed predecessors, these Song-period soldiers walked around the city, drinking and looking for trouble. Yet compared with their predecessors, Song soldiers were perhaps a little less openly combative against their superiors, at least until the point of mutiny.[53]

Important officials shared Hong Mai's assessment of the military camp, and they warned that trouble in the military camp could spread to the rest of the town and even threaten the state. The official Zhang Fangping (1007–1091) argued that poverty among military families led to potential unrest and mutiny.[54] The scholar-official Su Shi (1037–1101) warned that the lack of discipline in the camp led to widespread drinking and gambling among soldiers, as well as to desertion.[55] A letter by Su Shi mentions his participation in a local project for the building of barracks for local militias, improving their living conditions so they would not harm the local population.[56] In part due to growing urbanization, Song officials realized that military poverty became both a military and a social problem, and that it posed a threat not only within the military but also to other parts of society.

Extracting Value from Military Families

The role assigned to military families by the state and its agents extended beyond the supplying of men to the military. Song officials debated the possible impact of families on soldiers' performance and suggested that

51. *Yijian zhi*, *dingzhi*, *juan* 19, *chenzu tang dian*, 698.
52. *Yijian zhi*, *dingzhi*, *juan* 2, *liu daochang*, 551.
53. More about soldier mutinies in chapter 6.
54. *Chang bian*, 163.6.3928; Zhang Fangping, *Lequan ji*, 18.15.151.
55. Su Shi, *Dongpo quanji*, 64.18a–19a.70.
56. Su Shi, *Su Shi quanji jiaozhu*, 54.5987–90.

the presence of families increased soldiers' motivation to fight.[57] The official Wang Yan[1] argued that men with families would be more suitable and reliable for patrolling the streets of the town.[58] Whereas Song officials often spoke of soldiers as weak, cowardly, and criminal, some of them found soldiers to be less inclined to such bad behavior when accompanied by their families. In the eyes of the elites, families had a humanizing effect on soldiers, even if they considered those families a tool to be used, not a thing to be preserved or protected.

The presence of families in the military camp provided the Song state with other potential benefits. Military families resided in military camps, making them readily available for use as hostages. When soldiers committed a crime, their families could be subject to punishment. In very severe cases, including inciting mutiny and desertion during battle, the entire family of a soldier could be executed.[59] This was a severe punishment, and the decision to execute families lay with the emperor.[60] Another punishment for families of troublesome soldiers was the enslavement of their households, particularly women. This could

57. During the Jingkang reign period (1125–1127), when organizing the defense of the capital against the Jurchens, Li Gang (1083–1140) told the emperor, "Now the parents, wives, and children of [the soldiers of] the six armies all reside in the capital, and [the soldiers] are willing to defend them to the death" (*Song shi*, 358.11243). The Southern Song official Li Mingfu argued that local forces would be highly motivated because of the presence of their wives and children (Yang Shiqi, *Lidai mingchen zouyi*, 435.99.29b.758), and another Southern Song official argued that soldiers would be more reliable in times of crisis if they rotated together with their families (Yang Shiqi, *Lidai mingcheng zouyi*, 442.337.46a-b.443).

58. Wang Yan[1] claimed the soldiers in charge of law enforcement had not been replaced for a long time, became familiar with the streets of the town, and began committing crimes. He asked that instead men with good conduct and families replace them, with each performing this duty for one month, never to do it again afterward (*Song huiyao*, *bing*, 3.10, Qiandao 3rd year, 4th month, 19th day).

59. Military laws promulgated in 1127 called for the execution of soldiers' entire families when they committed particularly severe crimes: soldiers who deserted in battle and returned to their camp to cause mayhem; soldiers who incited mutiny; and those who led others in desertion (*Song huiyao, xingfa*, 7.29a.6748, Jianyan 1st year, 6th month, 14th day). The soldiers first to flee when going to combat were to be executed with their entire families (*Yaolu*, 6.180).

60. Song Taizu sometimes spared the families of mutineers and sometimes executed them. In 965 Song Taizu spared the lives of unruly soldiers and their families, wishing to avoid great bloodshed (*Song shi, juan* 257.8953). In 969, nineteen men who

include tattooing of the women.[61] The targeting of families explains the words of the official Xue Changru (1000–1061) in response to soldiers plotting a mutiny: "You all have parents, wives, and children. How can you do this?"[62] Xue's implied threat to the soldiers' families put an end to the unrest.

The mass scale of desertion made it one of the most troubling problems in the Song military.[63] Here, too, military families could be useful for the state. Soldiers would be less likely to desert if that entailed leaving their families in the camp.[64] When soldiers deserted, their wives could be detained in the camp as hostages.[65] In some cases, the state put families of deserters to work and allowed for the recruitment of their sons to military service.[66] When desertion left a postal station understaffed, a

---

had been implicated in the mutinous plots of a military official were executed along with their families (*Chang bian*, 10.4.232–33).

61. After Li Zhaoliang repressed the Baozhou mutiny, he divided the women of the rebellious soldiers between the various armies and took some of them into his own household. He released those only after fearing prosecution, yet the emperor did not pursue the matter (*Song shi*, 464.13563; *Chang bian*, 152.6.3697–98). In 1071, following a mutiny in Qingzhou, punishments to soldiers' families included the enslavement of the old, the sick, the young, and the women; tattooing of the males followed by their assignment to prison citadels; enslaving the old and sick in their home circuits; and the tattooing of all slaves, the males on the left hand, the females on the right hand. Later, an edict ordered to examine and grant release, pending on good behavior, in the cases of enslaved family members who shared a house with the soldier and of men over age twenty who had already been tattooed and conscripted to Jingxi. Those sent to the army were to be given money, and those already registered to Hubei were not to be transferred (*Chang bian*, 221.49.5383, 222.20.5403–4).

62. Fan Zhen, *Dongzhai jishi*, 4.35–36.

63. For more on desertion, see You Biao, "Lun songdai shibing taowang."

64. The official Zhang Jie (1027–1102) said: "As for people's constant emotions, do they not have love for parents, wives, and children? Unless in cases of repeat offenders who are not tolerated in their own camp, or of men charged with a crime and escaping punishment, or men who robbed state or private property, would they agree to leave their parents, wives, and children, and hide among the mountains and the forests and the wilderness?" (*Chang bian*, 493.7.11710).

65. An edict from 1031 orders an amnesty to the wives of deserters who were being detained in their camps (*Chang bian*, 110.3.2554).

66. In 1018 an edict approved that in cases of desertion from the dikes at Yangwu, the deserters' families in the camp should be put to work and given money and food. If they had sons willing to join the army, they were to be measured and registered (*Chang bian*, 95.2.2195).

common-enough problem, soldiers' wives could be ordered to deliver documents, a tough and dangerous task.[67] Officials used the presence of women in military spaces to regulate and discipline the soldiers. Physical threats to the wives of soldiers could keep soldiers in line and motivate them to work harder. In 1133, when soldiers in the Yongzhou postal stations did not respond to orders quickly enough, their superiors burst into the soldiers' quarters and tied up their wives.[68]

When the authorities needed a greater workforce, they could call upon the families of soldiers to perform specific tasks. In 965 the male relatives of soldiers were enlisted for ditch digging to create a small lake in the imperial city.[69] The official Li You (982–1044) had the "camp wives" (*yingfu*) assist in caring for victims of a famine.[70] When not called on by the government, families of soldiers still had to struggle to overcome the soldiers' low pay and the hard labor required of soldiers. In 1007 the wives and children of soldiers in Yizhou (in modern Guangxi) helped the soldiers cut wood in rainy and windy weather.[71] A memorial from 1137 describes the labor of the military family: the wife cleaned the soldier's armor, the son collected firewood, and on winter days the soldier repaired buildings in the camp.[72]

The Song army was a professional military, composed of full-time salaried soldiers who served for most of their productive lives. The Song government spent on average about 80 percent of its budget on military expenses, most of it on salaries.[73] That figure represents only a partial calculation of the true cost of the military. By assisting the labor of soldiers, the military families paid a share of the costs of keeping a huge standing army, as well as the costs of raising future soldiers for the state. Military families became a semi-official extension of the military. This provided the state with some financial benefits, but it came at the cost of low morale, crime, desertion, and mutiny.

67. This according to a report from 1142 by the Bureau of Military Affairs (*Song huiyao, fangyu*, 11.8, Gaozong, Shaoxing 12th year, 5th month, 29th day).

68. *Song huiyao, fangyu*, 1.53, Gaozong, Shaoxing 3rd year, 7th month, 14th day.

69. *Song huiyao, fangyu*, 1.11, Taizu Qiande 3rd year, 4th month, 13th day.

70. *Song shi*, 301.9995.

71. *Chang bian*, 66.18.1472. The official's harsh policies drove the soldiers to mutiny.

72. Xu Mengxin, *Sanchao beimeng huibian*, 180.9.357.

73. Mote, *Imperial China*, 114–15.

The Sex Trade and the Military

Once the military family lost the income of the soldier, whether it resulted from discharge, death, or desertion, the burden of making a livelihood fell on the women. The pressure on lower-class women of military families to seek employment outside of the household made them mobile and visible in the military camp, whether as entrepreneurs or as commodities. The growing market in the Song era provided some opportunities for women with business acumen, and in Hong Mai's stories military widows turned to the illegal production and sale of alcohol to make a living.[74] The economic growth of Song times also meant the commodification of women who were bought from families in need and sold to become courtesans and concubines. Within the military camp, prostitution became a source for supplementing the family's income. Some soldiers sold their wives. Others had their wives and daughters work as prostitutes in the marketplace.[75] As the sex trade blossomed within the Song empire, courtesans became a feature of life in the military camp. Courtesans lived in proximity to soldiers, as their neighbors and relatives, or as "camp courtesans," a special designation of the Song period.[76] Courtesans and prostitutes sold their services in the camp marketplace, where they became the object of drunken brawls among soldiers.[77]

74. *Yijian zhi, zhigui, juan* 3, *wu liu jingdu*, 1287–88; *Yijian zhi, zhigeng, juan* 9, *Chen xiaoyao*, 1207.

75. In 1135, facing problems in food supply, soldiers sold their wives to sustain themselves (*Yaolu*, 41.893–4). In 1162 the great Southern Song thinker Zhu Xi reported that some soldiers were so poor they had to collect firewood, weave sandals, and collect night soil to survive. The extremely poor among them even made their wives and daughters put on makeup and work by the market gate as prostitutes to get food (Zhu Xi, *Huian ji*, 11.36–37.184).

76. The sister of the soldier Long Ze was a courtesan (*Yijian zhi, zhiding, juan* 9, *long ze chen yongnian,* 613–14); the Quzhou (in modern Zhejiang) soldier Wang Xian lived in the same alley as the twenty-year-old courtesan Li Rou (*Yijian zhi, zhijia, juan 4, Li Rou*, 741). In 1136 a group of camp courtesans joined the crowd greeting a new official. A bull rushed out and killed one of the courtesans (*Yijian zhi, yizhi, juan* 13, *niu chu chang*, 294).

77. *Yijian zhi, jiazhi*, juan 9, *yu weng xiang ren*, 76.

The making of soldiers into officials' private servants became a perennial problem in Song administration. A similar process happened with women, and camp courtesans were vulnerable to sexual harassment and assault by officials.[78] The distinction between public money and an official's personal expenses was often hard to make. The same holds true for the humans whose lives the official controlled, both soldiers and state courtesans. When the human body became state property, the official found himself having to decide the proper usage for female bodies whose owners had low social standing and over whom the official had almost absolute power.

One of Hong Mai's stories illustrates how a woman from a military family could end up being sold. He tells of an official who ran into an old man and his daughter sobbing by the side of the road. The old man, a freshly discharged soldier who had served in the military for twenty years, had been robbed of his discharge papers. He had to give his daughter to the official in return for money to sort out his legal problems that resulted from losing his papers.[79] Of course, the female's fate in this story can be viewed as an example of upward social mobility, but the story also makes clear the poverty and vulnerability of military families, how those translated into the selling of the female family members, and the injury caused to a family by the sale of a daughter.

When the need arose, the state itself reached out and used the bodies of soldiers' wives for its own ends. In the final days of the Song, when the Song military grew desperate for manpower, it used soldiers' wives for seducing potential victims for impressment into military service.[80] Another way of luring people into the army, as well as covering up the true scale of desertion in a unit, consisted of having new recruits take on the identity of deserters. In addition to the deserter's identity, the replacement also re-

78. Liu Huan (1000–1080) was demoted for indulging himself with camp courtesans. A letter he left for a camp courtesan was the cause of his downfall (*Song shi*, 324.10493; *Chang bian*, 114.10.2672). The official Wang Xiao was dismissed for both his low skills and improper conduct that included harassing the camp courtesans (*Song huiyao, zhiguan*, 72.7, Xiaozong Chunxi 9th year, 8th month, 13th day), and the official Xue Shunyu was discharged for taking liberties with the camp courtesans on a regular basis (*Song huiyao, zhiguan*, 73.46, Ningzong Jiading 5th year, 9th month, 1st day).

79. *Yijian zhi, yizhi, juan* 2, *jiang jiaoshou*, 195–97.

80. *Song shi*, 193.4822.

ceived the deserter's wife and property.[81] The state and its agents treated soldiers, their identities, and their families as interchangeable parts that could be torn apart and reassembled according to need.

Access to military men and resources offered Song officials many opportunities to supplement their income: skimming soldiers' income, hiring out soldiers to contract work and pocketing their salaries, and turning soldiers into their own private servants. State courtesans, like soldiers, were a resource that officials could use. Song officials often crossed the line between the public and private and came to use soldiers and courtesans as their personal property, like the official in 1209 who was dismissed for taking his liberties with government courtesans and stealing from the soldiers' grain supplies.[82]

The growing monetization of the economy during the Southern Song increased the economic pressure on military families. Soldiers' families tended to live in urban areas and relied on a salary paid in grain, in cloth, and in cash. During the Southern Song, however, more of the soldiers' salary was paid in cash. This made military families very vulnerable to price fluctuations, especially inflation, a serious problem during the Southern Song. When military families lacked money and food, due to arrears, corruption, or simply due to the low salaries, members of military families took advantage of the opportunities available in the military camp for those who could earn money using their bodies: selling artisanal skills, renting out labor, and participating in the sex trade.

Helping the Family: Welfare Institutions

From its early days, the Song state supported the families of soldiers who fell in combat. Support could come in various forms: a single payment, short-term installments, or a permanent stipend.[83] The state did not assure

81. Yu Yunwen (1110–1174) warned that some military units, intent on hiding the high rates of desertion, recruited men under names of deserters. The new recruits received the deserters' entire family and property (Yang Shiqi, *Lidai mingchen zouyi*, 439.224.10b.404).

82. *Song huiyao, zhiguan*, 74.34, Ningzong Jiading 2nd year, 7th month, 28th day.

83. In 1001, following a battle, the emperor ordered to provide support for the families of soldiers who died (*Chang bian*, 50.6.1083–84). In 1043 families of soldiers

support for all military families, however. In one case, the state allocated a daily ration of rice to the grandparents, parents, and wives of fallen soldiers who had been left without male sons. The state ordered the payments to continue for the rest of their lives, but women who remarried had their payments stopped.[84] The large amounts of labor carried out by the Song military meant that the military suffered a large part of its military casualties not in battle but during labor. The state provided some assistance to military families whose men had been killed while doing labor: soldiers were crushed during construction, drowned performing river work, and perished delivering mail across the Song's intricate system of postal stations.[85]

Families of active-duty soldiers also often found themselves in dire financial straits. Early Song leadership already showed itself aware of the need to provide welfare to military families to maintain the Song's military strength.[86] State assistance became especially necessary when soldiers traveled on duty for extended periods of time. In one case, soldiers left half their food rations for their families before leaving, but this left the soldiers without sufficient food for themselves. At this point the emperor intervened and ordered special assistance.[87] When Emperor Zhenzong gave a gift of coal to military families during a very heavy snow, the

who died in battle in Dingchuan were to be given two months' worth of salaries (*Chang bian*, 141.29.3381). In 1044 the state decided to give a monthly allowance of rice to soldiers who had been discharged due to injuries as well as to the families of fallen soldiers (*Chang bian*, 150.20.3638).

84. Emperor Shenzong gave this order in 1074 (*Chang bian*, 150.45.6158).

85. In 1012, when twelve soldiers were crushed to death during construction, the emperor ordered to compensate their families with gifts of money and silk (*Chang bian*, 77.6.1761). In 1024, when soldiers drowned during labor on the rivers in Yizhou[2] (in modern Henan), officials marked them as deserters. The emperor ordered that the names of the drowned be documented and money given to their families (*Chang bian*, 102.2.2367). In 1121 Emperor Huizong ordered assistance to families of postal-station soldiers who died on the road (*Song huiyao, fangyu*, 10.37, Huizong Xuanhe 3rd year, 8th month, 12th day).

86. In 987 Zhao Yuanxi (966–992), Emperor Taizong's second son, advocated for the support of military families as part of a few measures meant to strengthen the army (*Chang bian*, 28.3.633–34).

87. In 1007 Emperor Zhenzong ordered this special assistance to soldiers in Jingdong (*Song huiyao, shihuo*, 42.4, Zhenzong Jingde 4th year, 7th month).

families of deployed soldiers received half the amount.[88] In another case, Emperor Renzong sent officials to inquire about the welfare of military families of soldiers who had been away for long periods. The emperor had the officials provide the military families with medical and burial assistance as needed.[89]

By the middle of the twelfth century, the state started showing concern also for discharged soldiers and their families. In 1157 the emperor approved a plan to help soldiers transition to farming after discharge, also with the purpose of protecting their families from poverty.[90] Zhou Bida (1126–1204) reported that soldiers discharged due to medical reasons were begging together with their families in the marketplace, holding up their military papers. Zhou expressed concern that this might affect the morale of soldiers passing by, and he suggested taking measures to assist the discharged troops.[91]

When the scholar Huang Gan (1152–1221) spoke about soldiers' welfare, he did so in very concrete terms. Huang explained that families prevent convict-soldiers from becoming repeat offenders, but soldiers' low income did not allow them to find wives. Huang Gan argued that crime within the military and desertion could be reduced by increasing soldiers' monthly income and assisting them with marriage and childbirth expenses, medicine, housing, and family support during soldiers' deployments.[92] Such a detailed proposal suggests the growing maturity and complexity of military welfare institutions during the late twelfth and early thirteenth centuries.

The need to assist families of discharged soldiers came at a time when military families became an important component of the urban landscape of the Song empire—especially in Hangzhou during the Southern Song period. Hangzhou had a huge beggar population, as large as a quarter of a million, and many among them discharged soldiers.[93] Because urban

88. This took place in 1012, following a heavy snowfall in the capital that lasted for many days (*Song huiyao, li*, 62.33, Zhenzong Dazhongxiangfu 5th year, 12th month).

89. This took place in 1040 (*Song huiyao, bing*, 5.3, Renzong Kangding 1st year, 4th month, 9th day).

90. *Song huiyao, shihuo*, 1.39, Gaozong Shaoxing 27th year, 5th month, 11th day.

91. Zhou Bida, *Wenzhong ji*, 1148.140.11a-b.548.

92. Yang Shiqi, *Lidai mingchen zouyi*, 439.224.47b–48b.422–23.

93. Takahashi, "Nansō Rin'an no kasō-min to toshi gyōsei," 123–124.

poverty was also military poverty, when Wu Zimu (1161–1237) described the various welfare mechanisms in Hangzhou, he described them as targeting both commoners and soldiers.[94] Inequality and poverty in urban spaces increased social tensions. The military poor had to pass through a marketplace laden with goods they could not afford.[95] When soldiers resorted to stealing, it also took place within the city.[96] The urban poor population of the Song period included a large component of poor military families. This made state welfare mechanisms important not only for the poor but also instrumental for social stability in the city and for the welfare and safety of all other urban residents.

Conclusion

Military families resided in military spaces, at the heart of the state's coercive power. The semi-official status of military families created a strong link between them and the state. Elite families too had to struggle to become associated with the state through participation in the examinations and the prospect of attaining office.[97] Yet, whereas securing official positions was one component out of a broad range of resources available for elite families, military families came to rely mostly on soldiers' salaries for survival. The state took advantage of its position. When the need arose, it used military families as laborers, as hostages, and as replacements. Without changing its spending in a dramatic or long-term manner, the state could increase its workforce on a temporary basis, then release the military families back to their lives.

The military family stands at the intersection of some of the most important trends of Song social, legal, military, and economic history. It was a product of the penal-military complex, the Song state's extremely ambitious project of social engineering. Military families were

94. Wu Zimu, *Meng liang lu*, 590.18.21b–23b.153–54.

95. Fang Hui, *Tongjiang ji*, 6.12.

96. *Song huiyao, xingfa*, 5.2, Taizong Taipingxingguo 9th year, 2nd month, 15th day.

97. For more on rising participation in the examination system during the Song, see Chaffee, *Thorny Gates of Learning in Sung China*.

both catalysts and products of Song urbanization. In their attempts to survive, military families participated in the growing markets of the Song period, as laborers, producers, and smugglers, and through the participation of women in the burgeoning sex and entertainment trade. Soldiers and their families came to form a unique social group, highly visible in urban areas, but the physical and social boundaries of their world were permeable. Other urban commoners were their neighbors, coworkers, lovers, and spouses. They too lived in the shadow of the penal-military complex.

The state and its agents displayed an ambivalent attitude to military families. Song elites perceived the Song military as a criminal, violent space. As the families of soldiers, military families became guilty by association. However, military families also appeared to exert positive influences on soldiers since Song rhetoric concerning families often fell in line with what some might call Confucian rhetoric. Song scholar-officials could not dismiss the ties of love and affection between soldiers and their relatives; this was a human aspect that could not be denied. Moreover, military families had their uses. They produced soldiers, and the state could use families to intimidate soldiers into being better soldiers and laborers. On the other hand, breaking up military families undermined soldier morale and could even bring about mutiny. This provided military families some protection despite the low status of soldiers.

The development of permanent welfare institutions for soldiers reveals that with time military families won more and more recognition from the state. When the state and its agents drafted laws and edicts that concerned the military, military families were also on their minds. Although the soldiers were all male, the military was not a purely masculine space. The state recognized the parents, wives, siblings, and children of soldiers as semi-official members of the penal-military complex. The state saw soldiers as members of nuclear families, and it took that fact into consideration when it drafted its decisions on military matters.

Modern-day scholars have pointed out that beyond Confucian rhetoric and ideals, larger social, economic, and political developments had a tremendous impact on women's roles in Middle Period China.[98] The

98. Bossler, *Courtesans, Concubines, and the Cult of Female Fidelity*; Ebrey, "Women, Money, and Class."

same holds true for the Song empire's military families. Women of the penal-military complex had no "inner chambers," and they shared the living conditions of soldiers. The state's labor demands of soldiers extended to women, who also provided labor for the Song's economic boom. Poverty put a great strain on military families, which sometimes had to sell or rent the bodies of female members to survive. Although the state often used Confucian rhetoric, this only served to highlight the dominance of other factors in shaping the lives of military families. This should lead us to contemplate what place, if at all, Confucian values held at the bottom of society.

CHAPTER 6

Resistance in the Military

Desertion, Mutiny, Deception, Mutilation

In the government yard of Linhai (in modern Zhejiang), an archer in the local militia was shouting drunkenly.[1] The district defender Shu Dan (1042–1104) flogged the drunk soldier with the bamboo rod, yet the soldier did not submit. The heavy cane was brought out, and the flogging recommenced. With a voice growing increasingly fierce, the soldier stated he was willing to have his back flogged as well. Shu Dan shouted at the clerks, ordering them to flog the man's back. The soldier cried out again with a loud voice, "You dare not behead me!" Shu Dan lifted his blade and beheaded the soldier. This impromptu execution impressed Shu Dan's superiors, who recommended him when the court called for new talent. Even the great minister Wang Anshi was delighted with this official who was stern in appearance, of broad learning, and eloquent in speech. Shu Dan was promoted.[2]

This anecdote about the direct and violent interaction between Shu Dan and a soldier paints the picture of a man who operated in two separate kingdoms. One is the kingdom of elite men. In that kingdom Shu Dan was a learned and eloquent individual. The other kingdom was that

1. A version of this chapter appears as a chapter in *State Power in China, 900–1325*, Patricia Buckley Ebrey and Paul Jakov Smith, eds (Seattle: University of Washington Press, 2016). Republished by permission of the copyright holder, the University of Washington Press.

2. Zhu Yu, *Pingzhou ketan*, 1.118–119 (32).

of the military camp, where violence reigned supreme, and where shouted curses replaced eloquent speech. Learned though he was, Shu Dan educated the soldier with the bamboo rod, the heavy cane, and finally, the blade.

As this anecdote shows, the authority of officials was met with defiance by members of the Song empire's largest underclass, its soldiers. The army is one of the most prominent manifestations of state power, both as a reflection of the state's power and as an organization that regulates almost every aspect of soldiers' lives. Stories of mutinies and resistance to the Song state's military institutions show the limits of state power, the points at which it was resisted by those who dwelled in the social and spatial margins of the state. Soldiers, militia men, and candidates for conscription resisted the military institutions in various ways: avoiding conscription, desertion, insubordination, self-mutilation, fraud, and mutiny.

Mutinies were relatively clear instances of resistance, violent events where soldiers collectively gave voice to their displeasure with their superiors. However, the term "resistance" carries a broad meaning here, similar to that invoked by James C. Scott and including also the acts of everyday violence through which commoners and soldiers attempted to avoid direct conflict with the state and its agents. Scott finds that such actions by peasants in 1970s Malaysia stem from their own world of values and traditions, and his formulation applies well to both the commoners and soldiers of the Song period.[3]

The numbers and circumstances of troops varied over time and space. The burden of service in the local militias tended to be especially heavy along the border with the Xia during the great military campaigns of the eleventh century. Life also grew tougher for soldiers in the final years of the Northern Song as the military system fell into a state of disrepair. Still, some broad generalizations can be made about the Song period. Service in the militias tended to be highly unpopular. As for the regular forces, although there were many different unit and troop categories in the Song military, soldiers were regarded as a distinct social group that occupied a low place in the social hierarchy. Their life was extremely punishing. They resisted.

3. Scott, *Weapons of the Weak*, 27–43.

Soldiers Are Dangerous: The Policy of Zero Tolerance

Already during the reign of the first Song emperor, voices in court warned of the dangers that soldiers posed.[4] Yet the first Song emperors were both military men who had a firm base of support within the military. As lords of an army of conquest, they employed violence on a regular basis toward military rivals, nonmilitary populations, and, if necessary, toward their own soldiers as well. However, the use of violence against soldiers tended to be measured, and when possible, the emperors left room for compassion, sometimes even sparing mutineering soldiers from death.[5]

By the mid-eleventh century, powerful civil officials, the graduates of the examination system, came to dominate the court.[6] These civil officials warned the throne of the arrogance of soldiers and argued for a strong hand in military administration.[7] The same scholar-officials who perceived soldiers as dangerous, violent creatures also wrote, interpreted, and implemented military policies and regulations. During the same period that scholar-officials received improving treatment and growing protections from the penal law, soldiers lived under their own legal code, far harsher than the laws governing commoners.[8] In practice, the military enforced

4. *Chang bian*, 12.10.274–75.

5. In 967 an imperial army officer led his troops in mutiny. Over ten thousand people in Jiannan (in modern Yunnan, Sichuan, Guizhou, and Gansu), including soldiers' families, became implicated. Instead of executing them, Taizu used clemency to put an end to the mutiny (*Song shi*, 257.8953). In 983 Taizong set a prize on capturing soldiers who broke into commoners' homes. More than a hundred soldiers were captured. Reluctant to kill them all, Taizong had them imprisoned in their prefecture instead, and he later released them and provided them with money (*Chang bian*, 24.14.562–63).

6. Scholars now recognize that the dominance of civil officials did not begin immediately with the founding of the Song, but it took about fifty years from the founding of the dynasty before civil officials dominated the court at the expense of generals. See Deng Xiaonan, "Tan Song chu zhi 'yu wuchen dushu.'" 45–55; Chen Feng, *Beisong wujiang qunti*, 348–52; Lorge, *Reunification of China*, 278–86.

7. See discussions by Shi Jie, Li Jing, Ouyang Xiu, and Sima Guang: Shi Jie, *Culai shi xiansheng wenji, bingzhi*, 9.102–3; *Chang bian*, 157.16.3799–3800; Ouyang Xiu, *Ouyang Xiu quan ji*, 18.933–34; Sima Guang, *Chuanjia ji*, 33.7b–9a.316–17.

8. McKnight, "Law and the Military in the Sung," 1.

the law lightly in cases of military officials, but it punished soldiers heavily.[9] Many crimes were punishable by death, including feigning sickness, trickery, self-mutilation, selling or losing one's armor, and leaving the camp alone.[10] Military laws differed from regular laws in both severity and quality: they intervened more deeply in the lives of the governed (dictating their location and movement, modifying their bodies, regulating labor and effort), they demanded capital punishment for many infractions, and they punished crimes unique to the military (i.e., desertion). For soldiers and their family members—millions of people—being part of the Song world meant living under military law.

In addition to the draconian military law, the state gave officials a relatively free hand to discipline their soldiers, even at the cost of breaking the law.[11] Executing soldiers allowed an official to show one's mettle. With a well-timed execution, an official could gain both authority over those below and appreciation from above.[12] The officers thought little of Qinzhou prefect Li Ji (960–1030) until he decided the case of a soldier charged with stealing a silver hairpin from a woman in the marketplace. Li Ji ordered his execution almost as an afterthought, resuming his reading immediately after pronouncing his judgment, thereby winning

9. Zhang Ming, *Songdai junfa yanjiu*, 137–62.

10. This according to the *Wujing zongyao,* an eleventh-century military compendium (Zeng Gongliang, *Wujing zongyao*, 14.11a.456, 14.14a.458, 14.15b.458, 15.3b.461).

11. An officer in Bingzhou (in modern Shanxi) flogged to death another officer's soldier. When this was reported, Zhang Yong (945–1015) warned that if they executed an officer over the matter of one soldier, the soldiers would slight their superiors and cause trouble. He added that their specific situation was even more dangerous because they had thousands of soldiers stationed there in a border area filled with non-Han groups. Zhang suggested that the officer be beaten with a rod and transferred. Instead, the emperor had the officer executed. Later the soldiers there killed an officer, pulling out his heart and internal organs. According to the account, the court then realized Zhang had been right (Wang Pizhi, *Shengshui yantan lu*, 2.20–1). A cavalry soldier who lost his bow was to be released due to an imperial amnesty, but the official Li Zhaoliang said, "A careless Imperial Guard cannot be pardoned." The soldier was demoted and sent to penal servitude. According to the account, the imperial army became disciplined from then on (*Song shi*, 464.13563–64.)

12. Zhang Yong had a clerk executed, thereby winning the obedience of the military officers (Wu Chuhou, *Qingxiang zaji*, 10.106–7); Zhao Gai cemented his authority by having a soldier who had run away and broken into a private residence beheaded in the marketplace (Wang Gui, *Huayang ji*, 60.2, p. 442).

the respect of his officers and even making a name for himself in court.[13] A garrison soldier in Shu went on a crime spree of robbery, arson, assault, and murder before turning himself in. The official Xue Gongkui executed the soldier on the spot, and the public allegedly praised him for it.[14]

Harsh laws and punishments employed in military life were important for weeding out potential troublemakers. A soldier who argued with a superior could be subject to execution. A brawl could be followed by a round of beheadings.[15] A soldier who cursed while being flogged was subject to beheading.[16] Officials were praised for their courage when they remonstrated with the emperor or when they spoke up against other powerful officials. For officials, the act of speaking up fulfilled ideals of honesty and courage. Soldiers had no such recourse. Soldiers spoke out with curses, and the officials did not praise them for their courageous and sincere behavior. Instead, their curses were answered with swift executions in the marketplace.

There are stories of compassion and forgiveness where officials spared soldiers who committed minor offenses. Wang Huaji (944–1110) spared a soldier a flogging after the soldier failed to rise to attention. After a soldier holding a candle had scorched Han Qi's whiskers by mistake, Han Qi tried to make sure the soldier would not be flogged for it.[17] In these examples of leniency, the fine qualities of officials occupy the center stage. The military setting serves as the background, the space where the kind-

13. Sima Guang, *Sushui jiwen*, 6.79–80.

14. Fan Zhen, *Dongzhai jishi*, 4.35.

15. Cao Wei (973–1030), the son of the general Cao Bin (931–999), executed an old soldier for arguing with him in a minor incident (Sima Guang, *Sushui jiwen*, 2.25–26); soldiers of the imperial Myriad Victories (Wansheng) and Dragon Vicious (Longmeng) Battalions had been gambling. The game ended in a fight with soldiers tearing apart roof beams to hit each other. The troops began to panic, but the official Li Zhaoliang caught, arrested, and beheaded the unruly soldiers, flogging the ringleaders first. According to the account, this terrified the entire army (*Song shi*, 464.13563).

16. An anecdote praises the famous officials Han Qi and Wen Yanbo for their heroic demeanor while ordering the execution of soldiers. Han Qi remained composed while Wen Yanbo grew angry at the soldiers' wickedness. The alleged offense: cursing their superior during a flogging (Shao Bo, *Shaoshi wenjian houlu*, 20.155). Also see anecdote in the beginning of the chapter.

17. Sima Guang, *Sushui jiwen*, 8.97; Ding Chuanjing, *Songren yishi huibian*, 8.356.

ness of these men manifested. Yet in the background of these stories, a truth is revealed. In these military spaces, harsh discipline and cruelty were the daily bread of most soldiers. An insolent soldier could be beheaded. Flogging was the lot of those who failed to respond fast enough or made a misstep. As for compassion, those who recorded these instances must have felt such behavior had been exceptional enough to provide proof of an official's outstanding character.

Bad Living Conditions

Soldiers led hard lives. Their monthly salaries, a combination of grain and cash (cloth was not given every month), could be higher than the income of many poor commoners, but soldiers' salaries were also subject to heavy skimming by their superiors. During the Southern Song, cash became a larger component of soldiers' salaries, increasing their exposure to the high inflation rate.[18] The high levels of skimming and inflation make it difficult, if not impossible, to judge soldiers' standards of living according to their salaries. However, descriptions of life in the military open a window into the material reality of soldiers' households.

Northern Song reports about life in the military camps reveal a landscape marked by misery, poverty, and hunger. Many soldiers and their families received insufficient food, and they had to share cramped living quarters.[19] Some soldiers had to sell their clothes, sometimes literally

18. Ihara Hiroshi argues that soldiers enjoyed reasonable living standards. Ihara bases this observation on the assumption that had soldiers lived poorly, "the Song government could not have sustained its military organization" (Ihara, "Numerical Indices," 9); Wang Yunchang calculated the real income of Song soldiers. He concludes that while some of the early and mid-Northern Song soldiers had a relatively high income, most suffered from harsh living conditions. Wang explains that this became even worse during the Southern Song (Wang Yunchang, *Songdai jundui jingying wenti*, 253–59).

19. In 1032 the court approved a request by Attendant Censor Li Hong (*jinshi* 1008), who spoke of the bad state of the soldiers from Chuanxia (in modern-day Sichuan and Shaanxi) who had been sentenced to serve in the border area in Shaanxi. Li reported that the soldiers tended to be old, lame, and thin, and that they shared a single room with their wives (*Song huiyao, xingfa*, 4.18 Tiansheng 10th year, 10th month, 16th day). In a similar report from the year 1048, Zhang Fangping warned that a

selling the shirts off their backs and wearing paper instead.[20] Malnourishment made soldiers too weak to wear their armor.[21] Soldiers who worked on the waterways died from overwork, thirst, and disease.[22] The abolition of the Rotation System under the New Policies only served to increase poverty in the military.[23] Reports on soldiers' poverty during the final years of the Northern Song, a time of intensifying military decline, mention soldiers who had to work outside the camp to supplement their income. Even imperial soldiers were reduced to performing menial labor outside the camp to support themselves. Some imperial soldiers bribed their superiors to avoid training, so they could have time to work.[24] In some cases, hunger drove soldiers to sell their weapons and military equipment in exchange for food.[25]

Reports on soldiers' lives during the Southern Song reflect a continued state of poverty among soldiers and exploitation by their superiors.[26] According to one official's report, regulations limited the lighting of fires

---

soldier's salary barely covered even his uniform costs. As a result, the soldiers' wives and children went cold and hungry (*Chang bian*, 163.6.3928); Zhang Fangping, *Lequan ji*, 18.15.151.

20. Wang Anshi spoke of this problem in 1071 (*Chang bian*, 222.19.5403; *Song shi*, 194.4843–44).

21. Early in the Qingli reign period (1041–1048), Fan Zhongyan argued that malnourished soldiers became too weak to carry their armor, and as a result they deserted and were ultimately beheaded (Tian Kuang, *Rulin gongyi*, 108–9).

22. In 1016 Emperor Zhenzong ordered medical treatment for the soldiers in Hangzhou after great numbers of them who worked in the water contracted a foot disease and many of them died (*Chang bian*, 88.41.2019). In 1023 great numbers of soldiers working the rivers in the height of summer died of thirst (*Chang bian*, 100.1.2324). In 1076 Shenzong spoke of large numbers of soldiers assigned to digging a canal in Huainan. The southern men working there were too weak to handle the daily workload. Many of the soldiers became very ill, but they still had to be carried to the workplace for inspection. Many died on the way (*Chang bian*, 173.71.6688.).

23. Under the new system, soldiers no longer went on bandit-hunting expeditions outside of their area and lost the bonuses attached to this duty. As a result, the soldiers did not get enough food and clothing (*Chang bian*, 312.6.7574).

24. According to an account from 1126 (Wang Zao, *Jingkang yaolu jianzhu*, 7.792).

25. In the spring of 1126 there were reports of soldiers who traded their weapons, shields, and body armor in the marketplace for cooked food. The government succeeded in confiscating over 4,200 military items from the commoners who had purchased them (*Song shi*, 197.4921).

26. According to the official Cheng Bi (1164–1242) (Cheng Bi, *Luoshui ji*, 2.18a–21a.236–37, *lundui zhazi*).

in the camps to between three and five in the afternoon, leaving soldiers without access to a warm drink of water at the end of the day. Soldiers were overworked and burdened by the costs of their own equipment (such as straps of leather, bow equipment, and arrows). The heavy burden of labor forced the soldiers' wives and children to assist the soldiers in carrying out their duties.[27] Military housing continued to be lacking in both quantity and quality.[28] Poverty in the military camps reduced the soldiers to collecting firewood, weaving sandals, collecting night soil, and sending their wives and daughters to work as prostitutes.[29] One official, Li Ruyi, won himself the nickname "Li Straw Shoes" because the poorest of his soldiers had to make him a pair of shoes on a daily basis.[30]

The monetization of soldiers' bodies and labor exacerbated the harsh conditions of military life. Because the Song military used salaried soldiers for labor, soldiers had a monetary worth both as names on a register and as units of labor. Soldiers' superiors used them to generate income through a variety of ways: skimming their salaries, tampering with the measurements for distribution of grain, renting out soldiers' labor outside of the camp, and forcing soldiers into taking loans or selling parts of their income.[31] Arrears in soldiers' payments could last for years.[32] One method for extracting money from soldiers, known as *zuocang*, included buying back surplus grain from the soldiers. The officials often made those sales mandatory, and they purchased the grain at below-market prices. In addition, although the regulations limited the purchase to surplus

27. According to an account from 1137 (Xu Mengxin, *Sanchao beimeng huibian*, 180.9.357). For more on the participation of the family in military labor, see chapter 5.

28. In 1186 the Bureau of Military Affairs reported that in Wenzhou (in modern-day Zhejiang) the housing shortage forced soldiers to find dwellings among the common people (*Song huiyao, bing,* 6.26, Chunxi 13th year, 1st month, 6th day).

29. This according to the Southern Song thinker and official Zhu Xi in 1162 (Zhu Xi, *Huian ji*, 11.36–37.184).

30. Yue Ke, *Ting shi*, 14.167–68.

31. In 1080 the censor Man Zhongxing reported that in the units working on the dikes, clerks extorted bribes from the staff of the moat forts and the soldiers. The clerks beat and harassed the soldiers, who had to borrow money from the state to bribe their superiors (*Chang bian*, 303.54.7386). For tampering with measurements, see *Chang bian*, 67.12.1504; *Song huiyao, shihuo,* 62.9, Renzong Tiansheng 7th year, 3rd month.

32. In 1080 Lü Wenqing (d. 1099) complained about problems with soldiers' pay in 216 imperial battalions in the Kaifeng area as well as River Clearing (Heqing) and postal-station prefectural battalions. According to the account, this situation continued for years without being investigated (*Chang bian*, 305.22.7418).

grain, officials often purchased greater amounts, leaving soldiers with insufficient food for survival.[33]

A shortage of food stood at the heart of much of the discontent and bitterness of army life. The Song military supplied great numbers of troops and their families across great distances, with the biggest challenge being the supplying of the standing armies in the border regions.[34] For that purpose, the state accumulated and stored grain for up to two or three years, depending on the region and kind of grain stored.[35] Yet the armies rarely received the full amount of grain allotted to them, especially in the units ranked lower in the military hierarchy.[36] Moreover, the soldiers' superiors within the battalions also often skimmed the soldiers' food stores. Even if the distribution of grain was timely, the grain given out was still old, often rotten, and less than promised.[37] The daily meal of old grain was one of the most unbearable elements of military life, a constant source of displeasure and anger among soldiers, and in a few cases it was the rotten grain that pushed soldiers to the point of mutiny.

Escaping the Register: Northern Song Local Militias

Resistance to military policies and institutions began as soon as people found themselves threatened by military registration and conscription. In times of military tension and conflict, the state embarked on large con-

33. Wang Yunchang, *Songdai jundui jingying wenti*, 274–75. Wang Yunchang finds the earliest mention of *zuocang* in Renzong's reign, but it continued to be a problem during the Southern Song as well.

34. See Cheng Long's study of supply logistics in the Northern Song's northwest border zone, *Beisong xibei zhanqu liangshi.*

35. Su Zhe, *Le cheng ji*, 38.840; *Chang bian*, 8.16.1527, 60.32.1341. Zhuang Chuo explains that wheat did not hold as long as rice (Zhuang Chuo, *Jile bian*, 1.38).

36. In 1047 Emperor Renzong ordered the granary officials to give soldiers food in a sufficient amount. Apparently, authorities accumulated grain for years before shipping it. Even then, only the imperial Superior Armies in the capital received their full food allowance. The Middle and Lower Armies received 80 to 90 percent of the food (*Song shi*, 194.4843).

37. Zhang Xiaoxiang, *Yuhu ji*, 14.10a–11a.614–15; *Song huiyao, shihuo,* 62.10, Renzong Qingli 7th year, 2nd month.

scription campaigns for the local militias of the threatened border zones. These conscription campaigns triggered popular mass resistance among local commoners who feared both the short-term disruption and long-term consequences of militia service. This took place already during the early decades of Song rule when, as a response to the military crisis with the Liao empire to its north, the Song state established large militias in the border area. Many commoners, reluctant to serve in the militias, preferred to flee their homes and turned to banditry instead.[38] This scene repeated itself numerous times during the Northern Song as commoners continued to find a variety of ways to avoid militia service.

The government dramatically increased the size of its militias following the outbreak of the Song-Xia conflict in 1038. This time, the Song state organized militias in the northwest border zone. Terrified of being tattooed for the militias, some men fled their villages and hid in the wilderness. Others "drilled holes in their limbs" to escape military service.[39] Other strategies included splitting households and joining the wives' kin, hiring people to assume one's identity, and trading identities with one another. The prominent official Han Qi complained that tattooing militia members on the back of the hand did not allow the state to distinguish clearly between militia members and other local men, making it difficult for the state to keep track of local militia members. Instead, Han Qi asked to have them all tattooed on the face and transferred to the imperial armies.[40]

The popular mood in the border regions had a powerful effect on the court. Tattooing the commoners who served in the militias was a sensitive and controversial issue among the population at large. Officials, including Han Qi himself in 1040, relayed to the throne the unpopularity of military tattoos among commoners. Following Han Qi's petition, Emperor Renzong halted tattooing completely among Shaanxi militias.[41] In

38. See the report the official Li Weiqing (943–999) made in 987 regarding the hardships of Henan commoners (*Chang bian*, 28.3.633–34).

39. *Chang bian*, 124.13.2928.

40. *Chang bian*, 138.10.3311–12. Chinese people used similar strategies of resistance to conscription during the Warlord Period of the early twentieth century (Lary, *Warlord Soldiers*, 16–17).

41. In 1040 Han Qi reported a state of great trepidation among the people of Shaanxi, who feared that registration for the Indomitables militias meant tattooing and

1041, in the Hedong border circuit, the government reduced the burden of tattooing from facial tattoos to arm tattoos after large numbers of local men fled from service in the local militias.[42] In one case, when the state calculated the fiscal cost of transferring militia men to the regular armies, it also factored in the anger and resentment of the men transferred. The record implies that a joining bonus was necessary for preventing the new recruits from a violent backlash.[43]

Another wave of unrest in the border regions began with the New Policies (1069–1085), the large reform effort that included the registration of the empire's households into *baojia*, mutual-surveillance units. The *baojia* reform expanded the local militia model, with the idea that militias would eventually supplant the regular armies. Under this reform, resistance to conscription to militias continued, and the descendants of militia members attempted to dodge service by dividing up plots and assuming other surnames or fake identities.[44] Other strategies commoners used to avoid *baojia* service included various manipulations of the household size: driving adopted children and sons-in-law out of their homes, marrying off widowed mothers, and splitting households between sons. Some men resorted to self-mutilation: poisoning their eyes, cutting off their fingers, or burning their skin to exempt themselves.[45]

Officials in the Song court, aware of the hostility to military policies among border zone residents, tried to tailor their policies to create mini-

---

conscription for the regular army. As a result, Emperor Renzong ordered that Han Qi avoid tattooing the arms and faces of the commoners conscripted to the militias (*Chang bian*, 126.37.2978–79). The official Li Gou (1009–1059) argued that people would not consent to being tattooed (Li Gou, *Xujiang ji*, 28.2a.238).

42. In 1041, after Li Zongyi (*jinshi* 1019) reported that many men of the local militias fled to avoid having their faces tattooed, it was decided to only tattoo the hands of the Indomitables of Hedong circuit when conscripting them into the regular army (*Chang bian*, 134.11.3189).

43. When Han Qi led the conscription of about fifty to sixty thousand militia members into the regular armies, he objected to giving them the customary joining bonus. Later, fearing an angry backlash from below, he reversed his position (*Chang bian*, 138.10.3311–12; 138.11.3312).

44. In 1070 the military commissioner's office at Qinfeng circuit reported that the children and grandchildren of men from the Staunch Guards (Baoyi) militias divided up their plots, assumed other surnames, and hardly ever held on to their true identities (*Song shi*, 191.4735–36).

45. *Song shi*, 192.4783–84.

mal resistance. Wang Anshi, the architect of the reforms, argued that the disturbances caused by the *baojia* reform simply reflected the old fear of tattooing for the regular militias.[46] Wang suggested steps to allay the fears of the commoners: avoiding sudden changes to the *baojia* service cycle and administering the *baojia* system through the Ministry of Agriculture instead of the Ministry of War.[47] Wang Anshi's offered solutions focused on changing the perception, not the essence, of the government's military policies.

Following the fall of the Northern Song in 1127, the newly established Southern Song government had to relinquish much of its control over the military and allow for the establishment of more autonomous armies and local defense forces. For the remainder of its existence, however, the Southern Song government reasserted its authority whenever possible.[48] The bodies of military men reflected those patterns of resistance and negotiation, revealing a similar logic to that of the Northern Song period. When men refused to serve in militias, the government spared militia members facial tattoos.[49] When press gangs scoured the marketplace for candidates for service, men cut off their own fingers.[50] When the government grew weak, it mutilated less. When the people's position weakened, they mutilated themselves preemptively.

The residents of the border regions had a long memory, and the traumas of conscription were passed on from generation to generation. Each conscription campaign, each reorganization of the military system, meant that the state once more focused its gaze on its military register. The commoners understood the basic cycle of military manpower policies. They knew that conscription campaigns tended to follow in the footsteps of

46. In 1071, when Emperor Shenzong asked about disturbances caused by the reform, Wang Anshi explained that the people feared being tattooed for the Warriors for Righteousness militias (*Chang bian*, 221.26.5375). Wang Anshi was likely referring to the conscription and tattooing of the men of Shaanxi and Hedong for the Warriors for Righteousness militias and the imperial Defending Victory Battalions (*Chang bian*, 221.64.5391–92).

47. *Chang bian*, 235.7.5697, 235.29.5710.

48. For more on this process, see Huang Kuan-chong, *Nansong difang wuli.*

49. During the first Song-Jin war, the government spared militia members facial tattoos to avoid estranging the local population (Li Xinchuan, *Jianyan yilai chaoye zaji*, 1/18.478.412–13).

50. Li Xinchuan, *Jianyan yilai chaoye zaji, yi ji*, 7.615.

natural disasters, and they took appropriate steps to delay, confuse, and escape the government.[51]

Song political history is often told as a dramatic factional conflict between reformers and conservatives, but the reactions of commoners to conscription campaigns tell a different story. Officials in court hotly debated military policies, but from a commoner's point of view a pattern emerged: appearing on any kind of military register could be disastrous. No matter how the political winds shifted, the men appearing on the military registers would be the first candidates for shuffling, transferring, or reinforcing wherever the need arose. The political pendulum swayed between reform and counter-reform, between reformers and conservatives, but all roads led the commoners in the border regions toward the army. Therefore, commoners made avoiding the register their main goal, whether by changing their identities, hiding, or self-mutilation.

Desertion

Once men became soldiers, one of their more common ways of resisting the military institutions was through desertion. The scale of desertion during the Song period grew to such heights that desertion became a famous trait of the Song military.[52] Already in the early Song, there were concerns in court that soldiers openly abandoned their generals and led their comrades in fleeing combat.[53] Desertion during combat was common enough to lead to the promulgation in the mid-eleventh century of a new law that called for the execution of soldiers whose general died in battle.[54] Yet desertion continued to haunt the military. In one famous in-

51. The official Sima Guang noted in 1064 that whenever they faced a flood or a famine, the commoners would begin preparations for a conscription campaign: they would split their households, sell their fields, and drift away and work as tenants (*Chang bian*, 203.2.4918).

52. For more about desertion in the Song military, see You Biao, "Lun songdai shibing taowang"; Zhang Ming, "Liangsong shibing taowangfa xintan"; Zhu Dejun, "Songdai xibei diqu taobing wenti."

53. The emperor discussed this in 1003 (*Chang bian*, 54.18.1194).

54. *Chang bian*, 134.24.3208, 153.13.3719.

stance, during the first Song-Jin war, a few thousand Song soldiers fled at the sight of just a few Jurchen cavalry.[55] Despite the reorganization of the Song military under the Southern Song, the military continued to suffer from high rates of desertion. One Southern Song official explained that the soldiers, sent to campaign at the height of winter with no parting feast, lacking in clothing and food, would flee as soon as they caught sight of the enemy.[56]

Beyond collapse and desertion on the battlefield, the labor armies of the Song also suffered from high rates of desertion. Soldiers fled work in great numbers, leaving their superiors with insufficient manpower.[57] Soldiers could flee in large groups as well. In one case, a group of a thousand corvée soldiers tried to escape together instead of reporting for duty.[58] In 1089 one investigation of the Yellow River Conservation Office revealed that of about sixty-three thousand soldiers sent there, 1,319 had died and 3,691 had fled.[59] The soldiers who deserted, some of them convicts, often joined bands of bandits, already largely composed of deserters.[60] The Song underworld was heavily militarized.

Reports on the situation in the Song's postal system, also operated by soldiers, reveal a system deeply crippled by desertion. Soldiers often deserted due to arrears in payments, and the state had to repeatedly issue pardons for postal-station deserters in the attempt to lure them back into the army.[61] Soldiers in these remote postal stations often deserted for lack

55. Zong Ze, *Zong zhongjian ji*, 1.12a-b.11.

56. This according to the official Cao Yanyue (1157–1228) (Yang Shiqi, *Lidai mingcheng zouyi*, 338.1b).

57. In 1070 the Song mobilized great numbers of prefectural soldiers to repair a series of forts in the Shaanxi border area. So many soldiers fled from Shaanxi circuit that the remaining manpower could not handle the transport of grain and fodder. The military mobilized additional manpower by transferring men who had been working on the waterways (*Chang bian*, 218.70.5309).

58. This took place in 1079 (*Chang bian*, 299.27.7281).

59. *Chang bian*, 422.12.10216.

60. In 1076 Emperor Shenzong commented on the groups of bandits troubling Hebei and Jingdong, many of them men who had been sent to penal servitude in the River Clearing Army and then deserted (*Chang bian*, 277.6.6768). In 1184 the official Luo Dian explained that in each case of banditry there must have been a deserter involved (Ma Duanlin, *Wenxian tongkao*, 168.20a.735).

61. The court issued various edicts to this effect in 1182, 1191, and 1203 (*Song huiyao, fangyu*, 11.30, Xiaozong Chunxi 9th year, 9th month, 13th day; *Song huiyao, fangyu*, 11.34,

of clothing or food.[62] The practice of *zuocang*, forcing soldiers to sell back their food at a low price, drove postal station soldiers to desertion.[63] Soldiers late on their mail delivery sometimes preferred to desert rather than face the consequences, possibly a beheading.[64] Shortage of manpower in the postal system compounded the issue. Desertion left the remaining soldiers with a heavier workload, which led to higher death rates, which led to increased desertion.[65] In some postal stations, soldiers' wives also delivered documents because only two or three soldiers remained. Some postal stations resorted to providing shelter to bandits and other men of dubious backgrounds to make up for lost manpower.[66] Hunger drove so many soldiers to desertion that in some postal stations only a single soldier remained.[67]

The criminalization of soldiers contributed to desertion, but the soldiers who deserted found themselves stigmatized further. The tattoos on deserters' faces left them with limited options, and many had no choice but to become bandits.[68] Captured deserters, if not executed, received a

Guangzong Shaoxi 2nd year, 11th month, 27th day; *Song huiyao, fangyu*, 11.36, Ningzong Jiatai 3rd year, 11th month, 11th day).

62. *Song huiyao, fangyu*, 10.38, Huizong Xuanhe 7th year, 2nd month, 16th day; *Song huiyao, fangyu*, 10.53, Gaozong Shaoxing 3rd year, 7th month, 14th day.

63. In 1108 an edict addressed the problem of postal-station soldiers who did not earn enough to meet their living expenses. The officials bought back food from them and did not leave them enough. Soldiers deserted, and none were recruited in their place. They had to hire commoners to provide transportation services for the state, yet those commoners ended up working without pay as well (*Song huiyao, fangyu*, 10.28, Huizong Daguan 2nd year, 3rd month, 14th day).

64. Hong Mai tells of a soldier who returned three days late from a mission. He was saved from a beheading only thanks to the intervention of the kind official Wang Shengxi. Wang argued that should they execute the soldier for being late, the next time a soldier would be late, he would prefer to desert rather than return (*Yijian zhi, guilin zouzu*, 1776–77).

65. According to a report from 1101 (*Song huiyao, fangyu*, 10.26, Huizong Jianzhongjingguo 1st year, 1st month, 9th day).

66. The Bureau of Military Affairs reported this in 1142 (*Song huiyao, fangyu*, 11.8, Gaozong Shaoxing 12th year, 5th month, 29th day).

67. *Song huiyao, fangyu*, 11.9, Gaozong Shaoxing 12th year, 6th month, 8th day.

68. You Biao, "Lun songdai shibing taowang," 98; When Zong Ze (1059–1128) served as commandant of Guantao (in modern-day Hebei), he executed all the deserters

special tattoo.[69] The deserter tattoo joined the growing list of characters on a soldier's face, further proof that there was a man who was dangerous, ugly inside and out. The fear of deserter tattoos deterred some deserters from turning themselves in. In one case, the government compromised and issued special amnesties that exempted deserters from facial tattoos.[70] If during the early tenth century warlords used tattooing to prevent desertion, in the Song empire tattoos contributed to desertion. And if soldiers deserted because of the harsh military life, they remained in hiding because of the harsh consequences of desertion.

Desertion and the Illegal Transfer

Putting a stop to desertion was complicated by the monetary value attached to soldiers, as officials had their own vested interest in having many soldiers under their authority. The more soldiers in a unit, the greater its budget. A high number of soldiers brought additional rewards for their superiors. The state used the meeting of military manpower quotas as one of the standards for assessing officials, and it distributed rewards and punishments accordingly.[71] Moreover, soldiers had a monetary value as units of labor. Generals and officials rented out the labor of their soldiers for a profit. Some soldiers even set up their own businesses, paying a portion of the money back to their superiors.[72]

The mass scale of desertion and the monetary value of soldiers led to a new problem: the creation of false military registers. After all, to generate income for officials, soldiers did not have to be physically present in their battalions if their names remained in the register. Some

---

he caught. The account adds that because of Zong Ze's actions, the area had no bandits (Fang Shao, *Bozhai bian*, 3 juan version, 1.74).

69. *Chang bian*, 467.30.11154.

70. This took place in 1036 (*Chang bian*, 118.17.2786).

71. Ouyang Xiu, *Ouyang Xiu quanji*, 421–22.

72. For more on the economic aspects of the Song military system, see Wang Yunchang's study *Songdai jundui jingying wenti*. McKnight also mentions the huge labor value of the military system (*Law and Order in Sung China*, 333).

officials who wanted to receive the award for a fully staffed unit hid the true scale of desertion among their troops.[73] This provided the officials with another benefit, because they could continue collecting the wages for the missing soldiers from the central government.[74] Officials who hid the numbers of deserters in their units became a recurring problem during the twelfth and thirteenth centuries.[75] In one case, an investigation turned up 3,497 documents of deserters kept by their units to cover up their departure.[76]

The phenomenon of empty registers and fake identities offered opportunities for officials and soldiers to cooperate in deceiving the central government. Officials who drove soldiers to desertion by overexploiting their labor could supplement the numbers by bringing in other deserters to stand in their place.[77] The deserters could improve their duty or location, sometimes also receiving an additional "signing bonus" when they joined

73. This according to the official Zhang Jin in 1172 (*Song huiyao, zhiguan*, 10.10, Xiaozong Qiandao 8th year, 8th month, 5th day).

74. In 1132 Han Xiaozhou (1075–1150) argued that officials did not report deserters so they could collect their salaries (*Song shi*, 370.11690). In 1121 Shen Jizhong reported that officials did not remove deserters from the register so they could keep on collecting their grain rations. When they caught deserters, they did not punish them according to the full extent of the law (*Song huiyao, xingfa*, 7.27, Huizong Xuanhe 3rd year, 4th month, 1st day); Zhu Xi argued that generals and officials in charge of provisions used the false military registers for self-enrichment (Zhu Xi, *Huian ji*, 26.50b–51a, 576).

75. In 1121 a memorial reported on the heavy military expenses in Hebei, where officials who benefited from the military budget did not remove deserters from the registers (*Song huiyao, xingfa*, 7.27, Huizong Xuanhe 3rd year, 4th month, 1st day); Zhu Xi argued that a large part of the Song's military income went to officials who used the empty registers for their own ends (Zhu Xi, *Huian ji*, 26.30b–31a.576); Yuan Xingzong (d. 1171) explained that after soldiers had deserted, officials kept the units understaffed on purpose in order to keep collecting the salaries of the missing soldiers (Yuan Xingzong, *Jiu hua ji*, 7.15b). In 1221 the Bureau of Military Affairs reported that after soldiers had deserted, their units hid the fact and continued to claim their salaries (*Song huiyao, zhiguan*, 32.55, Ningzong Jiading 14th year, 2nd month, 18th day).

76. The official Li Daxing (b. 1126) investigated circuits who held on to the documents of soldiers who deserted. He had 3,497 such certificates destroyed (*Song shi*, 395.12049).

77. In 1184 the Bureau of Military Affairs reported that officials embezzle clothing and grain from postal soldiers, rent out their labor, leading them to desert, and then replace them with deserters and loafers (*Song huiyao, fangyu*, 11.30, Xiaozong Chunxi 11th year, 9th month, 8th day).

the new unit.[78] The officials gave the deserters clothes, food, and a new name.[79] Sometimes, they even received the family and property of soldiers who had deserted.[80] The state regarded this phenomenon as "illegal transfer."

In the decades that spanned the end of the eleventh century and early twelfth century, illegal transfer became a serious problem. The government vacillated between a flexible pragmatic approach and a harsh moralistic approach. The government issued numerous decrees, for a while legalizing the transfers, then attempting to stop the problem with a strict implementation of rewards and punishments. At the same time, it relaxed some of the regulations that drove soldiers to desertion.[81] Repeated attempts to address this problem in the last forty years of the Northern Song period failed to resolve the issue.[82]

78. In 1083 the prefect of Ansu Military Prefecture (in modern-day Hebei), Pan Xiaochao, argued: "When imperial soldiers desert, those who turn themselves in can do an illegal transfer, thus escaping penal servitude. The prefectural soldiers who commit a crime and desert can transfer illegally without being caught. To escape hard labor, they go to a place with lighter labor duties. To escape harsh and distant places, they transfer to closer locations. The payment and grain given to them are wasted. This results in growing shortages of artisans in the construction forts." (*Chang bian*, 334.13.8032).

79. According to Hu Quan (1102–1180) (*Hudan'an xiansheng wenji*, 27.20).

80. Yang Shiqi, *Lidai mingchen zouyi*, 224.5b-a.

81. In 1082 the official Du Chang (d. 1104) asked that soldiers in Shaanxi who transferred illegally between units be tattooed and placed in the local prefectural armies. His request was approved and extended to all circuits (*Chang bian*, 325.42.7823). In 1109 an official of the Bureau of Military Affairs warned of the many problems created by a law that had been promulgated by Shaanxi circuit penal superintendent Wu Anxian (b. 1043). The law allowed deserters from the imperial and prefectural armies to transfer to a different battalion and have their tattoos altered accordingly. The official warned that the law allowed officials to compete for the soldiers, artisans, and craftsmen of another unit or agency. It also allowed some units to cover up the true numbers of deserters in their ranks by assigning the new people the names of soldiers missing from their own units. Instead, the official asked for a stricter implementation of rewards and punishments to prevent illegal transfers. His request was approved (*Song shi*, 193.4813). In 1121 Emperor Huizong relaxed the laws governing soldiers who deserted when late in delivering documents for fear of punishment (*Song huiyao, fangyu*, 10.37, Huizong Xuanhe 3rd year, 8th month, 12th day).

82. In 1091 the Ministry of Justice reported a request by the Bureau of Military Affairs that the soldiers of the Fengxiang superior prefecture (in modern-day Shaanxi) Baoning Pick (Jianzhong baoning) Battalion be forbidden to transfer to other units and have their tattoos altered (*Chang bian*, 458.29.10961). In a 1097 memorial, Jingyuan cir-

As it attempted to address the problem of desertion and illegal transfers, the Song state gradually made desertion an official criterion for assessing military officials. Deserters, like soldiers in the camp, came to have a monetary value. Already in the early eleventh century the Song state was rewarding law enforcement soldiers for each deserter and bandit they captured.[83] This remained the practice during the Southern Song period as well.[84] The Southern Song government continued expanding the reward system. During the first Song-Jin war, they set rewards for those who informed on deserters.[85] In the late twelfth century, the Song state set a system for rewarding and punishing military officials according to numbers of deserters in units under their command.[86] The Southern Song government recognized desertion as a chronic problem by establishing a permissible ratio of desertion in military units, ranging from 5 percent to a third and even a half of a battalion's manpower.[87] Attempts to combat illegal transfers were also reflected in changing tattooing pat-

cuit (in modern-day Gansu and Ningxia) military commissioner Zhang Jie (1027–1102) spoke against deserters transferring between different units. As a result of Zhang Jie's request, a decree ordered that the newly built forts and outposts of Shaanxi and Hedong circuits would not accept deserters as transfers (*Chang bian*, 493.7.11710–11). In 1106 and 1120 the eunuch-general Tong Guan urged the government to put a stop to the illegal transfer (*Song shi*, 193.4812–13, 4815).

83. In 1018, after the official Zhou Renmei complained that law-enforcement soldiers only get punished for failing to catch deserters and bandits and receive no rewards for it, the emperor approved his request to reward the soldiers 200 cash for each deserter or 500 cash for each bandit (*Song huiyao, zhiguan*, 48.126, Zhenzong Tianxi 2nd year, 8th day; *Song huiyao, bing*, 3.2, Zhenzong, Tianxi 2nd year, 8th month).

84. In 1170 it was decided to reward or punish patrolling inspectors according to the numbers of deserters they captured (*Song huiyao, zhiguan*, 59.25, Xiaozong Qiandao 6th year, 9th month, 19th day).

85. A reward of ten strings of cash was promised to those who inform on deserters (*Song huiyao, xingfa*, 7.29, Gaozong, Jianyan 1st year, 6th month, 14th day).

86. In 1082 great numbers of deserters during combat led to the punishment of two officials (*Song huiyao, zhiguan*, 66.17, Shenzong Yuanfeng 4th year, 12th month, 15th day).

87. In 1084 it was decided to provide faster promotion tracks for emissaries in charge of tea in Sichuan in whose units the rate of desertion fell below 5 percent (*Song huiyao, zhiguan*, 43.67, Shenzong Yuanfeng 7th year, 11th month, 22nd day). In 1113 the transportation commissioner for the East and West Zhe circuits laid out the parameters for awarding officials for their contribution of manpower to the transportation network. The rules included statements such as, "If deserters are less than a third [of the total number of soldiers]" and "If they sent the required [number of troops] but more

terns, as the Song state tried to limit soldiers' mobility between units by increasing the size and amount of information within military tattoos of labor troops.[88]

The crime of illegal transfer resulted directly from military policies that incentivized both soldiers and officials to collaborate against the state. The Southern Song state could not stop the illegal transfer, and officials continued to take in deserters under assumed names, sometimes using them as servants.[89] The competition for manpower became even fiercer as some battalions turned to other battalions to recruit their soldiers or to capture back their own deserters. One such attempt ended up in a big brawl in the marketplace between soldiers from two different units.[90]

Other Forms of Resistance

Because military service was centered on the soldier's body, some soldiers tried to escape service through self-mutilation. Soldiers used their sickles and axes to cut off their own toes or broke their own arms and legs in the hope of gaining a transfer to a better location.[91] Other soldiers committed crimes just so they could be banished to a different, more convenient

than half deserted . . ." (*Song huiyao, shihuo*, 43.8, Huizong Zhenghe 3rd year, 1st month, 29th day).

88. In 1186 an official asked that the shoulder tattoos of postal-station soldiers be bigger, clearly stating each soldier's prefecture, subprefecture, and unit. The emperor forbade units from receiving into their ranks soldiers who had deserted from other units. When giving out the payments, except soldiers present in the postal station as per the usual troop rotation, the officials were to inspect the tattoos on the soldiers' arms (*Song huiyao, fangyu*, 11.32, Xiaozong Chunxi 13th year, 2nd month, 4th day); on the changes in the content and size of tattoos during the Southern Song, see Sogabe, "Sōdai no shi-hai ni tsuite," 11–12.

89. Xie Shenfu, *Qingyuan tiaofa shilei*, 11.6a.

90. In 1175 an official spoke against generals who build their own armies and against armies who tried to recruit other units' soldiers (Yang Wanli, *Cheng zhai ji*, 120.26a-b.543); Zhu Xi, *Huian ji*, 96.11b.292; *Song shi*, 368.11454.

91. In 1012 there were reports that River Clearing soldiers used sickles and axes to cut off their own toes to gain a transfer to a neighboring prison citadel. Another edict from the same year reported that soldiers broke their own arms and legs to avoid corvée or to transfer to a better location (*Chang bian*, 77.4.1755, 78.26.1773).

location. Considering the relative dangers and burdens of life in the penal-military complex, some soldiers saw flogging and a facial tattoo as an acceptable price for a transfer.[92]

Soldiers did not blindly obey their superiors. Even without directly opposing their superiors, soldiers could simply fail to carry out orders or feign illness.[93] Soldiers stole from the boats carrying supplies.[94] They defied their superiors and went outside the camp to take advantage of economic opportunities, selling artisanal skills, engaging in commerce, and smuggling salt.[95] When delivering post, the soldiers would steal, swap, hide, or lose the mail, as well as open mail and insert blank pieces of paper instead or leak out the contents of the messages.[96] Convicts on their way to their place of banishment would escape en route, and the local authorities would be too timid to handle those who did arrive.[97]

A list of soldiers' crimes from 1091 reveals how deserters extended the networks of soldiers well beyond the military camp and into the bandits' stronghold. The list included robbery, theft, murder, arson, breaking inmates out of prison, hiding criminals, providing assistance to passing bandits, giving bandits weapons, and leaking information about plans to capture bandits.[98] Deserters continued to hover at the edges of military spaces, seeking opportunities for pillage or vengeance against former superiors.[99] Fearful of stirring up trouble, whenever they captured a deserter-

92. See the cases of prefectural River Clearing soldiers in the year 1028 who stole wood to gain a transfer: *Song huiyao, xingfa,* 4.15, Renzong Tiansheng 6th year, 1st month; *Song huiyao, xingfa,* 4.16, Renzong Tiansheng 7th year, 7th month, 4th day; *Song huiyao, fangyu*, 14.13, Renzong Tiansheng 7th year, 7th month.

93. Chen Shichong, *Suiyin manlu*, 3.28–29; *Chang bian*, 333.42.8021–22.

94. *Song huiyao, shihuo*, 42.21, Shenzong Zhiping 4th year, 10th month, 17th day.

95. *Song huiyao, shihuo*, 26.18, *yanfa* 5, *zalu*, Gaozong Shaoxing, 3rd year, 10th month, 11th day; *Chang bian*, 223.37.5434; Su Shunqin, *Su xueshi ji*, 10.15b-16a.67.

96. *Song huiyao, fangyu*, 10.38, Huizong Xuanhe 5th year, 7th month, 14th day; *Song huiyao, fangyu*, 11.8, *yichuan* 2, *jidipu xia*, Gaozong Shaoxing 12th year, 5th month, 29th day; *Song huiyao, fangyu*, 11.25, Xiaozong Qiandao 9th year, 2nd month, 14th day; *Song huiyao, fangyu*, 11.34, Guangzong Shaoxi 4th year, 10th month, 2nd day.

97. *Song huiyao, xingfa*, 4.64, Ningzong Jiatai 4th year, 1st month, 23rd day.

98. In 1091 the judicial commission of Hedong East circuit listed crimes committed by soldiers working on the dikes (*Chang bian*, 468.25.11186).

99. Gao Qiong (935–1006) foiled a plot by deserters to rob the prefect's entourage when he left the town (*Song shi*, 289.9692). In 1018 the deserter Huo Xing attempted to kill an official. The deserter attacked the official ferociously, and the military officer

bandit, some clerks would prefer to avoid a thorough investigation of his past.[100] Soldiers had their own support networks inside and outside their battalions. Officials had to consider that deserters were likely hiding beyond the camp walls, watching their movements, and waiting for their opportunity. Bands of deserters may have lacked the power to save soldiers from their predicament, but they could still avenge them.

Mutiny

When despair, fear, and anger reached levels that soldiers could not bear, they rose in mutiny. Soldier mutinies were public collective actions that openly protested the terms of life, payment, and service in the Song military. The Song period experienced a high frequency of such mutinies. Records of these events tend to be brief, but the scale and location of one mutiny that broke out in Baozhou (in modern Hebei) in 1044 caused enough concern in court to generate more detailed records. Through these accounts it is possible to examine the different stages in a soldiers' mutiny.

THE BAOZHOU MUTINY

The military garrisons in Baozhou had a long tradition of lawlessness. The battalion stationed at Baozhou was originally formed by recruiting bandits from the river islets in Tongzhou (in modern-day Jiangsu), as well as pirates from Liangzhe and Jiangnan circuits, and was reinforced with deserters. In the early 1040s, likely due to the military conflict with the Tanguts and the rising demand for combat troops, the battalion was elevated to the rank of an imperial battalion.[101] However, in 1044 the controller general Shi Daiju (*jinshi* 1023) decided to put an end to what he saw as waste: paying the soldiers special bonuses even though they did not go out on patrol missions. Shi asked the fiscal commissioner to stop

---

who rescued the official and carried him away sustained multiple stab wounds in the process (*Chang bian*, 95.14.2199).

100. This was the situation around the capital Kaifeng during the early twelfth century (*Song shi*, 354.11168).

101. *Song shi*, 187.4598.

payment of those special bonuses.[102] This exacerbated the tense relationship between the imperial soldiers, commanded by a eunuch, and the local civil officials.

The threat to the soldiers' income did not go unnoticed. When soldiers of the imperial Cloud Wings (Yunyi) Battalion began to talk about a mutiny, Prefect Liu Jizong became concerned and ordered that all the weapons used for practice be stored away.[103] Around the same time, Shi Daiju was drinking and gambling with Wei Gui, the supervisor of militia.[104] The two began to quarrel in front of a displeased crowd of soldiers. Drunk, Wei Gui cursed at Shi Daiju: "You can only pride yourself on having successfully reduced the soldiers' income!" The soldiers, upon hearing this, became furious.[105]

The incident between Shi and Wei took place before the distribution of uniforms, a dangerous moment in times of tension. Soldiers entered the officials' quarters with drawn blades. Shi Daiju took his family and fled through the east gate into the camp of the Unrivalled (Wudi) Battalion. Liu Jizong also brought his family into the camp. Together they used the Unrivalled troops to close the city, and they led the imperial Miraculous Guards (Shenwei) Battalion through the east gate to confront the mutineers. When the tide turned against the officials, Shi Daiju and Liu Jizong climbed the town walls to flee the rebels. Liu Jizong tried to cross the moat and drowned. Shi Daiju hid within the defensive structures by the walls, where he was killed by the mutineers.[106] The soldiers put Shi Daiju's head on a tree and shot arrows at it every morning until there was no room left. At that point they would pull the arrows out and start shooting at it again.[107]

102. *Chang bian*, 5.3676; Sima Guang, *Sushui jiwen*, 4.50; 11.134–35. The promotion of the battalion into imperial status might be responsible for the discrepancy between the battalion's duties and customs and the duties usually assigned to imperial battalions.

103. The Cloud Wings Battalion was promoted to imperial status in 1000 CE and merged with the Unrivalled Battalion that appears in this story (*Song shi*, 183.4572–73).

104. Supervisor of militia (*jianya*) according to Sima Guang; military director-in-chief (*dujian*) according to Li Tao.

105. *Chang bian*, 151.5.3676.

106. Shi Daiju hid within the abatis, a form of fortification or obstacle made from sharp sticks pointing outward.

107. Sima Guang, *Sushui jiwen*, 4.50.

The soldiers then faced the task of choosing a leader. They first chose the official Wang Shouyi as their leader, but when he refused, the soldiers killed him, spearing him through the heart and out his back. The mutineers then threatened Wei Gui, who agreed to lead them on condition that they listen to him. The soldiers agreed, and Wei ordered that they not touch the granary or kill without reason and convinced them to return their loyalty to the Song. According to Sima Guang, Wei Gui had the soldiers' ears.[108]

The initial round of violence was then followed by a round of siege and negotiations. According to one historical account by Li Tao, officials who came to quell the uprising spoke to the rebels on the walls. Some of the soldiers wanted to surrender, but, as more troops joined, the rebels stood firm in their resistance.[109] According to Sima Guang, the court sent the official Tian Kuang who stood under the walls of the town and called out to the soldiers. Still, the soldiers remained suspicious and would shoot anyone who came near. Palace eunuch Guo Kui called out to the soldiers and tried to reassure them of the court's trustworthiness.[110]

Sima Guang also tells us that the eunuch Yang Huaimin took advantage of the negotiations to settle a rivalry with Fiscal Commissioner-in-Chief Zhang Wenzhi, who had previously tried to take Yang's position and give it to a military official. Yang Huaimin reported to the emperor that the soldiers agreed to surrender in return for Zhang's head. The emperor agreed to the soldiers' demands and sent an imperial commissioner to behead Zhang. The official Fu Bi ran into the imperial commissioner on his way there and sent him back, alerted the emperor to the fact that this was probably a personal grudge, and warned of the problems that could be created by executing a senior official to satisfy mutinous soldiers. Zhang Wenzhi was demoted instead.[111]

The *Song shi* contains another account of these negotiations in the biography of the official Li Zhaoliang. The biography states that during the Baozhou uprising, the emperor sent Wang Guo to accept the soldiers' surrender. The soldiers clung to the wall and cried out: "If you bring infantry commander Li, we will surrender." Li Zhaoliang came with a few dozens of

108. *Chang bian*, 151.5.3676; Sima Guang, *Sushui jiwen*, 4.50, 11.134–35.
109. *Chang bian*, 5.3676–77.
110. Sima Guang, *Sushui jiwen*, 4.50–51, 11.134–35.
111. Sima Guang, *Sushui jiwen*, 4.51; *Chang bian*, 152.3.3696–3697.

his entourage, none wearing armor or carrying a shield or bow. They knocked on the town gates and shouted to those on top: "For those who come to surrender, I guarantee that no harm shall come to them. Otherwise, no creature here will be left alive." Soldiers began climbing down the city wall using the rope, and the next day the rest opened the gates and surrendered.[112]

After the rebels surrendered, they left the town. The last to leave were caught and executed. Some of the officials were punished for cutting the food rations of the battalion and for not being on the alert for mutinous soldiers.[113] The *Song shi* adds that later on Li Zhaoliang divided the women of the mutineer households between the various armies and took some of them into his own household.[114] According to Sima Guang's account, after the mutineers surrendered, one leader was buried alive but the others were not investigated.[115] The *Chang bian* describes a more gruesome end, with 429 men buried alive.[116]

THE PATTERN OF SOLDIER MUTINIES

As in the case of the Baozhou mutiny, conflicts over payment and treatment were among the most common causes for other soldier mutinies in the Song military. Soldiers on campaign plotted against cruel or incompetent officials and generals.[117] Excessive floggings drove soldiers to mutiny, as did threats to the welfare of soldiers' families.[118] Soldiers protested

112. *Song shi*, 464.13563.
113. Sima Guang, *Sushui jiwen*, 11.134–35.
114. *Song shi*, 464.13563.
115. Sima Guang, *Sushui jiwen*, 4.50–51: 11.134–35.
116. *Chang bian*, 151.35.3688.
117. Wang Zhongzheng (1030–1101), an official in charge of one of the main military forces of the 1081 campaign against the Xi Xia, was inexperienced in military matters. Wang, lost and fearful in the wide open spaces of Tangut country, forbade starting fires at night for fear of discovery by the Tanguts. The rear guard's food had not been fully cooked by the time night fell, and many of the soldiers who ate it fell ill. The angry soldiers began plotting to murder their commanding officers and scatter back (Sima Guang, *Sushui jiwen*, 14.182–83). In 1081 Song soldiers murdered the cruel official Li Ji[1] while they were all besieged by the Tanguts (Shao Bowen, *Shaoshi wenjian lu*, 10.101–2), In the failed campaign to retake the Sixteen Prefectures, Emperor Taizong pushed the soldiers so hard he caused the army to turn on him (Wang Zhi, *Moji*, 1.5).
118. A mutiny almost erupted in Kelan (in modern-day Shanxi) because of an official who had flogged soldiers (*Chang bian*, 156.15.3786). The high work quotas set by the

the dismissal of a popular general.[119] Changes in the remuneration system triggered mutinies.[120] Soldiers who feared hard labor, sometimes numbering in the thousands, refused to go to work.[121] A sudden discharge could lead to widespread anger among the troops who found themselves facing a threat to their livelihood.[122]

There were times when mistreatment of soldiers' officers by officials triggered the outbreak of a mutiny.[123] The officers, indispensable for managing the troops, stood above soldiers in authority and pay, but they were still vulnerable to abuse by officials. That officers could be punished by flogging set them apart from officials and placed them closer to the soldiers.[124] A close relationship between soldiers and their direct superiors could also lead an officer to start a mutiny in the attempt to shield his soldiers from a cruel official.[125]

As part of the collective nature of mutinies, soldiers mobilized each other by making their anger public—shouting a curse, revealing a truth, spreading rumors through the ranks. Then came the stage of plotting.

---

official Liu Yonggui in 1007 forced the soldiers to bring their wives to fell trees in the mountains in the wind and the rain. Later, soldiers murdered the hated official (*Chang bian*, 66.18.1472–73).

119. The soldiers under the command of Liu Guangshi resented his dismissal and turned on the official sent by the government (Luo Dajing, *Helin yulu*, 2.28).

120. The cancellation of a bonus to the imperial Dragon Riders (Longqi) Battalion triggered the mutiny in Baozhou, although the cruel behavior of a military official contributed to the hostile atmosphere (Zheng Xie, *Yunxi ji*, 20.4b–5a.296); Bao Zheng, *Bao xiaosu zouyi*, 4.12b–13a.119; *Minggong shupan Qingming ji*, 11.436–37.

121. In 1077 Wang Xiu and nine other soldiers from the Formidable Martiality (Xiongwu) Second Ballista Battalion were accused of inciting the soldiers to refuse to go and transport wheat. The deputy troop commandant Niu Sui was accused of not having tried to stop them. A decree ordered the beheading of Wang Xiu at the camp's gate and the banishment of the other nine. Niu Sui was to be flogged a hundred times and demoted to the Caozhou Clerk Reserves (*Chang bian*, 282.7.6900–1).

122. See these two cases from 1059 and from the twelfth century: *Chang bian* 190.4.4578–9; *Song shi*, 417.12495.

123. The Wang Jun mutiny erupted after the official allowed his servant to lord over the military officers, and he also had soldiers flogged on his servant's word (*Chang bian*, 45.26.980); Zeng Gong, *Longping ji*, 20.12b–13a.201.

124. In 1004, when his superior used a minor pretext to flog him, the Fengzhou (in modern-day Shaanxi) base citadel officer Liang Fu led six of his followers in killing the superior and escaping (*Chang bian*, 58.4.1273).

125. When the cruel conduct of Liu Yonggui caused widespread resentment among the troops in Yizhou, it was an officer who led them in mutiny (*Song shi*, 290.9706).

Soldiers discussed their plans: how to break into the armory and which officials should be killed first. If officials caught wind of such plans, they had an opportunity to act quickly, before the core group of mutineers could strike first and call for the rest of the soldiers to join them.[126]

As the unrest was brewing, officials with insight and sensitivity could defuse the situation in a timely manner. When Wen Yanbo held a banquet late into the night, the soldiers in his escort ignored orders and began tearing down a stable to use for firewood. The collapse of discipline led Wen and the military officials he was entertaining to realize their lives were in mortal danger. There were no minor infractions of discipline in the Song military, and such behavior signaled lack of regard for consequences, potentially a mutiny. Wen Yanbo defused the situation by showing concern for the soldiers who suffered in the cold and allowing them to continue, all while maintaining a calm and carefree attitude.[127] By making a timely concession while displaying confidence, Wen Yanbo may have saved the lives of all officials in attendance that night.

If officials exposed a mutinous plot at an early stage, they could still convince the soldiers to stop, even if they backed their words with the prodding of an iron whip.[128] When officials succeeded in quashing the mutiny before it began, a grisly public execution of the ringleaders could be deemed as a satisfactory solution. Such was the fate of eleven imperial soldiers of the Cloud Wings Battalion who were cut in half at the waist in 1045 after being implicated in a mutiny plot.[129] After all, small instances of unrest within the military were a common matter, and frugality called for bloodbaths to be reserved for special occasions.

126. In 1005 the officials in Shangzhou (in modern-day Shaanxi) uncovered a plot by soldiers to rob the armory and kill their superiors. They acted before the mutiny began (*Chang bian*, 59.9.1328). In 1052 Guo Shenxi (997–1074) was awarded for proving himself capable at suppressing soldiers who tried to instigate disorder in the ranks by executing one and tattooing two others (*Chang bian*, 173.9.4180).

127. Sima Guang, *Sushui jiwen*, 10.118.

128. This took place in Kelan fort (in modern-day Shanxi) in 1045. The officer who spun the iron whip was promoted (*Chang bian*, 156.15.3786).

129. In 1045 the soldier Liu Jin confessed to following others in a mutiny plot. As a result, eleven soldiers of the imperial Cloud Wings battalion were executed, including the soldiers Wang Zong and Qi Lan, by cutting them in half at the waist (*Chang bian*, 157.15.3799).

When anger and fear spread among the soldiers, moments of contact between officials and soldiers became highly volatile. The appearance of disorder and resentment in the drilling arena was considered especially dangerous.[130] The tensest moment of all was the point of payment: food, money, sometimes cloth. Soldiers who found the portions of grain to be below the standard stormed out.[131] Soldiers who did not receive their pay began airing out their grievances publicly, setting up the atmosphere for violent action.[132] At this point, when soldiers began acting publicly against their superiors, the camp stepped closer to the verge of mutiny.

Soldiers often rallied around the issue of the low quality of their food, especially because the logistical problems of feeding millions of people (soldiers and family members) meant that old and rotten grain became a standard aspect of the food supply system.[133] The most officials could do was to strike the right balance between getting rid of the old food (by giving it to the soldiers) and distributing food of a reasonable quality. Some chose to quell dissent by being generous with the "good stuff" even though that meant going against regulations.[134]

130. See these cases of lack of discipline while drilling that took place in 1075, 1080, and 1090: *Chang bian*, 271.18.6636, 303.49.7384–85, 449.26.10792–93.

131. In 1063 soldiers in the Palace Army Duty Group (serving in the palace and capital) asked for grain. Their superiors distributed grain using false measurements. The soldiers refused to accept it and left. Emperor Renzong ordered that an official should inspect the measurements and punish accordingly if they were not up to standard. Soldiers who asked for payment beyond the regular cycle or raised a clamor were to be handled according to military law (*Song shi*, 194.4843).

132. In 1059, when soldiers in Jing (in modern-day Gansu and Ninxia) did not receive their pay, they cursed the controller-general and started complaining to each other, stirring up a riot. After the authorities beheaded two of the rioters and tattooed three others, the riot ended. They also punished the clerk responsible for the delay in the soldiers' pay (*Chang bian*, 190.5.4579).

133. When Zhao Gai (995–1083) served as prefect of Hongzhou (in modern-day Nanchang, Jiangxi), Prefectural Supervisor Rao Shi, a man who allegedly delighted in causing strife, brought in a local man named Hu Shunzhi. The two tried to raise the tensions between Zhao Gai and his soldiers by warning him that soldiers of the imperial Returning to Moral Civilization (Guihua) Battalion were plotting a mutiny because they had had enough of the old and bad food. Zhao Gai refused to listen to them (Wang Gui, *Huayang ji*, 60.2.442).

134. Guo Chengyou was demoted in 1050. The charges against him included the giving of new grain to raise morale among the troops (*Chang bian*, 168.7.4046).

As was often the case in the Song military system, officials tried to resolve the rotten food problem with a numeric formula, and they sought for the optimal ratio of rotten grain to good-quality grain that would allow disposing of older grains but would still not be repulsive enough to trigger unrest. Due to the small amount of available fresh food, the ratio of old food could be high, 20 percent or even 50 percent. When the food quality fell too low, the situation could escalate very quickly. Soldiers raised a clamor in the granary, drawing blades. At this moment there was still time for officials to act quickly: punish the wrongdoer responsible for the bad food, sometimes also the soldiers who complained, but at the same time address the soldiers' grievance by improving the food quality.[135]

In addition to soldiers' regular salary, on special occasions, such as the Great Ritual (Da li), the state gave presents to soldiers around the empire. The official Ouyang Xiu voiced his concern that soldiers became far too accustomed to receive gifts without cause, and he warned that denied those gifts, soldiers turned to action: they gathered together, cried out, and brandished their weapons.[136] Ouyang Xiu described what he saw as a dangerous development in soldiers' culture: that they came to view their terms of employment as rights, and that they became capable of organizing around that principle.

135. The official Wang Deyong (987–1065) tried to come up with balanced formulas of 80 percent good food and 20 percent rotten food. When soldiers raised a clamor over the bad food they received, Wang Deyong went to the granary and scolded the clerks for not following his orders. He resolved the situation by flogging both the person in charge of rice distribution and the soldiers who complained about it (Sima Guang, *Sushui jiwen*, 4.46). In 1193 Wang Mingqing served as notary of the administrative assistant to the military commissioner of Ningguo military prefecture (in modern-day Anhui). According to precedent, whenever they distributed food, the soldiers and officials would gather in the granary. Wang Mingqing went to the granary, and when he arrived at the gate, he saw a group of soldiers leaving with an unpleasant expression. He inquired about it, and the soldiers explained that the controller-general Zhou Shixiu suggested using the previous year's rice for half of their rations. The soldiers resented the rotten rice, and they brandished their spears in the hall, spoke out in anger, and went to report the matter to the prefect, followed by many other soldiers. Wang Mingqing stopped them by promising only fresh rice from that moment on (Wang Mingqing, *Yuzhao xinzhi*, 4.66.69).

136. *Ouyang Xiu quan ji*, 9.412.

When soldiers raised a clamor and demanded rewards, the state tended to react violently, with floggings and beheadings.[137] However, during sensitive political moments of dynastic transition, officials showed a willingness to listen to the soldiers' claims. Following Emperor Yingzong's coronation in 1064, the soldiers of Jingnan were disappointed with the low-quality silk they received. The town stood on the brink of mutiny, but a brave superior saved the day when he convinced the soldiers to accept the silk with an impassioned plea.[138] Following the ascension of Zhezong in 1186, soldiers disappointed with the gift of money broke into the local government office with drawn blades. The official resolved the situation with a combination of immediate payment and punishment of the leaders.[139]

Once mutiny had begun, one of the first actions mutineers would undertake was breaking into the storehouse to seize weapons.[140] They then went about wreaking their vengeance on hated superiors and their families.[141] At the same time, the soldiers chose a leader: a soldier, an officer, or an official. If officials refused to join, the soldiers killed them.[142]

137. This took place in Sichuan in 971 (*Song shi*, 2.34).

138. Wei Tai, *Dongxuan bilu*, 11.123–24.

139. *Song shi*, 351.11093.

140. Cases of soldiers breaking into military storehouses for weapons include the Guanghua mutiny in 1043 (Sima Guang, *Sushui jiwen*, 11.133–34) and the Beizhou mutiny in 994 (*Song shi*, 5.95). A mutiny plot in 1045 in the Yongning military prefecture (in modern-day Hebei) included a plan to break into the weapons storehouse (*Chang bian*, 157.15.3799). In the Baozhou mutiny, the official Liu Jizong, concerned about unrest among the troops, ordered that all the weapons used for practice be stored away (*Chang bian*, 151.5.3676).

141. In the Baozhou mutiny, soldiers targeted the family of an official. During the late Southern Song, following a soldier mutiny, the Gaosha prefect Ma Guangzu had to hide in a back garden with his family scattered in a few different hiding spots. His wife hid with a clerk who used the opportunity to sexually assault her (Zhou Mi, *Guixin zashi*, 4.177).

142. Mutineers killed Liu Pan and his mother (Xiong Ke, *Zhognxing xiaoji*, 16.14a-b.958), In the Yizhou mutiny (in modern-day Guangxi), soldiers killed the hated prefect Liu Yonggui and the supervisor of militia Guo Jun, and chose Controller-general Lu Chengjun to serve as their general (*Chang bian*, 66.18.1472). In 1006 in the Yizhou[1] mutiny, soldiers killed Fu Zhaoshou, drove out Niu Mian, and chose Wang Jun as their leader (*Song shi*, 6.111).

In some mutinies, mutineers sought to replace a cruel leader or bring back a beloved leader who had been falsely accused or dismissed.[143]

Once the mutiny was already in progress or came close to erupting, turning to brute force alone could be dangerous for their superiors. When the soldiers in Guanghua Military Prefecture in 1043 received dry, hard bread, they suspected their official Han Gang was giving away their food, drink, and pay. They began tossing the hard bread at the official's quarters. When Han Gang responded with violence, the unrest turned into a mutiny and Han Gang had to flee for his life.[144] Initial attempts at quashing the Baozhu mutiny also failed.[145]

Even as mutineers took up arms, officials and officers still scrambled to halt the mutiny. This sometimes involved a brave and respected superior who confronted the soldiers. The official Huangfu Jian (1000–1075) took a softer approach to a mutiny. Realizing that the cruelty of a general drove the exhausted soldiers to mutiny, Huangfu opened the city gates and allowed the soldiers to scatter. He then went out of the city himself to plead with the deserters to "return" to the Song. By nightfall, most soldiers turned themselves in, and the clerks took charge of capturing the rest. The whole matter came to a conclusion within ten days.[146]

Even as a mutiny was well underway, the state and the mutineers could continue negotiations. Reports of the Baozhou mutiny describe a failed round of talks between soldiers on the city walls and officials below, followed by a successful offer of terms by the general Li Zhaoliang. Both sides took the negotiations seriously. At one point in the Baozhou mutiny, the emperor agreed to give the soldiers the head of an official despised by the mutineers.[147] Though there could be no room in official rhetoric to justify any kind of action against the dynasty, the reactions of officials and the court reveal that soldier mutinies had an air of legitimacy. Problems the soldiers pointed to needed to be resolved. Incompetent, corrupt, and cruel officials needed to be disciplined and removed for the military to function.

143. Soldiers turned on the cruel Zhu Fu to restore the capable Zhao Shujin to leadership of Xiuzhou (Wang Mingqing, *Huizhu lu, di san lu*, 2.327.250–51).

144. Sima Guang, *Sushui jiwen*, 11.133–34.

145. Sima Guang, *Sushui jiwen*, 4.50.

146. Liu Ban, *Peng cheng ji*, 38.6b–7a.372.

147. Sima Guang, *Sushui jiwen*, 4.51; *Chang bian*, 152.3.3696–97.

It is a common trope to imagine the Chinese imperial bureaucracy as a Confucian hierarchy, extending from the bottom (in the case of the military, soldiers), through ranks of superiors, all the way to the Son of Heaven on his imperial throne. Song mutinies tell a different story. Rather than a pyramidal hierarchy, it is possible to see here a few different players communicating directly with each other: the leaders of common soldiers, local administrators, and the central government.

Soldier mutinies usually led to grim endings with a string of executions in the marketplace. The Baozhou mutiny was followed by enslavement of family members and the burying alive of mutineers. In 994 a Beizhou soldier who had led his comrades in rising was crushed to death.[148] The authorities beheaded large groups of soldiers and sometimes their families too.[149] The Qingzhou mutiny was followed by executions for the main conspirators, as well as tattooing, enslavement, and assignment to military service for the soldiers and their relatives.[150] The state executed a few hundred of the Gaosha mutineers, and one clerk was burned alive, but they also punished the wrong-doing officials.[151]

Soldier mutinies ended in defeat, but that did not mean they failed completely. Song sources do not exonerate the soldiers from all responsibility for mutinies. The sources conclude that the soldiers in Baozhou were bandits and hard to control, and that in Jianchang they acted in an arrogant manner and their demands had no end.[152] Yet the sources also place a large share of the responsibility for mutinies on the shoulders of cruel, corrupt, and incompetent officials. Soldiers who resisted sometimes had some of their demands met, and the state investigated some of the crimes the soldiers complained about.[153] Usually, the state issued a pardon

148. *Song shi*, 5.95.

149. In 994 the Kuizhou (in modern-day Chongqing) soldier Xie Rong and a hundred others were executed in the marketplace for rioting (*Song shi*, 5.87).

150. For debates on the punishments for the Qingzhou mutineers and their families, see Wei Tai, *Dongxuan bilu*, 5.54; *Song huiyao, zhiguan*, 65.38, Shenzong Xining 5th year, 12th month, 26th day.

151. Zhou Mi, *Guixin zashi*, 4.177.

152. Zheng Xie, *Yunxi ji*, 20.4b–5a.296; Xiong Ke, *Zhongxing xiaoji*, 16.14a.958.

153. When fifty-six fort soldiers left their jurisdiction to complain about issues in payment and money owed to them, the state had their leader beheaded, and they disciplined the other soldiers. However, they also investigated the problems with payment (*Minggong shupan Qingming ji*, 11.436–37).

for most soldiers involved. At times, officials removed the trigger for the violence. Yet there could be no appearance of a rebel victory, and officials still punished the ringleaders harshly and tattooed and enslaved their families. A mutiny had to be terminated with a moral spectacle of both terror and grace.

Conclusion

The conflict of officials and soldiers tells a story that does not conform with the perception of the Song as a Confucian age. No harmonious moral hierarchy existed in the military, and Confucian values did not trickle down from officials to soldiers. In the penal-military complex, the worlds of officials and soldiers met in a violent collision. Soldiers were no admirers of the refined scholar-officials, nor did they follow them blindly. They complained, fought with their masters, and resisted authority time and again. Officials, for their part, were quick to turn to coercion, violence, and terror. The Confucian values that made them so famous were not for all to share.

The eighth-century Tang empire saw the rise of professional soldiers who came to see military service as their "rice bowl."[154] Under the Song, soldiers became a much larger group but also suffered a decrease in their social status. Song soldiers, directly dependent on the state for their livelihood, continued to wage struggles centered on their salaries and labor conditions. Soldiers formed a group that believed it had rights as well as duties. Soldiers demanded that their superiors play by the rules, and they held the state accountable for what they believed it owed them: reasonable food, timely payments, fair treatment, and responsible and professional leadership.

Strong similarities existed between the attitude and behavior of militiamen in the border zones and those of regular soldiers: fear of tattoos, self-mutilation, and flights to the wilderness to join bandit gangs. Higher rates of military service in the north meant that in those regions more commoners had relatives who were soldiers or veterans of the regular armies. The commoner of the border zones might end up among soldiers,

154. Graff, *Medieval Chinese Warfare*, 212, 216, 239.

as conscripted temporary labor, as a transfer from the militias, or as a member in the bandit camp. The shared patterns of resistance suggest that the world of the penal-military complex extended far beyond the military camp, and many of its members did not serve in the army.

Song military law was extremely harsh, but the state's treatment of soldiers changed following effective resistance by soldiers. Funds were dispersed, wrongs corrected, and evil officials punished. Just like in other aspects of Song administration, the officials and court used an uncompromising moralist rhetoric, but they also showed flexibility and pragmatism once the hard approach had failed.[155] Officially, there was no room for labor disputes in the Song armies. In practice, the court recognized the legitimacy of some of the soldiers' claims and allowed for the finding of solutions that would satisfy the soldiers. Officials drafted the policies of the government in the capital, but the court also allowed for input from the Song's underclass—input given through violent resistance.

The social trajectory of the poor was radically altered by military events. The Mongol conquest in the late thirteenth century led to the establishment of a new military system across the former territories of the Song empire, and the military institutions that gave birth to the tattooed soldiers of the Song ceased to exist. This new social class centered on the tattooed soldiers was forged through both exploitation and resistance within and against the Song state's penal-military complex. With the collapse of the Song's military institutions at the end of the thirteenth century, this social group also faded into darkness.

155. See Rossabi's study on the Song dynasty's pragmatism in foreign relations, *China among Equals*.

CHAPTER 7

Loyalist Tattoos and Tattooed Generals

How lonely the death of Yue Fei![1] What befell him in the dark of the emperor's prison? One account of the downfall of the Southern Song general reaches a tragic height in a famous scene. After Grand Councilor Qin Gui (1090–1155) had Yue Fei and his sons arrested, he sent He Zhu to elicit a confession from Yue Fei. Yue Fei, the great general who not long before saved the empire from ruin, now faced torture and death together with his son. Yue Fei, the Song empire's greatest warrior, tore the shirt off his body and showed his back to He Zhu. On Yue Fei's back were tattooed four large characters: "Exhaust one's loyalty in service of the state" (*jinzhong baoguo*). Upon seeing this, He Zhu realized Yue Fei was innocent of treason.[2] Shortly thereafter Yue Fei and his son who served under him were tortured and murdered in prison. Such was the sad end of Yue Fei's life, and with it also died the hope for restoration of Song rule in the lost northern portion of its empire. The myth of Yue Fei the great loyalist was born.

Within the story of the great loyalist, or more specifically, within his tattoo, hides another story, that of the struggle between tattooed soldiers and the state. This struggle revolved around two phenomena that reached

1. A previous version of this chapter appears as the article "Loyalist Tattoos and Tattooed Generals in the Song Dynasty," *Frontiers of History in China* 11, no. 2 (July 2016): 247–258.

2. *Song shi,* 365.11393.

a climax during the first Song-Jin war: the rise of tattooed men from the rank and file to senior positions of leadership, and the practice of tattooing statements of loyalty to the state and its ruler on the bodies of fighting men. By the time Yue Fei was born in the late twelfth century, such tattoos had deep roots, going back centuries.

Loyalist Tattoos during the Tenth Century

Tattoos with statements of loyalty appeared as early as the beginning of the tenth century, the last years of the Tang dynasty. In the year 906 the late Tang warlord Liu Rengong, notorious for his cruelty, pressed into service all men, aged fifteen to seventy, in the area under his control. The tattoos of the conscripted men varied according to social standing. Most men were tattooed on the face with the inscription "Deciding Hegemony Battalion" (Dingba du), whereas men of a higher social standing were tattooed on the arm with the inscription "Serving the ruler with all my heart" (*yixin shizhu*).[3] During these mass campaigns of violence and terror, loyalty was not freely given but tattooed on the skin. Liu Rengong gave elite men a concession, tattooing their hands instead of their faces. This did not change the basic rationale behind tattooing, though. The warlords of the early tenth century were military men who used tattooing to create large armies. In the process, the status and bodies of elite men both suffered great injuries. There was a lesson here for elite men of the Song period: military men and their tattoos needed to be disciplined.

Loyalist tattoos continued to receive a cold welcome in the early days of the Song. Huyan Zan (late tenth century) was a military man, described as rash and ferocious, a sworn enemy of the Khitans. Huyan Zan tattooed his body with the inscription "Kill the Khitans with devotion" (*chixin sha qidan*), and he burned the same inscription on the bodies of his wife and retainers. He had his saddle and saddle blanket and the tools he used embroidered and inscribed similarly in red and black, and he also had each of his sons tattooed with the inscription "When leaving, forget home for the sake of the state. When going to battle, put aside death for the sake

3. Xue Juzheng, *Jiu wudai shi*, 135.1801–2; Ouyang Xiu, *Xin wudai shi*, 39.424.

of the ruler" (*chumen wangjia weiguo, linchen wangsi weizhu*). Huyan's ways did not earn him praise from his superiors for being loyal and brave but instead almost led to his execution for "being strange and deluding the masses." When the emperor commuted his death sentence, Huyan argued that his journey to exile would be a popular event, hinting that his appearance was a curious spectacle.[4] Huyan's story takes place in the early Song period, but Huyan and his tattoos were the social and cultural products of the preceding Five Dynasties period, of a world run by military men who were free to tattoo themselves. By Song Taizong's reign (976–997), loyalist tattoos calling for the killing of the enemy and the sacrifice of one's family and life for the ruler were no longer embraced and respected but rather frowned upon.

Loyalist Tattoos and Rebel Tattoos during the Northern Song

Northern Song military tattoos usually designated the name, place, and number of a battalion. Battalion names had many different themes: functional, temporal (time of the battalion's founding), and martial. Some military tattoos expressed loyalty, such as "loyal and brave" (*zhongyong*), but the context of conscription was often coercive or semi-coercive (the conscript had no other way to make a living). Most of the men who wore the tattoos were illiterate. Some of them belonged to non-Han communities, suggesting an even greater degree of estrangement between the language and the tattooed subject.[5] Words like "loyal and brave" stood for the power of the Song state, as well as the power of the literate over the illiterate. With the act of tattooing, the Song state established that power.

Under the Song, tattoos became a state prerogative, one of the clearest symbols and manifestations of state power. Soldiers who rose in mutiny reclaimed that authority by tattooing the local male population and

4. *Chang bian,* 33.3.739.

5. This was the case when in the year 1042 five thousand Frontier Tribal Troops were recruited into the Qingjian fort. The characters "loyal and brave" were tattooed on the backs of their left hands (*Chang bian,* 135.17.3229).

conscripting them into the rebel ranks.[6] Smaller bands of soldier-bandits who engaged in banditry rather than rebellion also tattooed commoners into their ranks.[7] Tattooing could be accompanied by the application of other treatments usually reserved for criminals, like head-shaving.[8] When soldiers tattooed commoners, they inducted them into a world that was both militarized and criminalized.

When rebels tattooed, they mimicked the state, like the tattoos on the soldiers' faces in the mid-eleventh-century rebel army of Wang Lun that read: "Heaven Sent Sagely Victorious Battalion" (Tian jiang sheng jie zhihui).[9] This tattoo, although patterned on Song military tattoos, still varied in content, stating that the battalion broke from the Song state and now belonged to Wang Lun. Some rebel tattoos stated explicitly their quarrel with the Song state. The mid-eleventh-century rebel Wang Ze tattooed all adult males in his area, aged twelve to seventy, with the inscription "The righteous army is defeating the Zhao house and attaining victory" (*yijun pozhao desheng*).[10] In addition to tattooing himself an army, Wang Ze set up his own government and declared a new reign period, the trappings of an independent state.[11]

6. In 994 Wang Ji'en took Chengdu from the rebel Li Shun a day before Li was about to capture the city's men, tattoo their faces, and place them in the military registers. Li Shun's plot was thwarted. Once the Song government quelled the rebellion, it had Li Shun's soldiers tattooed on their faces (*Chang bian,* 36.1.784, 95.12.2198).

7. In 1076 Shenzong commented on the problem of banditry in Dezhou (in modern-day Hebei and Shandong). In Cangzhou a bandit-soldier called Grand Guardian Kang gathered close to a hundred men on the run, and for nearly a year he operated in the vicinity of Jingdong and Hebei, robbing property and tattooing commoners into his army (*Chang bian,* 279.18.6833). The difference between rebels and bandits was often that of scale.

8. In the year 1000 the rebel Wang Jun, who held the city of Yizhou (modern-day Chengdu), forced the young and strong of the city residents, as well as Buddhist and Daoist monks, to become soldiers. Wang Jun's forces tattooed the backs of their hands, shaved their heads, and tattooed their faces. They were then given military equipment and forced to climb the walls together with the rebels (*Chang bian,* 46.15.994).

9. In 1043 Wang Lun led a hundred soldiers with these facial tattoos (Ouyang Xiu, *Ouyang Xiu quan ji,* 783).

10. Zhao was the surname of the Song dynasty's imperial family.

11. Wang Ze, originally from Zhuo prefecture (in modern-day Hebei), left it for Bei prefecture (in modern-day Hebei and Shandong), where a famine drove him to sell himself to be a sheep herder. He later registered with the Declaring Resolution

Rebels used tattooing as a symbol of defiance, as well as to claim dominion over the bodies of the subjects of the state. Tattooing reinforced social labels such as "good" and "bad," "respectable" and "despicable." In ordinary times, those of higher social standing were rewarded twice. They were exempt from the physical act of tattooing and gained a higher social standing over the tattooed group. Rebels and bandits used tattooing as an act of social leveling, to turn the social pyramid on its head. When the residents of the penal-military complex rose in rebellion, they made the whole world a prison and themselves its kings.

Di Qing: A Tattooed General of the Northern Song

By the founding of the Song in the middle of the tenth century, tattoos were becoming a mark of shame, and tattooed faces were relegated to stigmatized spaces and submissive positions. However, in times of military crisis the Song state needed a competent military with capable leadership. At moments such as these, new opportunities presented themselves to tattooed men. This was the case in 1038, when the war between the Song and the Tangut Xia state in the northwest forced the Song state to change its stance toward fighting men. During this time, Di Qing, a clerk who joined the army to escape prosecution, was serving as a tattooed soldier in the northwestern frontier. He acquired the reputation of being a formidable warrior who charged his enemies with his hair loose, a terrifying bronze mask on his face.[12] In the course of a few years, Di Qing became a general, the greatest military figure of his time. A short while later, he fell from grace and died. In the story of Di Qing's rise and fall, the lines inked on his skin take a prominent place.

Di Qing's appearance became a meaningful part of his life story, of both his fame and infamy. Besides his tattoos, his body bore the scars

---

(Xuanyi) Battalion as a minor officer. When he left Zhuo, his mother bid him farewell and tattooed the character "fortune" (*fu*) on his back. The tattoo added to his supernatural appeal (*Chang bian*, 161.11.3890).

12. According to one source, Di Qing was a clerk who joined the army after he had been implicated in a crime, though the nature of his crime is unclear (Wang Pizhi, *Shengshui yantan lu*, 2.16).

of many battles against the Tanguts.[13] People called him "Heavenly Emissary Di." After Emperor Renzong compared him to the legendary heroes Guan Yu and Zhang Fei, Di Qing received the nickname "Rival to Ten Thousand" (Diwan), and people said that he could beat off ten thousand men with a single foot.[14] People also described Di Qing as "truly a spirit of war."[15] With his hair worn loose, bronze mask, scarred body, and tattooed face, Di Qing was a man of the field and the military camp. His body made an impression that no civil official in court could match.

Following Di Qing's military exploits, the emperor summoned him to the capital and appointed him commissioner of the Bureau of Military Affairs, making him one of the most powerful officials in the Song government. Despite his high position, Di Qing's presence in the center of the political arena drew much ridicule, often focused on Di Qing's low social background and his tattoos. People commonly referred to Di Qing as the "scoundrel commissioner." His soldiers also adopted this nickname, although perhaps in a more admiring tone.[16] The official Yu Jing referred to him as "Commoner Qing."[17] The official Liu Yi chastised him, referring to him as "a tattooed soldier."[18] The official Wang Yaochen (1003–1058), his colleague in the Bureau of Military Affairs, mocked his tattoos, but a quick retort by Di Qing put Wang to shame.[19] One source claims Wang could never forgive Di Qing his meteoric rise, which placed Wang, a

13. During the war against the Tanguts, Di Qing participated in twenty-five battles and was injured by arrows four times in the span of four years.

14. Guan Yu and Zhang Fei were two generals of Liu Bei (161–223) during the Three Kingdoms period. They were legendary warriors. Guan Yu became a deity of war and is worshipped to this day. It was said of them that they could each single-handedly defeat ten thousand foes.

15. Sun Sheng, *Sungong tanpu*, 1.147.

16. Ding Chuanjing, *Songren yishi huibian*, 7.325.

17. *Chang bian*, 150.10.3629.

18. Qiang Zhi, *Han zhongxian gong yishi*, 23.

19. According to the anecdote, when Wang Yaochen served together with Di Qing in the Bureau of Military Affairs, he often mocked Di Qing for his tattoos, saying, "They are getting finer and more colorful." Ding Qing replied, "Do you not like them? I shall offer you a line [of the tattoos]." Di Qing's response put Wang to shame (Kong Pingzhong, *Tan yuan*, 4.313).

successful graduate of the examinations system, under the authority of a man who used to be a common soldier.[20]

Di Qing's appearance was an important factor in his popularity among both soldiers and commoners. In one case, when Emperor Renzong suggested that Di Qing remove his facial tattoos, Di Qing declined; instead he preferred to keep them as a symbol to motivate the soldiers.[21] Di Qing had strong support from the rank and file, and his refusal to remove his facial tattoo won him great popularity among soldiers.[22] His presence in the capital created a spectacle, as great numbers of people rushed to cheer him and blocked the streets trying to catch a glimpse of the famous general.[23]

Another story portrays Di Qing as a violent drunk, mocked by a courtesan for his tattooed face. In this story, Di Qing's shame and anger regarding his tattoos were compounded by resentment toward officials with whom he could never compete because he lacked an examination degree. The story then implies that Di Qing even entertained ambitions of usurping the imperial throne. Such stories circulated widely enough at the time to make Di Qing fearful, leading him to request to be removed from his post. The court sent him away to be prefect of Chen prefecture, where he died shortly thereafter.[24]

Di Qing reached one of the highest positions in Song bureaucracy, but despite the rumors that portrayed him as a usurper, during Di Qing's lifetime, the checks and balances of Song government prevented any one official from posing a direct challenge to the throne. In addition, Di Qing was politically and socially vulnerable in court. He did not fit in among civil officials, nor was he part of the networks of generals who gained their

20. Wei Tai, *Dongxuan bilu*, 10.111.

21. Fang Shao, *Bozhai bian* (3 *juan* version), 1.74; *Chang bian*, 172.13.4153.

22. Ye Mengde, *Shilin yanyu*, 7.103.

23. *Chang bian*, 183.8.4435.

24. Wang Zhi, *Moji*, 1.15–16; Wei Tai, *Dongxuan bilu*, 10.117; Ye Mengde, *Shilin yanyu*, 7.103. The *Moji* reports that Di Qing wore yellow clothes, a privilege reserved for the imperial family. The *Dongxuan bilu* reports that a mysterious light was shining at night from Di Qing's residence. This violated Kaifeng's fire regulations. When the official in charge went to investigate, the fire had long been extinguished. The official Liu Chang compared this to a similar incident with Zhu Wen, the warlord who murdered the last emperor of the Tang, founding his own Later Liang dynasty. The implication here is that Di Qing was a usurper.

appointment by virtue of their marriage and personal ties to the imperial clan. What frightened officials mostly was what his ascent symbolized: that there were armed and scarred and angry men below; that in that lower world these men, and not civil officials, had their dominion; and that military men could claim and walk the paths to power, marching out of the military camp and into the imperial court.

Di Qing's tattoos run through the heart of his life story. He had a face that did not belong in court, in high office, or in elite circles. The tattoos were a reminder of his military achievements and of the hardship he had to endure to reach success, but they were also an Achilles' heel, a target for ridicule, a mark of the low-born, animal-like men who lived in the military camps. Critiques of his appearance and demeanor were leveled not just at him but at an entire group of people who needed to know their place and stay there.

Rebel, Enemy, and Regular Army Tattoos in the First Song-Jin War (1125–1140s)

The outbreak of war with the Jin in 1125 and the collapse of the Song military created a huge demand for military manpower as various forces competed to capture and tattoo as many men as possible. Dispersed Song armies hunted down commoners and tattooed them as soldiers.[25] Tattooed convicts took advantage of the collapse of the penal system to escape and form their own armies, and some even used their new power as leverage for gaining an official position from the Song court.[26] As the

25. *Song shi*, 193.4818

26. Zhang Yu, originally a clerk from Pingyang superior prefecture (in modern-day Shanxi), had been tattooed for a crime, then escaped back and gathered a group of a few thousand men. At the time, Ci prefecture (in modern-day Hebei) was without defenses, and the local soldiers agreed to welcome Zhang Yu into the prefecture. The Jin forces raided the borders of the prefecture a few times but never actually passed through the area as part of their offensives. Zhang Yu was appointed audience usher and prefect of Ci. Eventually, when a Jurchen offensive was impending, Zhang Yu and his army escaped (*Yaolu*, 7.202). In 1127 the Hangzhou outlaw Chen Tong[1], after first feigning surrender, took over a city and tattooed and conscripted all the able men

state collapsed, the general Miao Fu kidnapped and tattooed men to increase his army while he attempted a coup against Emperor Gaozong, an episode that had a devastating effect on the emperor's faith in the imperial armies.[27]

The war with the Jin fractured Song suzerainty in many areas and shattered much of the Northern Song's military organization. Many new military forces stepped in. The most powerful one was the Jin military, but they were not alone. In some areas local resistance slowed down or repulsed Jin offensives. Dispersed Song armies, bandits, and rebels (these categories often overlapped) came together to form their own armies, whose relationship to the Song varied from nominal recognition to violent opposition. Because military tattoos were a prerogative of the Song state and a symbol of its authority, the shattering of the state robbed it of its monopoly over the tattooing needle, and new forms of military tattoos began to appear.

The escaped convicts who built their own armies during the war used their own new military tattoos. Huang Jin, a man of Shuzhou, was an escaped slave, a bandit, and a convict. During the first Song-Jin war, Huang Jin formed an army of soldier-convicts, altered the tattoos on their faces into the shape of two flags, and called them "the Army of Flag men." Later, after the Jurchen invasion, Huang Jin surrendered with his forces to the Song state and received an official position.[28] Ding Jin, a convict-soldier from Shouchun (in modern-day Anhui), escaped from the military. He took advantage of the outbreak of the war in 1127 to return home. He then organized the people of Sucun (in modern-day Henan, Kaifeng area) into a large army of tens of thousands of men with six dots

---

therein, numbering a few tens of thousands (*Yaolu*, 8.232); Du Yan, originally a military man, took Mizhou (in modern Shandong) in 1127. The official Zhao Ye had abandoned the city with his family. Later, Du Yan had him sliced to pieces, and then killed his family and had their heads displayed in the marketplace. Du Yan tattooed all the people in the city to increase his army (*Yaolu*, 10.277). In 1132 Lu De, a rebel soldier from Taiping prefecture (in modern-day Anhui), planned to have all the able-bodied men in the city tattooed, massacre the old and weak, and then take his new soldiers with him (*Yaolu*, 53.1102).

27. When Miao Fu attacked Shouchang subprefecture (in modern-day Zhejiang) in 1129, he pillaged the area and had the local men tattooed for his army (*Yaolu*, 22.550).

28. Wang Mingqing, *Yuzhao xinzhi*, 4.52.64.

or the two characters "entering the gang" (*ru huo*) tattooed on their faces.[29] Both Huang Jin and Ding Jin brought their armies to the Song side and received official positions as a reward. In Ding Jin's case, the Song state had his soldiers retattooed and reassigned.[30]

During the first Song-Jin war, irregular tattoos made appearances even within the Song state's own armies. Zhang Jun was one of the four legendary generals credited with saving the Song empire from destruction at the hands of the Jurchens. Zhang Jun, whose army had been following the Song court, had the strongest men in his army tattooed from buttocks to feet, giving rise to the nickname "decorated legs." The tattoo, based on tattoos of drifters in the capital, prevented Zhang Jun's soldiers from fleeing to other armies.[31] The "decorated legs" tattoos declared that this army was Zhang Jun's. Much like in the final years of the Tang dynasty, tattoos no longer bound the soldiers to the state but to a specific general. It is possible to find visual traces of Zhang Jun's "Decorated Legs" tattoos hidden within the famous painting *Along the River during the Qingming Festival* (*Qingming shanghe tu*) (figs. 4–5). This Song-period painting of Kaifeng contains two pairs of these men, with a tattoo pattern wrapping around their legs. The tattoos in Zhang Jun's army during the first Song-Jin war were very likely based on tattoos like those of the laboring men in the painting.

The Jurchens too competed with the Song state over the tattooing of Song subjects. According to a chilling description of the conduct of the Jurchen forces in the year 1131, the Jurchens kidnapped Song subjects, incarcerated them, and tattooed the character "official" (*guan*) above their ear. The Jurchens left their newly acquired slaves among locals, set a price on their heads, and sold them. The Jurchens later exchanged the rest of their captives for horses with the Tatars (Dada) and the Xia, and some were sold to places as far away as Mongolia, to the Shiwei people, and to Goryeo (modern-day Korea).[32] Commodities marked with Sinitic-script characters traveled from the Song empire to other parts of the Eurasian

29. *Yaolu*, 10.279. Perhaps there is a correlation between the two tattoos since the characters *ru huo* require six brush strokes.

30. *Yaolu*, 12.315.

31. Zhuang Chuo, *Jile bian*, 3.84.

32. *Yaolu*, 40.880. The Shiwei were related to the Khitans.

FIG. 4. Pair of tattooed laborers pushing a cart. Detail of Zhang Zeduan, *Along the River during the Qingming Festival* (*Qingming shanghe tu*). Northern Song. Long scroll, ink and color on silk, ht. 24.8 cm, w. 528.7 cm. Courtesy of the Palace Museum, Beijing.

world: porcelain, currency, and books. Tattooed human bodies were another item on that list of commodities produced by the Sinitic-script empire of the Middle Period. For the contemporaries of the Song empire, this was one of the defining features of Song civilization.

The memory of the first Song-Jin war as a great trauma for the Song people contains a strong elite perspective. When Song elites were the victims, their plight was described as a crisis of the state, and their daughters, wives, and sisters needed protection from the savagery of the Jurchens who sold them into the international markets of twelfth-century East Asia. In days of peace, though, elites had been the beneficiaries of the commodification and degradation of human bodies, both as those who could

FIG. 5. Pair of tattooed laborers by a well. Detail of Zhang Zeduan, *Along the River during the Qingming Festival* (*Qingming shanghe tu*). Northern Song. Long scroll, ink and color on silk, ht. 24.8 cm, w. 528.7 cm. Courtesy of the Palace Museum, Beijing.

construct their elite status through the marking of the poor, and as consumers of the bodies of women, all under the guise of the rule of law, sophisticated cultural consumption, and economic growth.

Loyalist Tattoos during the Early Southern Song

In the chaos of the Song-Jin war, military tattoos came to contain more and more loyalist messages. These were no longer isolated incidents of eccentric individuals but entire armies that were tattooed with loyalist lines. One of the more notable instances of a loyalist tattoo during this period was the army established by Wang Yan, a Song general whose army disintegrated in the face of the Jurchen assault during the military disaster of 1127.[33] Wang Yan gathered seven hundred soldiers and continued to fight the Jurchens. To prove their loyalty, his soldiers allegedly volunteered to have their faces tattooed with the eight characters "Serving the state with devotion, swearing to kill the Jin caitiffs" (*chixin baoguo shisha jinzei*).[34] Wang Yan's army grew to ten thousand men, and because of the eight characters tattooed on their faces people referred to them as the Eight Characters Army.[35]

The facial tattoos of Wang Yan's Eight Characters Army declared loyalty and sacrifice for the Song state, but they had a practical use as well. Whether or not the soldiers were moved by their own sincere loyalty, tattoos could hinder Song soldiers from joining the Jurchen side. In times of peace, the marking of soldiers' bodies made it harder for them to escape and assimilate in commoners' society. With the outbreak of the first Song-Jin war, the collapse of Song rule in many areas provided soldiers with new choices, one among them the option to cross over to the side of the Jurchens. The great numbers of military officials and Song troops that did so proved it was a viable option. A standard military or penal tattoo would not have stopped the Jurchens from employing Song men. The entire spectrum of negative meanings attached to tattooed soldiers disappeared once a person moved over to the Jurchen side. Loyalist tattoos with insulting remarks about the enemy provided one solution to the problem of soldiers crossing over to the Jin. Such insults were no laughing matter. A hundred and fifty years later, in 1286, in the campaigns the Mongol armies waged against the Đại Việt kingdom, the Mongols captured Vietnamese soldiers with the two characters "kill the Tatars" (*sha da*) tattooed on their arms. The Mongols were furious at this and killed many of the prisoners.[36]

The newly established Southern Song court tried to make sense of those autonomous tattooed forces that fought against the Jurchens. In 1128

33. The famous tattooed general Yue Fei was one of the men under his command, but he left, taking some of Wang Yan's troops with him.

34. Xu Mengxin, *Sanchao beimeng huibian,* vol. 2, 113.11a.361; *Yaolu*, 9.256; *Song shi*, 368.11451–52. The *Yaolu* only mentions the first four characters of the tattoo.

35. *Yaolu*, 15.371–72.

36. Chen Jinghe, *Daietsu Shiki Zensho,* 358.

a grand councilor and a general debated in the Song court the meaning of tattoos inscribed on men's faces. The grand councilor warned the emperor that the men who claimed to defend the emperor were bandits. The general Zong Ze objected and argued that those were righteous and loyal gentlemen who, without regard for their own bodies, tattooed their faces as a declaration of support for the Song. Zong Ze warned that turning against these men and treating them as criminals would cause them to lose heart.[37] The account does not describe the content of the tattoos Zong Ze was defending, but the record suggests that those were loyalist tattoos as well. They certainly were not the standard military tattoos that designated an individual's position within the armies administered by the central government. The court, already concerned about the loyalty of these new military forces, eyed nervously armies that tattooed without the government's permission.[38] At the very least, local initiatives for tattooing were an indication of a degree of local autonomy that the Song government found troubling.

The early Southern Song court had reason to be concerned by military men with loyalist tattoos. Whether Wang Yan's Eight Character Army truly volunteered to have their faces tattooed or not, there is no question that Wang Yan fought for the Song court. Loyalist tattoos, however, were also used by armies that were much more loosely tied to the Song. The troops of the soldier Ge Jin tattooed their faces with the characters "Not failing the Zhao king" (*bufu zhaowang*), even though Ge Jin commanded a rogue army composed of dispersed troops who pillaged Bin and Di prefectures.[39] In 1130 rebel soldiers tattooed villagers they captured with the characters "Coming together to restore the Song" (*juji xingsong*).[40] By choosing loyalist tattoos, the soldier-bandits avoided an open break with the Song state, maintaining the possibility of a future pardon and maybe even a reward from the government. However, despite

37. *Yaolu*, 14.342–43.

38. Deng Guangming argues that Gaozong feared local defense forces led by commoners would eventually turn against the Song (Deng Guangming, *Yue Fei zhuan*, 19).

39. *Yaolu*, 14.350–51.

40. This took place when over two thousand rebel soldiers of Chaling subprefecture (in modern-day Hunan) pillaged the Yongxing subprefecture of Chenzhou (in modern-day Hunan) (*Yaolu*, 31.724).

their content, the context of early Southern Song loyalist tattoos was that of a collapsing state and of coercion.

Yue Fei

Times of war provided opportunities for lower-class men who could fight. In the decades before the Song's founding, men with tattooed faces and dubious pasts reached the highest positions of power.[41] The founding of the Song saw tattooed faces pushed away from political power. The collapse of the Northern Song in 1127 reversed that process yet again. New regular military units, roving military bands, rebels, bandits, and local defense militias all offered opportunities for men of all backgrounds. Bandits and men of violence were welcomed once again, treated with honor, and given official positions. One common saying at the time observed: "If you want to be rich, sell wine. If you want to be an official, kill people, set fire, and receive the summons."[42]

Yue Fei, a commoner of a relatively humble social background, was one of the many men who were drawn into the military during the first Song-Jin war. Yue Fei joined the army through the Volunteers (Xiaoyong) preferential service track. He was tattooed upon joining, probably on the back of the hand.[43] Yue Fei rose swiftly through the ranks and became the most successful general of his time. At some point in his career Yue Fei acquired a large back tattoo: "Exhaust one's loyalty in service of the state."[44] Yue Fei's success on the battlefield, coupled with his growing power and popularity, gradually made him a threat to the central court. He was summoned to the capital, arrested on trumped-up charges, tortured, and murdered in prison.

41. Ouyang Xiu, *Xin wudai shi*, 61.747.

42. Zhang Zhifu, *Ke shu*, 417. Arson was one of the crimes commonly associated with bandits, rebels, and other criminal types.

43. Yue Fei was tattooed upon joining the service of Zhang Suo (Xu Mengxin, *Sanchao beimeng huibian*, vol. 3, 207.2b–3a.95–96). See also the work by modern-day scholar Wang Zengyu, *Jinzhong baoguo*, 5–7, 10–11.

44. *Song shi*, 365.11393. Wang Zengyu argues that Yue Fei's mother tattooed her son's back with the famous inscription following the fall of the Central Plain to the Jurchens (Wang Zengyu, *Jinzhong baoguo*, 20–22).

Because Yue Fei became both a leader and a symbol of the military resistance to the Jin, his death followed the signing of a peace treaty that put an end to the first Song-Jin war. In later years, Yue Fei's tattoo became a symbol of his heroism, loyalty, and sacrifice for the state, yet during his own lifetime, his tattoo also stood for war, chaos, a weak state, and the rise of military men from the bottom of society.[45]

Yue Fei's famous tattoo was based on a popular theme, as loyalist tattoos were already spreading through the empire. Many soldiers from Wang Yan's Eight Characters Army ended up serving in Hangzhou, the new capital of the Song.[46] Many men of the "volunteer armies" (*zhongyi*) of the northwest had faces tattooed with loyalist tattoos such as "Kill the enemy and serve the state" (*shadi baoguo*). Following a request by military authorities, in 1137 the emperor limited access to the imperial palace of men whose faces had large character tattoos or scars caused by moxibustion.[47] This decision was at least partially reversed in 1144 when Li Yong, a former bandit who had become general, received a position in court. Li, who had two flags tattooed on his face (a penal tattoo), was received with suspicion when he tried to enter the court. Ultimately, Emperor Gaozong decreed those officials who had faces tattooed with big characters or scars would be allowed to have interviews with the emperor.[48]

The court made this decision in favor of officials with tattooed faces roughly two years after Yue Fei's death. This decision was a minor triumph for those men who had succeeded in climbing the military ranks; it did not extend to low-ranking soldiers as well, and the debates about the presence of tattooed men at court reveal that the fault lines between the tattooed and the clear-skinned remained. The soldiers whose faces were tattooed were not lauded as heroes. The military crisis opened new possibilities for social mobility, and the social and military reality of the front crept closer to the court, in terms of both physical proximity and

45. For more about Yue Fei, see Deng Guangming, *Yue Fei zhuan*; Gong Yanming, *Yue Fei pingzhuan*; Kaplan, *Yueh Fei*; Wang Zengyu, *Jinzhong baoguo*; Wang Zengyu, *Yue Fei xin zhuan*; Wang Zengyu, *Yue Fei he Nansong qianqi*. For a discussion of Yue Fei's place in the historical narrative, see Wilhelm, *From Myth to Myth*; Huang, *Shrines of Yue Fei*; Liu, Yüeh Fei; Matten, *Worship of General Yue Fei*.

46. Li Xinchuan, *Jianyan yilai chaoye zaji*, 1/18.468.402–3.

47. *Yaolu*, 112.2094.

48. *Yaolu*, 151.2851.

consequences, when compared with much of the Northern Song. Still, the military officials whose bodies bore testament to the fact that they had climbed the ranks were eyed with suspicion. Perhaps that time saw the beginning of a positive shift in the status of tattooed men, but they were still received with an awkward and cold embrace.

Yue Fei, *The Water Margin*, and "Real Men"

In his classic biography of Yue Fei, Deng Guangming describes how on one occasion Yue Fei was given a concubine. Once he had questioned her and realized she was unable to withstand the hard life of the military camp, he sent her away. Deng sees this scene as proof of Yue Fei's commitment to the cause of the Song state.[49] The literal content of Yue Fei's tattoo, declaring loyalty and sacrifice for the state, shaped our modern reading of Yue Fei's story, including anecdotes like the one of Yue Fei and the concubine. Yet Yue Fei's tattoo had another layer to it. As a military tattoo, it placed him in the social and cultural world of the penal-military complex. By placing Yue Fei's story in that world, one's view of Yue Fei the man changes as well.

A code for another reading of Yue Fei's tattoo can be found in the famous Ming novel *The Water Margin* (Shuihu zhuan), the most famous representation of the social types who resided in the Song's penal-military complex. *The Water Margin* is not simply the creation of elite authors during the sixteenth and seventeenth centuries. Modern-day scholars noted that although the story acquired its mature shape only during the late Ming, it has strong roots in the Song period: it describes real Song military institutions; the tales of the bandits and deserters within are based on traditions of storytelling that go back as far as the eleventh century; and the violence in the novel echoes old folk traditions, ones that predate elite interventions in the story.[50]

49. Deng Guangming, *Yue Fei zhuan*, 280.

50. Smith, "*Shuihu zhuan* and the Military Subculture of the Northern Song," 363–422; Jenner, "Tough Guys, Mateship and Honor"; Huang, *Negotiating Masculinities*, 111.

The novel's protagonists, some of them tattooed men themselves, embody a certain ideal masculine type, that of "real men" (*haohan*). Yue Fei's tattoo served also as a mark of membership in that world. What kind of men were *The Water Margin*'s "real men"? Martin Huang describes the defining masculine characteristics of the novel's protagonists: generous with money, drinking to excess, lacking sexual interest in women, and highly prone to use extreme violence.[51] Jenner describes them as men who seek violence for violence's sake.[52] *The Water Margin*'s huge success over the centuries made its protagonists well-known and popular characters throughout the Chinese world, and the novel became a foundational text for that tough and violent brand of masculinity.

Considered from this angle, when Yue Fei rejected the concubine, he did not display the behavior of a loyal subject but rather of a "real man": a man who showed little interest in women and sex, whose true bond was to his "brothers," and whose real passion lay in the pursuit of violence. Yue Fei embodied many other of the characteristics of a "real man." He was a warrior who was mighty in body and rode alone through enemy territory. He was the man who ripped the heart from his uncle's chest when the uncle tried to kill him with an arrow.[53] Yue Fei was the violent and dangerous drunk who beat one of his own lieutenants to within an inch of his life in an intoxicated fit.[54] When he caught a bandit who declared himself a "real man," Yue Fei personally released his bonds and made him a loyal deputy, prefiguring the behavior of Song Jiang, the bandit leader in *The Water Margin*.[55] His hot temper, his tattoos, his great strength, his sense of fairness, and his appreciation of courage—all would make him feel at home as a character in *The Water Margin*, a novel filled with heroes who were murderers, bandits, and deserters.

The seventeenth-century commentator Jin Shengtan argued that the only heroic quality of Song Jiang, the leader of the bandits in *The Water Margin*, was his ability to buy people's gratitude.[56] However, as previous

51. Huang, *Negotiating Masculinities*, 103–12.
52. Jenner, "Tough Guys, Mateship and Honor," 1–34.
53. Deng Guangming, *Yue Fei zhuan*, 88–89.
54. Deng Guangming, *Yue Fei zhuan*, 94.
55. Deng Guangming, *Yue Fei zhuan*, 102.
56. Huang argues that Jin's comment is "certainly to the point" (Huang, *Negotiating Masculinities*, 105).

chapters have shown, the Song military maintained discipline and loyalty through violence and the payment of salaries. Deserters formed gangs based on the same principles. Ironically, heroes of the poor are criticized for a masculinity that is too materialistic. This is certainly one of the genius elements of upper-class rhetoric, that it allows the rich to paint themselves as disinterested in the material world and therefore the most qualified to own, control, and handle the material goods and the bodies of lower-class people.

The Water Margin recalls another Song-period hero: the woman warrior Yang Miaozhen (ca. 1193–1250) who became the inspiration for *The Water Margin*'s heroine, Yizhang Qing (Hu Sanniang).[57] Yang and her husband, Li Quan (d. 1231), were individuals of a lower social background who carved out their own sphere of influence in Shandong between the Song, the Jin, and the Yuan empires. Unlike Yue Fei, Yang's and Li's local power base in Shandong and their ability to change sides provided them with a strong negotiation position with the Song and Yuan courts. Modern-day scholar Wu Pei-Yi argues that Yang Miaozhen's memory was marginalized in the centuries after her death because she did not display the conduct required of a chaste woman.[58] In both the cases of Yue Fei and Yang Miaozhen, lower-class masculinity and femininity were downplayed within their stories to create visions of loyal subjects and chaste women.

The world Yue Fei came from is still hidden from sight, as his memory was made to serve the narrative of a struggle among states and among peoples. When the nationalist gaze is turned to the past, it creates some of the most powerful images in Chinese history. Tortured in prison and executed by traitors on trumped-up charges, Yue Fei died a martyr not just for loyalty to the emperor but for loyalty to the state and the masses of people who depended on it for protection. A unified Chinese identity comes to life through the division of protagonists into brave patriots on one side, and traitors and cowards who sought peace at any price on the other. This division—in traditional historiography, in modern scholarship, and in popular memory—assumes the existence in the Song era of a monolithic identity in which all subjects were clearly marked by their

57. Wu, "Yang Miaozhen," 159.
58. Wu, "Yang Miaozhen." 167–69.

commitment to a Chinese Song state: "good" subjects were loyal to their state whereas the "bad" ones betrayed the state.

Yue Fei's tattoo became a symbol of his story, his sacrifice, and his heroism. Yet that symbol can also serve as a key to unraveling the old story of the martyr of the state. By moving the symbol to the fore, a different picture emerges with a different sort of hero. Yue Fei was also the man who came from a humble background and climbed the ranks by the force of his martial prowess. The animosity toward him reflects more than cynical power plays and fear of military power in the hands of a strong general. In both his appearance and his conduct, Yue Fei resembled more the men of the military camps than those at court. The playing out of the tensions between the highborn and lowborn in the court of the Song paved Yue Fei's road to his ignominious death.

The scene where Yue Fei tore off the shirt from his body and exposed his tattoo to his interrogator immortalized him in popular memory. But this grand gesture was more than just proof of the fact that Yue Fei's heart was indeed loyal and sincere. The unveiling of Yue Fei's body was also an unveiling of all that his body signified: his alienation from the men at court, the cruelty of army life and of a world at war, and the courage and pride of the men who served in the rank and file of the Song armies. To a modern-day observer, these four characters can be viewed as a call for unity of thought and action, the closing of ranks in the face of an approaching foreign foe. Yet Yue Fei's tattoo also tells a story of class division and defiance of upper-class values. In that sense, Yue Fei truly was a hero of the people.

CHAPTER 8

Twilight of the Age of Tattooing

In the middle of the thirteenth century, a forensic examiner approaches the corpse of an adult male. He strips it of its clothing and washes it. He then begins searching for tattoos, first on the frontal bones, then the face, the back of the hand, and finally, the nape of the neck. He notes their size and shape: a tattoo behind the ear for bandits, on the face for repeat offenders. A square shaped tattoo meant the convict had been punished with a beating. If its shape was circular, the convict had served time in penal servitude. He looks for signs of tattoos that had been removed. He records scars from beatings in his ledger, noting their age and the nature of the beating (such as the use of a thorny staff for flogging).[1] For the examiner reading the body of the deceased, tattoos and scars marked the main chapters of the latter man's life.

Tattoos continued to be an important trait of the Song state and civilization throughout the Southern Song period (1127–1279). The multitude of tattoos on hundreds of thousands of bodies during this period are only known to us through a relatively small number of references in texts and paintings. Assembled together, these references tell a story about life in the Song state following the great war with the Jin empire and the loss of the north. In this period of chronic military crisis, life in the penal-

1. The account is based on McKnight's translation of Song Ci's thirteenth-century instructions for forensic examiners (Song Ci, *Washing Away of Wrongs*, 90); the meaning of the penal tattoos is based on a 1085 edict (*Chang bian*, 362.25.8667).

military complex never went back to what it had been before the war. Echoes of that story can be found in the changing patterns of tattoos during the twelfth and thirteenth centuries.

The New Military Hierarchy of the Mid-Twelfth Century

With the removal of its great generals in the middle of the twelfth century, the Song central government—now based in the south—began to reassert its will over its military forces at the cost of decreasing some of its military power.[2] The military restructuring of the mid-twelfth century also brought about the rise of a new military hierarchy. Following a failed coup attempt by a general of the imperial armies at an early stage of the war, the imperial armies were no longer entrusted with imperial defense, and they gradually grew more like the prefectural labor armies in terms of capabilities, duties, and standing. Military positions within the diminished imperial armies were often empty sinecures, sometimes given to imperial relatives.[3] Other lesser military forces continued to exist beside the imperials: prefecturals, militias, and local law enforcement troops.

Instead of the imperials, new types of military tracks appeared at the top of the military hierarchy. The roots of this process go back to the early twelfth century, when growing shortages of military manpower led the Song court to create more appealing service tracks like the Volunteers and Policemen (Shichen).[4] Once the first Song-Jin war broke out in 1125, elite men, even civil officials, joined the ranks of the Volunteers, swelling their numbers substantially. Many of these Volunteers were elite men who took advantage of the crisis and registered their relatives and associates in the military, soldiers in name only, in order to cash in on the military crisis by collecting salaries. After the war, as the Southern Song state stabilized, Volunteers became a designation for the upper tier of soldiers within the

2. Huang Kuan-chong, *Nansong difang wuli*, 242.

3. Koiwai, *Sōdai heiseishi no kenkyū*, 298–300; Wang Zengyu, *Songchao junzhi chutan*, 205–10.

4. Wang Zengyu, *Songchao junzhi chutan*, 198–99.

Southern Song regular forces.[5] Below the Volunteers were the Ordinary Soldiers (Junshi). Policemen remained a separate service track of low-ranking military officials.[6] The Song military stationed its strongest fighting units in the capital and in other strategic positions along the Yangzi and in Sichuan.[7]

There are some indications for improvement in the terms and status of military service during the Southern Song, at least in certain military tracks. Volunteers were better paid than Ordinary Soldiers, and some stout and strong men refused to join the military unless it was for the Volunteers service track.[8] At the local level, elite men became more involved in organizing and leading local militias, implying a changing attitude to participation in military activities among elites.[9] At the same time, even though military salaries grew after 1127, this did not lead to improved living standards among all soldiers. Previously, payments of cloth and grain formed an important component of military salaries. During the mid-twelfth century, the Song state relied more and more on money, including paper money, to pay soldiers' salaries. This exposed military salaries to the Southern Song period's high levels of inflation. Even the Volunteers, the more lucrative military track, experienced a drop in real income.[10] Within the Volunteers, the standing of men could vary greatly, but most of the rank and file in the Southern Song military's fighting units were still Ordinary Soldiers who did not enjoy the same improved standing. The status of labor troops was even worse.

Skimming and fraud, as well as high levels of inflation during the Southern Song period, make it hard to analyze changes in soldiers' living standards and social standing by their salaries alone. The laws and regulations governing military tattoos suggest that important changes

5. Wang Zengyu, *Songchao junzhi chutan*, 118–19.

6. Wang Zengyu, *Songchao junzhi chutan*, 158.

7. Wang Zengyu, "History of the Sung Military," 243; Wang Zengyu, *Songchao junzhi chutan*, 227.

8. The modern historian Wang Zengyu argues that this means the Volunteers' social status was higher when compared with the Four Superior Armies (elite imperial armies), the top fighting forces of the Northern Song (Wang Zengyu, *Songchao junzhi chutan*, 204).

9. Hymes, *Statesmen and Gentlemen*, 6–11.

10. Wang Yunchang, *Songdai jundui jingying*, 253–54.

took place during and following the first Song-Jin war, drawing a line between the regular armies of the tenth and eleventh centuries and those of the twelfth and thirteenth centuries. Many among the Volunteers were exempt from tattooing, and this lower rate of tattooing suggests that there was some improvement in the status and life conditions of soldiers.[11] At the same time, this change was gradual and partial, as there was always a meaningful tattooed component among them.[12]

The content and location of Southern Song Volunteer tattoos provide stronger indications for some improvement in the status of fighting troops. The most striking difference was their location on the back of the hand rather than the face. One account states those tattoos were eight characters long: "Volunteers of the Pacification Commissioner's Office of X circuit" (*moulu anfusi xiaoyong*).[13] In content, they still expressed the soldier's military assignment, except the battalion was replaced with the circuit, a far larger military administrative unit. Both the location and the content of the tattoos reflect a "loosening" of the laws governing soldiers. During the Northern Song, in the regular armies, where the coercive power of the state was strongest, most of the soldiers had facial tattoos. In the militias, however, popular resistance to militia service meant that militia tattoos were relegated to the back of the hand, and sometimes tattoos were suspended completely.[14] The terms of debate had changed by the middle of the twelfth century, as hand tattoos became the norm in the regular armies. The migration of Volunteers' tattoos to a less visible and less painful location suggests a concession on the side of the government and some improvement in the status of soldiers.

Having the tattoo record the soldier's circuit rather than battalion could be seen as another concession by the state. The circuit was the highest military administrative unit, whereas the battalion was the basic operational unit in the Song military. Locking a soldier into the circuit rather than the battalion suggests that the central government of the Southern

11. Wang Zengyu, *Songchao junzhi chutan*, 203–4.

12. In 1235 the military conscripted and tattooed ten thousand men to fill in the missing quotas of the Volunteers (Anon., *Songshi quanwen*, 32.46b).

13. This was the pattern used when the Song military tattooed men for the Volunteers in 1192–1193 (Xie Shenfu, *Qingyuan tiaofa shilei*, 78.21b–22a).

14. For more on this topic, see chapter 6.

Song intervened less in micro-management of military manpower, placing greater authority in the hands of senior military officials. It also increased the size of the soldiers' "cage." Soldiers could, in theory, engage in "illegal transfers," moving between units in the same circuit, while the military assignment recorded in their tattoos still held true.

Changes in soldiers' status were not limited to the top tiers of the Song military, as they also took place in some of the labor battalions. One account relates that the migration of the military tattoo from the face to the back of the hand also took place in the postal-station battalions, one of the more infamous sectors of the military labor system. Due to the hard and dangerous conditions of service in the postal system, desertion was rife, and postal stations were, as noted in earlier chapters, chronically and severely understaffed. As a result, postal stations often took in deserters from other units. In 1186, as a response to these "illegal transfers," the government ordered to increase the size of postal-station soldiers' arm tattoos, and it made the distribution of food and clothing conditional on presentation of one's tattoos for inspection.[15]

The decision to increase the size of postal-station soldiers' arm tattoos attests to the changing lines of debate regarding tattooing. In the Northern Song, similar debates revolved around a choice of tattooing either the face or the back of the hand. Yet in the late twelfth century, when faced with problems of discipline, the government chose to increase the size of arm tattoos rather than have the faces tattooed. The changes in tattooing patterns suggest that during the military crisis of the early twelfth century, the "military" aspect of the penal-military complex grew in importance at the expense of the "penal" aspect, providing soldiers with a stronger negotiating position vis-à-vis the central government. At the same time, tattoos remained indispensable to the military system, and, in fact, became even more closely incorporated into it. The tattoo became the locus of the soldier's identity, the medium through which a soldier could be "seen" by the state, locking the soldier into a specific unit where he was supposed to receive his food, his clothing, and other forms of payment.[16]

15. This took place in 1186. *Song huiyao, fangyu*, 11.32, Chunxi 13th year, 2nd month, 4th day.

16. The principle resembles the strategy of locking citizens into work units (*danwei*) in the People's Republic of China under Mao.

Military tattoos were not an independent text but a part of a larger sequence of military manpower records. A mid-twelfth-century account explains that the time of a soldier's tattooing was one of the important details that appeared in each soldier's service record, together with his military camp, birthplace, and age.[17] Soldiers' names appeared on the military register, but their bodies were a part of the register, a "carbon copy" of a soldier's assignment. The moment of tattooing was the individual's rite of passage into the penal-military complex, his body becoming a copy of a state document, a reflection of the military register. Despite changes in tattoos' content and location, they remained a core trait of life in the penal-military complex throughout the Southern Song.

Tattoos were common enough in the armies of the early thirteenth century to become synonymous with the bodies of soldiers. A description of the Southern Song's failed Northern Campaign (Beifa) in 1206 recalls many of the images from Northern Song military life: failed logistics, hunger, despair, and suicide. According to one account, so many soldiers committed suicide by jumping into wells that, whenever people drew water from the wells, there would be tattooed skin floating on top of the bucket.[18]

By the late thirteenth century, soldiers in the fighting armies of the Song military were tattooed on their arms with their name and surname. This did not extend to prefectural and imperial armies, the lower armies of the Southern Song, where soldiers had their foreheads tattooed with six dots.[19] The emergence of an individual identity in military tattoos marks a significant shift in soldiers' status. Not just interchangeable parts in a machine, they had become officially recognized as human individuals. However, the fragmented structure of military administration allowed the government to limit such concessions to specific tiers and battalions.

The transition from facial tattoos to arm tattoos in some units was most likely a result of the severe military crisis of the Southern Song

17. This according to an edict from 1164. All these details were to be written down in three copies: one for the camp, one for the Ministry of Revenue, and one for the overseer-general. This was to be the practice in all the Song's armies (Ma Duanlin, *Wenxian tongkao*, 154.14b.460).

18. Yue Ke, *Ting shi*, 14.163–64.

19. Fang Hui, *Xu gujin kao*, 37.23b–24a.609.

period. War was changing in the early twelfth century, ever growing in scope and goals. Military defeats became less and less sustainable for the Song state. Coercion no longer sufficed, as the morale of the army became crucial for the survival of the state. However, this change was not consistent across the military hierarchy. Soldiers' humanity continued to be measured, ranked, and assigned the appropriate quota of suffering. Those most often assigned the greatest measures of pain and shame were the soldier-convicts for whom facial tattoos continued to be the standard.

Penal Tattoos in the Southern Song

Penal tattoos grew in detail and complexity during the twelfth and thirteenth centuries.[20] Throughout the Southern Song, some convicts were tattooed with two flags on their faces.[21] In some cases, the two flags were only part of a larger tattooing scheme. When bandits had their death sentences commuted, the two characters "spared beheading" (*mianzhan*) were tattooed on their foreheads, and two flags were tattooed on their faces.[22] In other similar cases, convicts had the characters "bandit" (*qiangdao*) tattooed on their foreheads, and the location and nature of punishment were tattooed on the sides of their heads.[23] Convicts sentenced for hard labor were tattooed with the inscription "assigned for hard labor in the military of X prefecture" (*pei zhoufu tunzhujun zhongyi*).[24] Bandits whose death sentences were commuted and replaced with hard labor had their

20. Sogabe, *Sōdai no shi-hai ni tsuite*, 11–12.

21. The rebel Huang Jin, mentioned earlier in this chapter, had two flags tattooed onto his face. In 1237 an army was created using criminals whose faces were tattooed with two flags (Zhou Yinghe, *Jingding jiankang zhi*, 39.5b.1971). A man who offended the infamous grand councilor Jia Sidao (1213–1275) was thrown into prison, where two flags were tattooed onto his face (Zheng Yuanyou, *Suichang zalu*, 8a.384).

22. Fang Hui, *Xu gujin kao*, 37.23b–24a.609.

23. *Song huiyao, xingfa*, 4.56, Chunxi 8th year, 5th month, 16th day.

24. According to an order from 1149 (*Song huiyao, xingfa*, 4.47, Shaoxing 19th year, 8th month, 22nd day).

own tattoo: "X Army/X Prefecture Hard Labor" (*moujun huo mouzhou zhongyi*).[25]

During the Southern Song, in a single military unit, one could see a diverse range of tattoos, ranging from the "very martial" (military tattoo on the hand) to the "very penal" (penal tattoo on the face). Deserter tattoos occupied a special position. Those were penal tattoos, but ones employed against soldiers who had deserted, a crime unique to the military. As a result, deserter tattoos contained both penal and martial elements. They included the seven characters of the soldier's military assignment, but they were located on the left side of their forehead instead of underneath the left thumb.[26] Severity of the offense was also factored in: a large penal tattoo for severe offenders, a tattoo of the military assignment for light offenders.[27]

Tattoos and flogging scars told the story of a person's past, but they also determined their future. After all, the state and its agents "read" the soldiers through their bodies. In one case, an official wrongly accused a man of using a false identity, claiming that he was in fact a convict who had been exiled and tattooed several times. The accused had his body inspected by a tattooist, and the lack of flogging scars saved his life.[28] A man with military tattoos would always be suspected of being a soldier, making discharge papers paramount for maintaining his freedom.

The penal-military biography inscribed by tattoos was an important textual genre of the Song period. In the early tenth century, both elite men and lower-class men documented their private histories. Elite men did so in the form of funerary inscriptions (*muzhiming*), written after their death, whereas the tattooed soldiers and thugs wrote "needle histories" on their own bodies. The Song state took over authorship of these "needle histories" and made them into records of pain and shame. Elite

25. According to an edict from 1181 (*Song huiyao, xingfa*, 4.56, Chunxi 8th year, 4th month, 15th day).

26. The Hunan Pacification Commissioner's Office requested to tattoo according to this scheme in 1197 (*Song huiyao, zhiguan*, 41.116, Qingyuan 3rd year, 3rd month, 25th day).

27. This policy was decided in 1167 (*Song huiyao, xingfa*, 4.51, Qiandao 3rd year, 10th month, 3rd day).

28. Huang Zhen, *Huangshi richao*, 76.1a–2a.770–71.

biographies were meant for the consumption of future generations, whereas the body-biographies of soldiers were meant for consumption only during their lifetime, and later they would rot away and disappear in graves that were often unmarked or unnamed.[29]

The Popular Tattooing Scene during the Twelfth and Thirteenth Centuries

In the last years of the Northern Song, a tattooed man made his way into the imperial entourage. The man, a descendant of an official, had tattooed himself during his unruly youth, and he was known by the title "the Tattooed Immortal."[30] The tattooed man was not alone, for Kaifeng of the early twelfth century had a bustling tattooing scene that stretched beyond the ranks of the military. In the Song capital, men tattooed themselves as a symbol of a rebellious and violent masculinity. The anecdote about "the Tattooed Immortal" suggests that tattooing generated enough interest in court to allow a tattooed man into the imperial entourage.

Perhaps part of the secret for the fascination of the court with tattooing lay in the distinct class flavor of tattooing, a practice associated with strong and violent men. The "Decorated Legs" tattoo, a pattern running down both legs, was popular among menial workers and drifters in early twelfth-century Kaifeng. During the first Song-Jin war, the "Decorated Legs" became military tattoos when the general Zhang Jun had his armies tattooed with those patterns.[31] Zhang Jun's choice to use these tattoos for his troops suggests that his own troops hailed from the same social universe as the laborers and thugs of the capital city. "Decorated Legs" tattoos were popular enough that they appear again, more than a century later, in a late Southern Song anecdote about Chen "Decorated Legs" (Chen Huajiao), who owned a noodle shop in Hangzhou.[32]

29. For a study of a Song period graveyard with soldiers' graves, see Sanmenxia Shi wenwu gongzuodui, *Beisong Shaanzhou louze yuan*.

30. Wang Mingqing, *Huizhu lu, houlu*, 2.133.98.

31. See chapter 7.

32. Wu Zimu, *Meng liang lu*, 13.5a.106.

The "Decorated Legs" might be the only Middle Period tattoo that was documented both textually and visually, as it is possible to see that pattern on the legs of laboring men in the famous painting *Along the River during the Qingming Festival* (*Qingming shanghe tu*). Large and complex tattoos, such as the "Decorated Legs" pattern, suggest the existence of a mature tattooing scene with professional tattooists and a clientele that extended to nonmilitary lower-class types. The appearance of these tattoos in both Kaifeng and Hangzhou more than a century apart attests to the continuity of the practice of decorative tattooing, and it also shows the cultural transmission of specific patterns and styles. Many of the men sporting the "Decorated Legs" tattoos were not soldiers, but they were still part of the same larger social group from which soldiers were often taken into the military as volunteers, conscripts, and convicts.

Together with military and penal tattoos, decorative, individually authored tattoos also appeared in the Song underworld. During the first Song-Jin war, there was a Shandong bandit named Liu Zhong, who called himself "White Felt Hat" (Bai zhan li). Liu tattooed his own forehead and was known at the time as "the painted-face beast." It is very likely that Liu Zhong was a former soldier. His tattoo was decorative, but the decision to tattoo the forehead may have been the result of an attempt to cover up a penal or military tattoo. Liu Zhong's success in taking over a military unit is another possible indication of some military experience.[33] The tattoo on his forehead may have been his own choice, but it still placed him in the social world of soldiers, deserters, and bandits.

The evidence for tattooing in local society during the Southern Song is not plentiful, but it still suggests that tattooing was a popular and well-developed practice. Tattooing, popularly referred to as "needlework" (*cixiu*), was popular enough for there to be tattooists who set up specialized shops. Tattooing also had a religious significance among groups known as "tattooed-bodies associations" (*jinti she*), and tattooed characters may have made roads into local religious practices.[34] In the cities there were criminal types with extensive tattoo work on their bodies, men

33. Liu Zhong trapped and killed a Song general with a false offer of surrender and then took over the general's soldiers (*Yaolu*, 19.444).

34. Fang Hui, *Xu gujin kao*, 37.23b–24a.609; Nai Deweng, *Ducheng jisheng*, 14a–15a; Wu Zimu, *Meng liang lu*, 1.9b–11b.

like Wu the Sixth (Wu Liu), who survived by doing odd jobs, hustling, and crime; and Zhu the Third (Zhu San), who participated in religious processions.[35]

The ideal of rebellious, violent, and "bad" masculinity expressed in tattoos was subject to curiosity and admiration even beyond the lower classes. In 1215 Zhao Xiyao, a member of the imperial clan, caused a scandal. He decorated his body with tattoos and surrounded himself with an entourage of underworld characters. Zhao Xiyao's status as a member of the imperial clan put him out of the reach of regular officials, and he had to be disciplined through the Chief Office of Imperial Clan Affairs (Taizong zhengsi).[36] The incident suggests that tattooing was forbidden for members of the imperial clan.[37] It also shows tattoos symbolizing a certain kind of forbidden yet desirable social power, a ticket into the world of strong, dangerous, and violent masculinity.

Visual representations of Song-period tattooed men are found in Song paintings and drawings. The tattooed men depicted are of a lower social standing, with some of them engaged in menial labor. Their tattoos are decorative, colorful patterns that cover extensive areas of their arms and legs. The tattoos peek out from under a sleeve or proudly cover the exposed bodies of laborers, showing enough detail to reveal the artist's fascination with them, but still occupying a marginal position within the grand context of the painting's narrative (fig. 6). There could only be a hint of the world from which tattoos came, leaving armed men with tattooed faces conspicuously absent from Song images.

The decorative tattoos appearing in Song paintings differ sharply from the standardized, often textualized, form of penal-military tattoos, but they also have much in common. In all these spaces, tattoos stood for a violent and aggressive masculinity. In lower-class society and in the underworld, men used their tattoos to tell stories about themselves, even if the state often did intervene, adding a "commentary" of penal tattoos. On the other end of the spectrum, the military tattoos of the regular

35. Hong Mai, *Yijian zhi*, *guizhi*, *Wu Liu jingdu*, 9.1287–88, *geshan paijun*, 8.1263–64.

36. *Song huiyao*, *dixi*, 7.31, *zalu*, Ningzong Jiading 7th year, 2nd month, 23rd day.

37. Imperial clan members occupied a special position in Song society. For more on the imperial clan, see Chaffee, *Branches of Heaven*.

FIG. 6. This advertisement for a play shows a man offering eye medicine to a tattooed man. *Selling Eye Medicine* (*Zaju "mai yanyao" tu ye*). Song Period. Ink and color, ht. 23.8 cm, w. 24.5 cm. Courtesy of the Palace Museum, Beijing.

armies, the nature of authorship changed. The state still authored the tattoos, but by adding the soldier's name, it expanded the story. It recognized that individuals had parents who had been named, and who had named their son in turn, making them coauthors of the tattoo. It recognized that the soldier was no longer just an interchangeable part, but a member of a family, and therefore, part of the larger human story that binds human society together.

The colorful decorative tattoos in Song paintings recall a few of the tattooed protagonists of the novel *The Water Margin*: Shi Jin, who had nine dragon tattoos running over his body, and Yan Qing, who sported many decorative tattoos. Shi Jin and Yan Qing were not soldiers, but they found themselves in the same gang of bandits with Lin Chong, a military-officer-turned-convict with a textual facial tattoo. The world of the penal-military complex was diverse, and many roads led to it. As this book has shown, not all its members were active soldiers. Some were peddlers, beggars, veterans, menial laborers, and bandits. Yet their paths often intertwined: in crowded alleys, in prison citadels, and in bandits' lairs.

These brief glimpses into the popular tattooing scene in the Song bring to mind some of the street scenes from ninth-century Chang'an, four hundred years earlier. Despite the Song state's rigorous attempts to make tattooing a state prerogative, tattooing as a local practice survived. Criminal types, religious associations, disgruntled youth, and those who sought the company and support of such social types continued to decorate their bodies. The relative silence of Song scholars on this aspect of life serves as a warning that descriptions of Song life may have been purged of many elements of life that Song elites viewed as inappropriate, dangerous, or meaningless.

The Mongol Conquest and the Twilight of the Tattooed-Soldiers

The Song empire's geopolitical environment changed dramatically with the rise of the Mongols under Genghis Khan and the destruction of the Jin empire in the early thirteenth century. The new military crisis led the Song state to reorganize its military, establishing three strong military commands on its threatened northern and western borders: Sichuan, Jinghu, and Huainan. The Song court allowed for these military commands to rise in power and influence, setting aside the checks and balances that had so far curtailed the power of the military.[38] This allowed for a single family, the Lü family, to monopolize military appointments in two of the three important military commands. When members of the family defected to the Mongols, the Song defense system collapsed.[39]

38. Wang Zengyu, *Songchao junzhi chutan*, 245–46.

39. See Fang Cheng-hua's study of the Lü family: "Military Families and the Southern Song Court."

As in the first Song-Jin war a century prior, the war between the Song and the Mongols provided men of more humble origins the chance the make their own fate. In the long drama that unfolded between the Song dynasty and tattooed men, a tattooed face was to have the last laugh. Xia Gui was a man of the late Southern Song. He was punished in his youth, and the penal tattoo of two flags on his face gained him the nickname "Xia the Flag Man" (Xia Qi'er). Later in his life, Xia Gui made his way up the ranks and was appointed general. He was a fierce and daring military commander, appreciated by his soldiers, who called him "Grandfather Xia" (Xia Yeye). His appearance must have been impressive, as Emperor Lizong (r. 1224–1264) ordered Xia's portrait made.[40] Ultimately, the tattooed general Xia Gui crossed over to the side of the Mongols and handed over the Huaixi region to them.[41]

When the Mongols advanced into Song territory, they captured soldiers and commoners and grouped them according to their skin: clear skinned, tattooed arms, and tattooed faces. The Mongols released many of the soldiers and made them into commoners. *The Record of the Pacification of the Song* (*Ping song lu*) presents the release as the benevolent Mongol response to the requests of their new subjects.[42] The Mongols also registered many other soldiers with tattooed hands as soldiers in the Mongol army. They were then assigned to Han units, and thereafter tattooing in the Mongol military was discontinued.[43] The Mongols continued to use penal tattoos, except they were done along ethnic and gender lines: tattooing of women and Mongols was forbidden.[44] Officials were not allowed to tattoo Mongols, and any tattoos on Mongol bodies had to be removed.[45] Tattoos continued to reflect and support the new social hierarchy, but they decreased in importance as the state was no longer engaged in projects of mass tattooing. The golden age of tattoos was over.

40. Anon., *Songji sanchao zhengyao jianzheng*, 3.259. Unfortunately, this image of Xia Gui's tattooed face did not survive.

41. Wang Yun, *Qiujian ji*, 50.14b.673; Liu Minzhong, *Ping song lu*, 2.15a.1055.

42. Liu Minzhong, *Ping song lu*, 1.9a–9b.1044; Song Lian, *Yuan shi*, 12.244.

43. Song Lian, *Yuan shi*, 13.269, 98.2519. According to the *Yuan shi*, 83.600 soldiers with "marked hands" were registered as Mongol soldiers (Song Lian, *Yuan shi*, 12.255).

44. Shen Jiaben, *Dayuan shengzheng guochao dianzhang*, 49.11.22a.

45. Song Lian, *Yuan shi*, 103.2633.

CONCLUSION

In the centuries that passed since the fall of the Song dynasty, soldiers, their families, and other members of the social world of the penal-military complex were relegated to the margins of the historical narratives of the Song period. The culture of scholar-officials, widely referred to as Confucian, came to represent Song society and culture in historical memory, and their textual, social, and institutional legacy became a famous cornerstone of Chinese culture and identity today. Yet the rise of the Song period's new elite, with scholar-officials as their heroic role model, involved the setting up of a professional paid army and the criminalization and degradation of the millions of men and women who lived in the shadow of the Song state's military and legal institutions. Elite symbols and rituals (the study of the classics, the journey of the examination candidate, the official's robes) stood for power over and exclusion of this large social group. Scholar-officials, wary of soldiers, drafted military laws and regulations aimed at social control and social engineering. When scholar-officials debated military policies, their thoughts were also on the soldiers who surrounded them, guarded them, and served them, and whose daughters and wives were available to them through the sex trade.

The civil-service system and the military system generated two different social worlds, but both were parts of the larger Song world, and they shared similar organizing principles: state-dependent semi-hereditary groups with a weak relationship to the locality (Rotation System for soldiers, law of avoidance for officials) whose status was reaffirmed by cycles of testing based on fixed standards. Both groups revolved around membership in organizations that had laws, practices, and culture that went far beyond any single locality, stretching throughout the empire. An individual could be promoted, demoted, or simply transferred to far-off places, yet remain within his organization. However, the similarities between the civil service and the military were those of mirror opposites, of two diametrically opposed groups. Both were systems for assessment of manpower. Yet whereas the examination system awarded successful candidates with degrees that marked them as society's best, within the penal-military complex the state tattooed soldiers and convicts to mark them as society's worst. Both groups were based on the idea of a meritocracy, but the civil-service path offered great rewards for merit, whereas in the military realm demerit took center stage, and punishments were part of the routine operations of the military camp.

Both the examination system and the penal-military complex formed the nucleus of far larger social worlds. The examination system became a pillar of elite status. Only a tiny group among examination candidates succeeded in passing the examinations, but many more achieved a measure of prestige by association with the examinations: whether by studying for the examinations themselves or through having a relative or associate who studied for the examinations. Membership in the penal-military complex too was often acquired by association, as tattooed soldiers were also members of a larger social circle: soldiers' families and neighbors, men who had spent time in the military as convicts, men likely to join the army, and military veterans. Many of these people found their way into that world later in life, but most of them were born into it, just as scholar-officials were usually born into elite families.

The development of the ideal of the scholar-official or literati of the Song period included the assumption that social mobility was possible, and that success was a true measurement of an individual's skills, effort, and character. In such a meritocracy, people of good qualities were supposed to succeed, and those of bad qualities were supposed to fail. Song soldiers embodied all the negative opposites of elite qualities. Literati described soldiers as criminal, lazy, and violent while at the same time they portrayed themselves as morally upright, hardworking, educated, and wise. The increasing use among elites of the rhetoric of social mobility involved the criminalization of the poor, with the downtrodden soldier as the necessary counterpart to the literatus.

Contemporary evaluations of the social transformation of the Song age assume a cultural-social trickle-down model. According to this model, if the Song elites were Confucian, then Confucian ideas and values trickled down from the top to the bottom of society, making all of Song society Confucian in the process. The trickle-down model is not limited to ideas; it also touches on social opportunities. According to this line of thinking, because the Song era saw the rise of a bigger, more open elite, it must have been a time of increased social mobility. The reality was that in the military realm opportunities for social mobility did not trickle down and neither did Confucian ideas. As the custom of military tattoos demonstrates, Confucian ideals and culture did not prevail in the military. Nor were they meant to. Upward social mobility through the army was possible but rare. It tended to take place when a military crisis forced the hand of the state. When such social mobility took place, it was not celebrated but rather frowned upon by scholar-officials.

Violence was an important aspect of Song life, especially in the lives of Song soldiers and their families. Within the historical narratives the systemic violence that permeated life in the penal-military complex was sanitized and rationalized. Abuse became discipline. Extraction of labor from soldiers became a virtuous act toward the commoners who had been spared labor. Mutilation became justice. Herding of marginal populations into military service became an act of benevolence. Yet the residents of the penal-military complex knew the truth of it: the floggings and the beatings, the tattooing, the hard labor, the forced marches, and the public executions were all the true hallmarks of their Song civilization.

The great project of creating this new social group involved the breakdown of social and physical boundaries, the disassembling of families and bodies to turn them into something new, greater than the sum of all its parts. As it embarked on this project, the Song state converted men into a set of measurable criteria that assessed the soldiers' bodies, skills, and the monetary worth of their labor. Within the penal-military complex, the Song state found a space where it gained vast experience in surveillance and control and where it experimented with new forms of currency and economic production. The tattooing, measuring, payment, and equipping of mass standing armies forms an important chapter in the history of Song institutions, economy, and technology.

The examination system became one of the most well-known traits of Late Imperial China. Despite a short interruption in the early Yuan period (late thirteenth–early fourteenth centuries), the examination system was adopted by the Mongol Yuan dynasty as well, and it remained the most famous and important institution of the Sinitic-script empires through the Ming and Qing periods and until the early twentieth century. The Song examination system's far-less-famous and far-more-sinister counterpart was forgotten, but it did not disappear completely, for even after Mongols abolished the practice of military tattoos, all later dynasties continued to employ penal tattoos. It was only in 1905 that the Qing dynasty abolished the examination system in the attempt to remove all obstacles to China's modernization. At the same time, the Qing discontinued the punishment of tattooing.[1] To this day, the examination system remains a symbol of Late Imperial China and its society and culture while the memory of penal tattoos faded.

In the centuries since the fall of the Song empire, military tattoos continued to make sporadic appearances in the Sinitic-script world. In 1357, the late years of the Yuan dynasty, an official formed a local army of rootless and hungry men and tattooed their backs with the inscription "Loyally Protecting the State, Swearing to Kill the Red Turbans" (*chixin huguo shisha hongjin*).[2] In the nineteenth century, Taiping rebel forces used tattoos to mark their captives and humiliate them.[3] During the Korean War of the twentieth century, Chinese Nationalists tattooed Chinese prisoners of war with anticommunist slogans to prevent them from returning to the People's Republic.[4] In all of these cases, as in the Song case, military tattoos were not a reflection of the inner world of those wearing them. As far as they represented identity, it was an external one forced on them by others.

1. Sogabe, *Sōdai no shi-hai ni tsuite*, 21.
2. Tao Zongyi, *Nancun chuogeng lu*, 27.343. The Red Turban Rebellions were a series of uprisings against the Mongols. The founder of the Ming dynasty was one of the leaders of this movement.
3. Meyer-Fong, *What Remains*, 73–81.
4. Young, *Name, Rank, and Serial Number*, 42–43, 70, 102–3.

The Military System and the Sex Ratio

Soldiers of the Song period were not alone in the process of becoming commodified objects. When men were being tattooed, put to work, and attached a monetary value, a similar process was taking place with women who appeared in the marketplace as courtesans and concubines of elite men. The sex trade continued to expand in the centuries following the destruction of the Song state, skewing the male-female ratio in lower-class society. During the Ming and Qing dynasties, as more and more families purchased concubines, there were growing numbers of young men who were unable to find a wife. These men, referred to as "bare sticks" (*guanggun*), became a serious social problem. These were the men who were more likely to travel, join secret societies, and support rebellions.[5] In times of dynastic crisis, such men posed a significant threat to the survival of the state.

The Song state's military system played an important part in its relative success in avoiding large popular rebellions like those that took place during the Yuan, Ming, and Qing dynasties. The Song state actively swept through lower society, assigning potential male troublemakers to military service. By keeping these men confined to the penal-military complex, it avoided the threat of large-scale popular rebellions and instead faced relatively small, isolated, and numerous cases of mutiny and insubordination. The bloody price for the disastrous campaigns of the Song military was not spread out evenly across society but was paid mostly by a specific sector of the population: families at the bottom of society. Although later dynasties allowed for the trade in females to continue, they did not build mechanisms for addressing the large numbers of young unmarried males. This may have decreased the amount of coercive violence the Sinitic-script states used in the short run, but it had disastrous consequences for them in the long run.

5. Jiang Quanbao and Jesâus J. Sâanchez-Barricarte, "Bare Branches and Social Stability," 538–61.

Social-Military History and National Identity

The antagonistic relationship between soldiers and their superiors had a great impact on the Song state's military strategy, tactics, and technology. Modern scholars tend to explain the Song military's reliance on large infantry armies in geopolitical terms. The Song empire lacked suitable pastures for raising war horses, and it compensated for that weakness by excelling in other areas: defense of walled cities, naval technology, and gunpowder weapons. Yet the Song state's military institutions were also shaped by strong social and economic changes. Song soldiers were salaried workers in a society displaying growing class divisions. Poverty drove many of them into service, as volunteers but also as convicts in a carceral system of a massive scale. As unfree laborers and combat troops, they had little share in victories, but they suffered greatly during defeats. The tactics and weapons used by the Song military offered advantages for managing a reluctant workforce. After all, horses provide their riders with a great degree of individual mobility, whereas walled cities and ships can resemble prisons.

The Song military used soldiers in ways that forced them to work together for survival. The technologies of defending walled cities, warships, and gunpowder shared a few elements: a large and diverse workforce was necessary to produce them, and they demanded teams to operate. In both walled cities and ships, the fates of the fighting men were bound together. Desertion was far harder than in the open field, and a loss in battle spelled disaster for the entire unit, forcing potential deserters and mutineers to cooperate. A millennium later, studies of soldiers' behavior in combat during World War II found that soldiers behaved differently when their conduct was directly related to the fate of other men (as in automatic weapons firing teams) or if their survival depended on each other's performance (as in members of bomber crews).[6] The Song military organization suggests that the Song government already understood this principle, that military technology is directly related to soldiers' morale and behavior in combat.

6. Lang, *Military Organizations*, 869.

The concept of a nation became one of the most powerful motivating forces in the mass armies of the twentieth century. Modern nation-states spent great resources on teaching their citizens from a young age that individual sacrifice for the sake of the nation was a natural and worthy deed. This notion played a meaningful part in military strategy, allowing generals of modern armies to order large numbers of people to march to their death.[7] The Song period still did not see the rise of a national consciousness that would justify sacrifice for the state by its soldiers. When the Song court demanded war of movement of its soldiers, it often found its plans frustrated, its armies scattered and slaughtered. Most often, though, the Song's scholar-officials tended to show a pragmatic attitude. They demanded obedience—even reluctant obedience—rather than love and devotion for the state from their rank and file. The Song state's military institutions reflect a keen awareness that violence, not love, made soldiers obey, and they drafted policies accordingly, generously measuring out violence and coercion, creating a cruel world tempered with a system of salaries and bonuses.

The high degree of violence within the penal-military complex reveals an important truth about Song society. The greater the degree of state violence, the weaker its level of cultural hegemony. In the Song state's box of administrative tools, tattoos represented the point where the hegemony of elite culture ended, forcing the state to stamp its mark on soldiers' bodies to place them firmly under its control. In this sense too, the Song state was a pioneer. The Yuan, Ming, and Qing empires, heirs to the Song as the rulers of the Sinitic-script world, continued to use penal tattoos. By the nineteenth century, states across Eurasia tattooed criminals: from India to Russia and France. A few Western states expanded the scope of tattooing from individuals to groups, employing tattooing and branding against populations considered inferior and external to the "positive" social order. In the United States, the branding of misbehaving slaves continued until the defeat of the South in the Civil War.[8] In

7. For more on the ideal of the war of movement and the relationship between culture, nationalism, and war, see Ousbi, *The Road to Verdun*, a study of the French army during the Battle of Verdun.

8. Bradley, "Body Commodification?"; Anderson, "Godna"; Morgan and Rushton, "Visible Bodies."

the mid-twentieth century, Nazi Germany tattooed Jews, Romani, homosexuals, and other groups they considered to be inferior and harmful. In all these modern cases, tattooing and branding marked the line where the state decided that its cultural hegemony ended, making way to brute force and coercion.

Soldiers and elite men did not share the same culture, but the Song empire they lived in still formed one coherent world. Sinitic script determined the contours of their world. Elites interacted with the sons and daughters of the penal-military complex as superiors, as masters, and as clients, but elite men and the men of the penal-military complex did not share the same "imagined community." The application of penal and military tattoos to an illiterate population by a small literate elite became one clear manifestation of the different, even opposing, ways social groups were tied to the Sinitic-script world. In the interaction between the literate and the illiterate, Sinitic script represented power, control, and exclusion.

What share did the residents of the penal-military complex have in the golden age of the Song? In the penal-military complex the benevolent Song state became a parasitic entity that preyed on society's weakest and most marginal groups. The cultural achievements of the Song age meant little for those who were never meant to be the producers or even consumers of culture but only uninitiated and unappreciated spectators. Economic growth brought no comfort to those who were its victims. Written out of history, their bodies become a map legend, the key to a tale etched in scar tissue and tattoo ink that runs throughout Song history and paints the picture of a shadow world to the world of the scholar-officials, a realm where the narratives of the benevolent age of the Song crumble. Turn the key to enter that dark kingdom, and you may not easily find your way back.

"Come, memory, let us seek them there in the shadows."

—Donald Justice, *On the Death of Friends in Childhood*

Chinese Character List

A

An Congjin 安從進
An Lushan 安祿山
Ansu 安肅

B

baimian yecha 白面夜叉
bai mudan 白牡丹
bai zhan li 白氈笠
Banzhi 班直
Bao Daocheng 包道成
baojia 保甲
Baojie 保捷
Baoyi 保毅
Baozhou 保州
Bei 貝
beifa 北伐
Beizhou 貝州
Bian 汴
Bin 濱
bing 兵
Bingzhou 並州
Bo 博
bufu zhaowang 不負趙王

C

Cai Jing 蔡京
Cai Tao 蔡絛
Cangzhou 滄州
canzhi tu 蠶織圖
Cao Bin 曹彬
Cao Wei 曹瑋
Cao Yanyue 曹彥約
Caozhou 曹州
Chaling 茶陵
Chang'an 長安
Chao Zhongshi 晁仲式
Chen 陳
Chen Fu 沈富
Chen Fuliang 陳傅良
Cheng Bi 程珌
Chengde 承德
Chen Huajiao 陳花脚
Chen Tong 陳峒

Chen Tong[1] 陳通
Chen Yaozuo 陳堯佐
Chenzhou 郴州
chixin baoguo shisha jinzei 赤心報國誓殺金賊
chixin huguo shisha hongjin 赤心護國誓殺紅巾
chixin sha qidan 赤心殺契丹
Chongjie 崇節
chongwen yiwu 崇文抑武
chumen wangjia weiguo, linchen wangsi weizhu 出門忘家為國臨陣忘死為主
Chuan 川
Chuankou 川口
Chuanxia 川峽
Chuan Xiaozhong 川效忠
Chuan zhongjie 川忠節
Ci 磁
cipei 刺配
cixiu 刺繡
ciziren 刺字人
Cui Zuwu 催祖武

D

dada 達靼
da li 大禮
Daming 大名
Daning 大寧
danwei 單位
daozei 盜賊
Dazhongxiangfu 大中祥符
De 德
Deng Jie 鄧楷
Dezhou 德州
Di 棣
Dianqian jun 殿前軍
Dianqian si 殿前司
Difang 提防
Ding 定
Dingba du 定霸都
Dingchuan 定川
Ding Jin 丁進
Di Qing 狄青
diwan 敵萬
Duan Chengshi 段成式
Duangong 端拱
Du Chang 杜常
Du De 杜德
dujian 都監
Du Yan 杜彥

F

Fan bing 蕃兵
Fan Chunren 範純仁
Fan Zhongyan 范仲淹
Fan Zuyu 范祖禹
Feimeng 飛猛
Feng Hui 馮暉
Fengjie 奉節
Feng Shixing 馮時行
Fengxiang 鳳翔
Fengzhou 鳳州
fu 福
Fu Bi 富弼
Fujian 福建
Fu Qiu 傅求
Fuyan 鄜延
Fu Zhaoshou 符昭壽
Fuzhou 福州
Fuzhou[1] 鄜州
Fuzhou weiyuan 府州威遠

G

gaici 改刺
Gao Li 高澧

Gao Qiong 高瓊
Gaosha 高沙
Gaozong 高宗
Gaozu 高祖
Ge Jin 葛進
Gengshufa 更戍法
Gongdi 恭帝
Gongjianshou 弓箭手
Gongsheng 拱聖
Gongshou 弓手
guan 官
guanggun 光棍
Guanghua 光化
Guangnan 廣南
Guangshun 廣順
Guantao 館陶
guangwei 廣威
Guan Yu 關羽
Guangzong 光宗
gui han 歸漢
Guihua 歸化
guinong 歸農
Guiyuan 歸遠
Guo Chengyou 郭承祐
Guo Jun 國均
Guo Kui 郭逵
Guoseng 郭僧
Guo Shenxi 郭申錫
Guo Wei 郭威

H

Han 漢
Han Gang 韓綱
Han Qi 韓琦
Han Xiaozhou 韓肖冑
Hangzhou 杭州
haohan 好漢
Hedong 河東
Henan 河南
Heqing 河清
He Ruo 何若
Heshuo 河朔
He Tan 何郯
He Zhu 何鑄
Hong Kuo 洪适
Hong Mai 洪邁
Hong Zhongfu 洪中孚
Hongzhou 洪州
Hu Quan 胡铨
Hu Sanniang 扈三娘
Hu Shunzhi 胡順之
Huyan Zan 呼延贊
Huai 淮
Huainan 淮南
Huaixi 淮西
Huan 環
Huang Chao 黃巢
Huangfu Jian 皇甫鑑
Huang Gan 黃幹
Huang Jin 黃進
Huanqing 環慶
Huo Xing 霍興

J

Ji 濟
Jia Changchao 賈昌朝
jian 賤
Jianchang 建昌
Jiang 江
Jiangbingfa 將兵法
Jiangnan 江南
Jiangyang 江陽
Jiankang 建康
Jiannan 劍南
Jia Sidao 賈似道
jianya 監押

Jianzhong baoning 揀中保寧
Jiaojun 教駿
jiedushi 節度使
Jin 晉
Jing 涇
Jingdongxi 京東西
Jinghu 荊湖
Jingnan 荊南
Jingyuan 涇原
Jingzhou 荊州
jinjun 禁軍
Jinling 金陵
jinti she 錦體社
jinzhong baoguo 盡忠報國
Jiyang 吉陽
juji xingsong 聚集興宋
Junshi 軍士
juntousi 軍頭司
junyuan 軍員

K

Kaixi beifa 開禧北伐
Kang 康
Kanpojijia 龕波給家
Kelan 岢嵐
Kong Du 孔都
Kui 夔
Kuizhou 夔州

L

Langzhou 朗州
Li 利
Liang 梁
Liang Fu 梁福
liang min 良民
Liangzhe 兩浙
Liao 遼
Liao Gang 廖剛
Li Chuyun 李處耘
Li Daxing 李大性
Li Fugui 李復圭
Li Gang 李綱
Li Gou 李覯
Li Hong 李紘
Li Ji 李及
Li Ji[1] 李稷
Li Jin 李進
Li Jue 李覺
Li Miao 李邈
Li Mingfu 李鳴復
Lingnan 嶺南
Linhai 臨海
Linzhou feiqi 麟州飛騎
Li Qian 李謙
Li Quan 李全
Li Rou 李柔
Li Ruyi 李汝翼
Li Shun 李順
Li Tang 李唐
Li Tao 李燾
Li Weiqing 李惟清
Li Xian 李憲
Li Yong 李用
Li You 李宥
Li Zhaoliang 李昭亮
Lizong 理宗
Li Zongyi 李宗易
Liu 劉
Liu Bao 劉寶
Liu Bei 劉備
Liu Chang 劉敞
Liu Daochang 劉道昌
Liu Guangshi 劉光世

Liu Huan 劉渙
Liu Jin 劉金
Liu Jizong 劉繼宗
Liu Rengong 劉仁恭
Liu Sanniang 劉三娘
Liu Shouguang 劉守光
Liu Wen 劉溫
Liu Yi 劉易
Liu Yonggui 劉永規
Liu Zhiyuan 劉知遠
Liu Zhong 劉忠
Longmeng 龍猛
Longqi 龍騎
Longwei 龍衛
Long Ze 龍澤
Lü 呂
luan 亂
Lu Chengjun 盧成均
Lu De 陸德
Lü Gongbi 呂公弼
Lunan 瀘南
Luo Dian 羅點
Luoyan du 落雁都
Lü Wenqing 呂溫卿
Lü Zuqian 呂祖謙

M

Ma Guangzu 馬光祖
mahu Du 麻胡杜
Mamu 馬牧
Mai Wenbing 麥文昞
Man Zhongxing 滿中行
Mei Xian 梅先
Mei Yaochen 梅堯臣
mianyifa 免役法
mianzhan 免斬
Miao Fu 苗傅
Miao Xi 妙喜
Mingzhou 明州
Mizhou 密州
moujun huo mouzhou zhongyi 某軍或某州重役
moulu anfusi xiaoyong 某路安撫司效用
muzhiming 墓誌銘

N

Nanchang 南昌
nei wai xiangzhi 內外相制
Ningguo 寧國
Niu Mian 牛冕
Niu Sui 牛遂
Nong Zhigao 儂智高
Nüzhe 女遮

O

Ouyang Xiu 歐陽修

P

Pan Xiaochao 潘孝綽
pei zhoufu tunzhujun zhongyi 配州府屯駐軍重役
Pengri 捧日
Ping Song lu 平宋錄
Pingyang 平陽
pi ruo 疲弱
pishumen tianwang 毗沙門天王

Q

Qi 齊
Qian 錢
Qiang 羌

qiangdao 強盜
qianggan ruozhi 強幹弱枝
Qiangzhuang 強壯
Qian Weiji 錢惟濟
Qiaoliang 橋樑
Qi Lan 齊闌
Qinfeng 秦風
Qing 慶
Qingbian jun 清邊軍
Qingjian 清澗
Qingli 慶歷
qingming shanghe tu 清明上河圖
Qin Gui 秦檜
Qingyuan 慶元
Qinzhou 秦州
Qi Yanguang 戚彥廣
Qi Yi 其乂
que'er 雀兒
Quegu 榷酤
Quzhou 衢州

R

Rao Jun 饒俊
Rao Shi 饒奭
Renzong 仁宗
ru huo 入火
Run Po 潤陂

S

san wang de 三王得
San ya 三衙
sha da 殺韃
shadi baoguo 殺敵報國
shang deng 上等
Shangguan Wan'er 上官婉兒
Shangjun 上軍
Shangzhou 商州
Shanxian 山險
Shaoxing 紹興
sha Yin 殺尹
Shaozhou 邵州
Shen Diao 沈調
Shen Jizhong 沈積中
Shenwei 神衛
shibing 士兵
Shi Changyan 施昌言
Shichen 使臣
Shi Daiju 石待舉
shisha Jinzei, bufu zhaowang 誓殺金賊，不負趙王
Shiwei 室韋
Shiwei qinjun 侍衛親軍
Shouchang 壽昌
Shouchun 壽春
Shouzhou 壽州
Shu 蜀
Shu Dan 舒亶
Shuihu zhuan 水滸傳
Shuilu yunsong 水陸運送
Shunzhou 順州
Shuzhou 舒州
Sima Guang 司馬光
Sima Kang 司馬康
Song Ci 宋慈
Song Jiang 宋江
Song Qi 宋祁
Song shi 宋史
Song Taizu 宋太祖
Sucun 蘇村
Sun Lan 孫覽
Su Shi 蘇軾
Su Song 蘇頌

T

Taiping 太平
Taipingxingguo 太平興國
Taizong 太宗
Taizong zhengsi 大宗正司
Tang 唐
Tang[1] 湯
Tang Jie 唐介
Tang Sheng 唐勝
taozou 逃走
tianfu 天福
Tian jiang sheng jie zhihui 天降聖捷指揮
Tian jia yu 田家語
Tian Kuang 田況
Tianwu 天武
Tian Xi 田錫
Tianxiong 天雄
Tieshi 鐵師
Tingshi 桯史
Tongdao 通道
Tong Guan 童貫
Tongzhou 通州
Tubing 土兵

W

Wang 王
Wang Anshi 王安石
Wang Deyong 王德用
Wang Fu 王福
Wang Gui 王珪
Wang Gui[1] 王貴
Wang Guo 王果
Wang Huaji 王化基
Wang Jian 王建
Wang Ji'en 王繼恩
Wang Jingchong 王景崇
Wang Jixun 王繼勳
Wang Jun 王均
Wang Lun 王倫
Wang Mei 王美
Wang Mingqing 王明清
Wang Shengxi 汪聖錫
Wang Shipeng 王十朋
Wang Shouyi 王守一
Wang Xian 王先
Wang Xiu 王秀
Wang Yan 王彥
Wang Yan[1] 王炎
Wang Yaochen 王堯臣
Wang Ze 王則
Wang Zhongheng 王仲衡
Wang Zhongzheng 王中正
Wang Zong 王宗
Wansheng 萬勝
Wanzhou 萬州
Weibo 魏博
Wei Gui 韋貴
Weijie 威捷
Weisheng 威勝
wen 文
Wen Di 文迪
Wen Yanbo 文彥博
Wenzhou 溫州
wu 武
Wu Anxian 吳安憲
Wudi 無敵
Wujing zongyao 武經總要
Wu Lin 吳璘
Wu Liu 吳六
Wuqi 武騎
Wusu 武肅
Wuxi 無錫

Wuyue 吳越
Wu Zetian 武則天
Wu Zimu 吳自牧

X

Xi 奚
Xi[1] 霫
Xia 夏
Xia Gui 夏貴
Xiajun 下軍
Xiang 襄
xiangjun 廂軍
xianwei 縣尉
Xiaoqi 驍騎
Xiaosheng 驍勝
Xiaoshun 効順
Xiaoyong 效用
Xiaozong 孝宗
Xia Qi'er 夏旗兒
Xia *yeye* 夏爺爺
Xie Rong 謝榮
Xie Si 謝四
Xihe 熙河
Xingguo 興國
Xining 熙寧
Xinzhou 信州
Xiong Er 熊二
Xionglüe 雄略
Xiong Ming 熊明
Xiongwei 雄威
Xiongweijie 雄威節
Xiongwu 雄武
Xiuzhou 秀洲
Xi Xia 西夏
Xuanyi 宣毅
Xuanzong 玄宗
Xue Changru 薛長孺
Xue Gongkui 薛公奎
Xue Shunyu 薛舜俞
xunjian 巡檢
Xu Yao 徐瑤

Y

Yan 兗
Yandai 堰埭
Yang 楊
Yang Chun 楊椿
Yang Huaimin 楊懷敏
Yang Jingzong 楊景宗
Yang Miaozhen 楊妙真
Yang Wanli 楊萬里
Yangwu 陽武
yan yao suan 眼药酸
Yanzi du 雁子都
Yi 益
yibing 義兵
Yijianzhi 夷堅志
yijun 義軍
yijun pozhao desheng 義軍破趙得勝
yingfu 營婦
Yingzong 英宗
Yin Yan 尹偃
yixin shizhu 一心事主
Yiyong 義勇
Yizhang Qing 一丈青
Yizhou 宜州
Yizhou[1] 益州
Yizhou[2] 滑州
Yongning 永寧
Yongxing 永興
Yongzhou 永州

Youchuan 郵傳
Youyang zazu 酉陽雜俎
Youyi 游奕
Youzhou 幽州
yuan 元
Yuanhe 元和
Yuanliao shengyuanzhi 員僚剩員值
Yuan Xingzong 員興宗
yuan zhan nandu 願戰南都
Yue Fei 岳飛
Yue Ke 岳珂
Yugan 餘干
Yu Jing 余靖
Yun 鄆
Yunqi 雲騎
Yunyi 雲翼
Yu Yunwen 虞允文
Yuzhang 豫章

Z

zhakou panche tu 閘口盤車圖
Zhan 詹
Zhang 張
Zhang Fangping 張方平
Zhang Fei 張飛
Zhang Gan 張幹
Zhang Jie 章楶
Zhang Jin 張津
Zhang Jun 張浚
Zhang Kang 張亢
Zhang Kemao 張克懋
Zhang Qixian 張齊賢
Zhang Suo 張所
Zhang Wenzhi 張昷之
Zhang Yan 章綖
Zhang Yong 張詠
Zhang Yu 張昱
Zhang Zhongxuan 張仲宣
Zhan Zhiyong 詹志永
Zhao Buyi 趙不易
Zhao Gai 趙槩
Zhao Kuangyi 趙匡義
Zhao Kuangyin 趙匡胤
zhaomu 召募
Zhaoshou duangong 招收端拱
Zhao Shujin 趙叔近
Zhao Siguan 趙思綰
Zhao Xiyao 趙希堯
Zhao Xiaoge 趙小哥
Zhao Xie 趙卨
Zhao Xing 趙興
Zhao Ye 趙野
Zhao Yuanxi 趙元僖
Zhe 浙
Zheng Chao 郑超
Zhenghe 政和
zhiai tu 炙艾圖
zhihui 指揮
Zhong E 种諤
Zhongjun 中軍
Zhong Shiheng 種世衡
zhongyi 忠義
zhongyong 忠勇
Zhou Bi 周祕
Zhou Bida 週必大
Zhou Renmei 周仁美
Zhou Shixiu 周世修
Zhou Taizu 周太祖
Zhou You 周祐
Zhuangyong 壯勇
Zhu Fu 朱芾
Zhu Jin 朱瑾

Zhuo 涿
Zhu San 朱三
Zhu Wen 朱溫
Zhu Xuan 朱瑄
Zi 梓
zidi 子弟
Zizhou 梓州
Zizhou[1] 資州
Zong Ze 宗澤
zuocang 坐倉

Bibliography

List of Abbreviations

Chang bian	Li Tao, *Xu zizhi tongjian changbian*
SKQS	*Yingyin Wenyuange Siku quanshu*
Song huiyao	Xu Song, *Song huiyao jigao*
Yaolu	Li Xinchuan, *Jianyan yilai xinian yaolu*
Yijianzhi	Hong Mai, *Yijianzhi*

Primary Sources

Anon. *Songji sanchao zhengyao jianzheng* 宋季三朝政要箋證. Beijing: Zhonghua shuju, 2010.

Anon. *Songshi quanwen* 宋史全文. In SKQS.

Anon. *Qunshu huiyuan jiejiang wang* 群書會元截江網. In SKQS.

Bao Zheng 包拯 (999–1062). *Bao xiaosu zouyiji* 包孝肅奏議集. In SKQS.

Cai Kan 蔡戡 (jinshi 1166). *Dingzhai ji* 定齋集. In SKQS.

Cai Tao 蔡絛 (fl. 11th c.–12th c.). *Tie wei shan congtan* 鐵圍山叢談. Beijing: Zhonghua shuju, 1983.

Cai Xiang 蔡襄 (1012–1067). *Duanming ji* 端明集. In SKQS.

Changsun Wuji 長孫無忌. *Tanglü shuyi* 唐律疏議. Beijing: Falü chubanshe, 1999.

Chen Fuliang 陳傅良 (1137–1203). *Lidai bingzhi* 歷代兵制. In SKQS.

———. *Zhizhai ji* 止齋集. In SKQS.

Chen Hu 陳鵠. *Xitang ji qijiu xuwen* 西塘集耆舊續聞. Beijing: Zhonghua shuju, 2002.

Chen Jinghe 陳荊和 ed. *Daietsu Shiki Zensho/ Đại Việt Sử Ký Toàn Thư* 大越史記全書. Tokyo: Tokyo Daigaku Toyo Bunka Kenkyujo Fuzoku Toyogaku Bunken Senta, 1984.

Chen Shichong 陳世崇 (1245–1308). *Suiyin manlu* 隨隱漫錄. Beijing: Zhonghua shuju, 2010.

Chen Shidao 陳師道 (1053–1102). *Houshan tancong* 後山叢談. Beijing: Zhonghua shuju, 2007.

Cheng Bi 程珌 (1164–1242). *Luoshui ji* 洺水集. In SKQS.

Ding Chuanjing 丁傳靖 (1870–1930). *Songren yishi huibian* 宋人軼事彙編. 2 vols. Beijing: Zhonghua shuju, 2003.

Duan Chengshi 段成式 (d. 863). *Youyang zazu* 酉陽雜俎. Beijing: Zhonghua shuju, 1981.

Fan Zhen 范鎮 (1007–1087). *Dongzhai jishi* 東齋記事. Beijing: Zhonghua shuju, 1980.

Fan Zuyu 范祖禹 (1041–1098). *Fantaishi ji* 范太史集. In SKQS.

Fang Hui 方回 (1227–1307). *Tongjiang ji* 桐江集. Nanjing: Jiangsu guji chubanshe, 1988.

———. *Xu gujin kao* 續古今考. In SKQS.

Fang Shao 方勺 (b. 1066). *Bozhai bian* 泊宅編. 1983. Reprint, Beijing: Zhonghua shuju 2007.

Gao Cheng 高承 (fl. 11th century). *Shiwu jiyuan* 事物紀原. In SKQS.

Gao Huisou 高晦叟 (fl. 12th century). *Zhenxi fangtan* 珍席放談. In *Quansong biji*, 3rd part, vol. 1. Zhengzhou: Daxiang chubanshe, 2008

Hong Kuo 洪适 (1117–1184). *Panzhou wenji* 盘洲文集. In SKQS.

Hong Mai 洪邁 (1123–1202). *Rongzhai suibi* 容齋隨筆. Beijing: Jinghua chubanshe, 2003.

———. *Yijian zhi* 夷堅志. Beijing: Zhonghua shuju, 1981.

Hu Quan 胡全 (1102–1180). *Hudan'an xiansheng wenji* 胡澹庵先生文集. China: From collection of Sun Huyun 孫胡澐. Qing Qianlong reign period, 22nd year (1757).

Huang Gan 黃幹 (1152–1221). *Mianzhai ji* 勉齋集. In SKQS.

Huang Zhen 黃震 (1213–1280). *Huangshi richao* 黃氏日抄. In SKQS.

Kong Pingzhong 孔平仲 (1044–1111). *Tan yuan* 談苑. In *Quan Song biji*, 2nd part, vol. 5. Zhengzhou: Daxiang chubanshe, 2005.

Li chi: Book of Rites. Translated by James Legge. New York: University Books, 1967.

Li Gang 李綱 (1083–1140). *Liangxi ji* 梁谿集. In SKQS.

Li Gou 李覯 (1009–1059). *Xujiang ji* 盱江集. In SKQS.

Li Shangjiao 李上交 (fl. 1051). *Jinshi huiyuan* 近事會元. In SKQS.

Li Tao 李燾 (1115–1184). *Xu zizhi tongjian changbian* 續資治通鑒長編. 20 vols. Beijing: Zhonghua shuju, 2008.

Li Xinchuan 李心傳 (1166–1243). *Jianyan yilai chaoye zaji* 建炎以來朝野雜記. Beijing: Zhonghua shuju, 2006.

———. *Jianyan yilai xinian yaolu* 建炎以來繫年要錄. 8 vols. Beijing: Zhonghua shuju, 2013.

Liang Kejia 梁克家 (1128–1187). *Chunxi sanshan zhi* 淳熙三山志. In *Song yuan fangzhi congkan* 宋元方志叢刊, vol. 8. Beijing: Zhonghua shuju, 1990.

Liu Ban 劉攽. *Pengcheng ji* 彭城集. In SKQS.

Liu Chang 劉敞 (1019–1068). *Gongshi ji* 公是集. In SKQS.

Liu Minzhong 劉敏中 (1243–1318). *Ping song lu* 平宋錄. In SKQS.

Liu Xu 劉昫 (887–946). *Jiu Tang shu* 舊唐書. Beijing: Zhonghua shuju, 1975.

Lu You 陸游 (1125–1210). *Weinan wenji* 渭南文集. In SKQS.

Luo Dajing 羅大經 (1196–1242). *Helin yulu* 鶴林玉露. Beijing: Zhonghua shuju, 1983.

Luo Jun 羅濬. *Baoqing siming zhi* 寶慶四明志. In *Song Yuan fangzhi congkan* 宋元方志叢刊, vol. 5. Beijing: Zhonghua shuju, 1990.

Ma Duanlin 馬端臨 (ca. 1254–ca.1323). *Wenxian tongkao* 文獻通考. In SKQS.

Mei Yaochen 梅堯臣 (1002–1060). *Tianjia yu* 田家語 ("The Peasant's Words"). Translated by Yi-tsi Mei Feuerwerker. In *Ideology, Power, Text: Self-Representation and the Peasant "Other" in Modern Chinese Literature,* Yi-tsi Mei Feuerwerker, 22–23. Stanford, CA: Stanford University Press, 1998.

Minggong shupan qingmingji 名公書判清明集. Edited by Zhongguo shehui kexueyuan Song Liao Jin Yuan shi yanjiushi 中国社会科学院宋遼金元史研究室. Beijing: Zhonghua shuju 1987.

Nai Deweng 耐得翁 (13th c.). *Ducheng jisheng* 都城紀勝. In SKQS.

Ouyang Xiu 歐陽修 (1007–1072). *Ouyang Xiu quanji* 歐陽修全集. Beijing: Beijing shi zhongguo shudian, 1986.

———. *Xin Tang shu* 新唐書. Beijing: Zhonghua shuju, 1975.

———. *Xin Wudai shi* 新五代史. Beijing: Zhonghua shuju, 1974.

Peng Cheng 彭乘 (fl. 1086). *Moke huixi* 墨客揮犀. 2002. Reprint, Beijing: Zhonghua shuju, 2004.

Qian Ruoshui 錢若水 (960–1003). *Song Taizong shilu* 宋太宗實錄. Lanzhou: Gansu renmin chubanshe, 2005.

Qian Yan 錢儼 (937–1003). *Wuyue beishi* 吳越備史. In SKQS.

Qiang Zhi 強至 (1022–1076). *Han zhongxian gong yishi* 韓忠獻公遺事. In *Quan Song biji*, 1st part, vol. 8. Zhengzhou: Daxiang chubanshe 2003.

Shao Bo 邵博 (d. 1158). *Shaoshi wenjian houlu* 邵氏聞見後錄. 1983. Reprint, Beijing: Zhonghua shuju, 2006.

Shao Bowen 邵伯溫 (1057–1134). *Shaoshi wenjian lu* 邵氏聞見錄. 1983. Reprint, Beijing: Zhonghua shuju, 2008.

Shen Jiaben 沈家本 (1840–1913), ed. *Dayuan shengzheng guochao dianzhang* 大元聖政國朝典章. Taibei: Wenhai chubanshe, 1964.

Shen Kuo 沈括 (1031–1095). *Mengxi bitan* 夢溪筆談. In SKQS.

Shi Decao 施德操 (fl. 12th c.). *Beichuang zhiguo lu* 北窗炙輠錄. In *Quan Song biji*, 3rd part, vol. 8. Zhengzhou: Daxiang chubanshe, 2008.

Shi Jie 石介 (1005–1045). *Culai Shi xiansheng wenji* 徂徠石先生文集. 1984. Reprint, Beijing: Zhonghua shuju, 2009.

Shi Su 施宿 (1164–1222). *Jiatai kuaiji zhi* 嘉泰會稽志. In *Song Yuan fangzhi congkan*, vol. 7. Beijing: Zhonghua shuju, 1990.

Sima Guang 司馬光 (1019–1086). *Chuanjia ji* 传家集. In SKQS.

———. *Sushui jiwen* 涑水記聞. In *Quan Song biji*, 1st part, vol. 7. 2003. Reprint, Zhengzhou: Daxiang chubanshe, 2008.

———. *Zizhi tongjian* 資治通鑑. In SKQS.

Sima Qian 司馬遷 (ca. 145 BCE–86 BCE). *Shi ji* 史記. Beijing: Zhonghua shuju, 1982.

Song Ci 宋慈 (1186–1249). *Xiyuan lu* 洗冤錄. Translated by Brian E. McKnight. In *The Washing Away of Wrongs: Forensic Medicine in Thirteenth-century China*. Ann Arbor: Center for Chinese Studies, University of Michigan, 1981.

Song Lian 宋濂 (1310–1381). *Yuan shi* 元史. Beijing: Zhonghua shuju, 1976.

Song shi 宋史. Compiled by Tuo Tuo 脫脫 (1313–1355). Beijing: Zhonghua shuju, 1977.

Su Shi 蘇軾 (1036–1101). *Dongpo quanji* 東坡全集. In SKQS.

———. *Su Shi quanji jiaozhu* 蘇軾全集校注. Zhang Zhilie 張志烈, Ma Defu 馬德富, and Zhou Yukai 周裕鍇, eds. 20 vols. Shijiazhuang: Hebei renmin chubanshe, 2010.

Su Shunqin 蘇舜欽 (1008–1048). *Su xueshi ji* 蘇學士集. In SKQS.

Su Song 蘇頌 (1020–1101). *Su weigong wenji* 蘇魏公文集. In SKQS.

Su Zhe 蘇轍 (1039–1112). *Lecheng ji* 欒城集. 3 vols. Shanghai: Shanghai guji chubanshe, 1987.

Sun Sheng 孫升. *Sungong tanpu* 孫公談圃. In *Quan Song biji*, 2nd part, vol. 1. Zhengzhou: Daxiang chubanshe, 2006.

Tao Gu 陶穀 (903–970). *Qingyi lu* 清異錄. In SKQS.
Tao Yue 陶岳 (*jinshi* 985). *Wudai shibu* 五代史補. Chengdu: Bashu shushe, 1993.
Tao Zongyi 陶宗儀 (fl. 1360–1368). *Nancun chuogeng lu* 南村輟耕錄. 1959. Reprint, Beijing: Zhonghua shuju, 1997.
Tian Kuang 田況 (1005–1063). *Rulin gongyi* 儒林公議. In *Quan Song biji,* 1st part, vol. 5. Zhengzhou: Daxiang chubanshe, 2003.

Wang Gui 王珪 (1019–1085). *Huayang ji* 華陽集. In SKQS.
Wang Mingqing 王明清 (1127–ca. 1215). *Huizhu lu* 揮麈錄. 1961. Reprint, Beijing: Zhonghua shuju, 1962.
———. *Touxia lu* 投轄錄. Shanghai: Shanghai guji chubanshe, 1991.
———. *Yuzhao xinzhi* 玉照新志. Shanghai: Shanghai guji chubanshe, 1991.
Wang Pizhi 王闢之 (*jinshi* 1067). *Shengshui yantan lu* 澠水燕談錄. Beijing: Zhonghua shuju, 1981.
Wang Pu 王溥 (922–982). *Tang huiyao* 唐會要. In SKQS.
———. *Wudai huiyao* in SKQS.
Wang Shipeng 王十朋 (1112–1171). *Meixi ji* 梅溪集. In SKQS.
———. *Wang Shipeng quanji* 王十朋全集. Shanghai: Shanghai guji chubanshe, 1998.
Wang Yinglin 王應麟 (1223–1296). *Yu hai* 玉海. In SKQS.
Wang Yun 王惲 (1227–1304). *Qiujian ji* 秋澗集. In SKQS.
Wang Zao 汪藻 (1079–1154). *Jingkang yaolu jianzhu* 靖康要錄箋注. Chengdu: Sichuan daxue chubanshe, 2008.
Wang Zhi 王銍 (fl. 12th c.). *Mo ji* 默記. Beijing: Zhonghua shuju, 1981.
Wei Tai 魏泰 (fl. 11th c.–12th c.). *Dongxuan bilu* 東軒筆錄. Beijing: Zhonghua shuju, 1983.
Wei Zheng 魏徵 (580–643). *Sui shu* 隨書. Beijing: Zhonghua shuju, 1973.
Wei Zhuang 韋莊 (836–910). *Wei Zhuang ji* 韋莊集. Beijing: Renmin wenxue chubanshe, 1958.
Wen Ying 文瑩 (fl. 11th c.). *Xiangshan yelu* 湘山野錄; *Yuhu qinghua* 玉壺清話. Beijing: Zhonghua shuju, 1984.
Wu Chuhou 吳處厚 (*jinshi* 1053). *Qingxiang zaji* 青箱雜記. Beijing: Zhonghua shuju,1985.
Wu Zimu 吳自牧 (1161–1237). *Meng liang lu* 夢粱錄. In SKQS.

Xie Shenfu 謝深甫 (*jinshi* 1166). *Qingyuan tiaofa shilei* 慶元條法事類. Beijing: Zhongguo shudian, 1984.
Xiong Ke 熊克 (ca. 1111–ca. 1189). *Zhongxing xiaoji* 中興小紀. In SKQS.
Xu Mengxin 徐夢莘 (1126–1207). *Sanchao beimeng huibian fu jiao kan ji* 三朝北盟會編附校勘記. Taibei: Wenhai chubanshe, 1962.

Xu Song 徐松 (1781–1848). *Song huiyao jigao* 宋會要輯稿. From the digital database at the Taiwan History Digital Library, http://thdl.ntu.edu.tw/.
Xue Jixuan 薛季宣 (1134–1173). *Langyu ji* 浪語集. In SKQS.
Xue Juzheng 薛居正 (912–981). *Jiu wudai shi* 舊五代史. Beijing: Zhonghua shuju, 1976.

Yang Shiqi 楊士奇 (1365–1444). *Lidai mingchen zouyi* 歷代名臣奏議. In SKQS.
Yang Wanli 楊萬里 (1127–1206). *Cheng zhai ji* 誠齋集. In SKQS.
Ye Mengde 葉夢得 (1077–1148). *Shilin yanyu* 石林燕語. 1984. Reprint, Beijing: Zhonghu shuju, 1997.
Ye Shaoweng 葉紹翁 (fl. 12th century–13th century). *Sichao wenjian lu* 四朝聞見錄. 1989. Reprint, Beijing: Zhonghua shuju, 1997.
Ye Shi 葉適 (1150–1223). *Ye Shi ji* 葉適集. Beijing: Zhonghua shuju, 1961.
Yingyin Wenyuange Siku quanshu 影印文淵閣四庫全書. 1,500 vols. Taibei: Shangwu, 1983–86. Reprint, 1,800 vols, Shanghai: Shanghai guji chubanshe, 1987.
Yuan Jiong 袁褧 (fl. 12th c.–13th c.). *Fengchuang xiaodu* 楓窗小牘. In *Quan Song biji*, 4th part, vol. 5. Zhengzhou: Daxiang chubanshe, 2008.
Yuan Xingzong 員興宗 (d. 1170). *Jiu hua ji* 九華集. In SKQS.
Yue Ke 岳珂 (1183–1234). *Ting shi* 桯史. 1981. Reprint, Beijing: Zhonghua shuju, 2010.

Zeng Gongliang 曾公亮 (999–1078). *Wujing zongyao* 武經總要. In SKQS.
Zeng Zao 曾慥 (fl. 1136–1147). *Gaozhai manlu* 高齋漫錄. In *Quan Song biji*, 4th part, vol. 5. Zhengzhou: Daxiang chubanshe, 2008.
Zhang Fangping 張方平 (1007–1091). *Lequan ji* 樂全集. In SKQS.
Zhang Hao 張淏. *Baoqing guiji xuzhi* 寶慶會稽續志. In *Song Yuan fangzhi congkan*, vol. 7. Beijing: Zhonghua shuju, 1990.
Zhang Ruyu 章如愚 (*jinshi* 1196). *Qunshu kaosuo houji* 群書考索後集. In SKQS.
———. *Qunshu kaosuo xuji* 群書考索續集. In SKQS.
Zhang Shunmin 張舜民 (*jinshi* 1065). *Huaman lu* 畫墁錄. In *Quan Song biji*, 2nd part, vol. 1. Zhengzhou: Daxiang chubanshe, 2006.
Zhang Tangying 張唐英 (1029–1071). *Shu tao wu* 蜀檮杌. In SKQS.
Zhang Xiaoxiang 张孝祥 (1132–1169). *Yuhu ji* 于湖集. In SKQS.
Zhang Zhifu 張知甫 (fl. 12th c.). *Ke shu* 可書. 2002. Reprint, Beijing: Zhonghua shuju, 2004.
Zhao Ruyu 赵汝愚 (1140–1196). *Song mingchen zouyi* 宋名臣奏議. In SKQS.
Zheng Xie 鄭獬 (1022–1072). *Yunxi ji* 鄖溪集. In SKQS.
Zheng Yuanyou 鄭元祐 (1292–1364). *Suichang zalu* 遂昌雜錄. In SKQS.
Zhou Bida 周必大 (1126–1204). *Wenzhong ji* 文忠集. In SKQS.
Zhou Hui 周輝 (b. 1226). *Qingbo zazhi* 清波雜誌. Beijing: Zhonghua shuju, 1994.

Zhou Mi 周密 (1232–1308). *Guixin zashi* 癸辛雜識. 1988. Reprint, Beijing: Zhonghua shuju 1997.

Zhou Yinghe 周應合 (1213–1280). *Jingding jiankang zhi* 景定建康志. In *Song Yuan fangzhi congkan*. Beijing: Zhonghua shuju, 1990.

Zhu Xi 朱熹 (1130–1200). *Huian ji* 晦庵集. In SKQS.

Zhu Yu 朱彧 (fl. 11th c.–12th c.). *Pingzhou ketan* 萍洲可談. Beijing: Zhonghua shuju 2007.

Zhuang Chuo 莊綽 (fl. 12th c.). *Jile bian* 雞肋編. In *Quan Song biji*, 4th part, vol. 7. Zhengzhou: Daxiang chubanshe, 2008.

Zhuang Zhou 莊周. *Zhuangzi jinzhu jinshe* 莊子今注今譯. 1983. Reprint, Beijing: Zhonghua shuju, 2006.

Zong Ze 宗澤 (1059–1128). *Zong zhongjian ji* 宗忠簡集. In SKQS.

Secondary Sources

Abramson, Marc S. *Ethnic Identity in Tang China*. Philadelphia: University of Pennsylvania Press, 2008.

Abu-Lughod, Janet L. *Before European Hegemony: The World System A.D. 1250–1350*. New York: Oxford University Press, 1989.

Alexander, Michelle. *The New Jim Crow: Mass Incarceration in the Age of Colorblindness*. New York: New Press, 2011.

Allsen, Thomas. "The Rise of the Mongolian Empire and Mongolian Rule in North China." In *Cambridge History of China, Vol.6, Alien Regimes and Border State, 907–1368*, edited by Herbert Franke and Denis Crispin Twitchett, 321–413. Cambridge: Cambridge University Press, 2008.

Alyagon, Elad. "Loyalist Tattoos and Tattooed Generals in the Song Dynasty." In *Frontiers of History in China* 11, no. 2 (July 2016): 247–78.

———. "Soldier Mutinies and Resistance during the Northern Song." In *State Power in China, 900–1325*, edited by Patricia Buckley Ebrey and Paul Jakov Smith, 277–306. Seattle: University of Washington Press, 2016.

An Guolou 安國. *Songchao zhoubian minzu zhengce yanjiu* 宋朝周邊民族政策研究. Taibei: Wenjin chubanshe, 1997.

Anderson, Benedict. *Imagined Communities: Reflections on the Origin and Spread of Nationalism*. Rev. ed. London: Verso, 2006.

Anderson, Clare. "Godna: Inscribing Indian Convicts in the Nineteenth Century." In *Written on the Body: The Tattoo in European and American History*, edited by Jane Caplan, 102–17. London: Reaktion, 2000.

Anderson, James A. "Treacherous Factions: Shifting Frontier Alliances in the Breakdown of Sino-Vietnamese Relations on the Eve of the 1075 Border War." In *Battlefronts Real and Imagined: War, Border, and Identity in the Chinese Middle Period*, edited by Don J. Wyatt, 191–226. New York: Palgrave Macmillan, 2008.

Birge, Bettine. *Women, Property, and Confucian Reaction in Sung and Yüan China (960–1368).* Cambridge: Cambridge University Press, 2002.

Boltz, Judith Magee. "Not by the Seal of Office Alone: New Weapons in Battles with the Supernatural." In *Religion and Society in T'ang and Sung China,* edited by Patricia Buckley Ebrey and Peter N. Gregory, 241–305. Honolulu: University of Hawai'i Press, 1993.

Bond, Henry. *Lacan at the Scene.* Cambridge, MA: MIT Press, 2009.

Bossler, Beverly Jo. *Courtesans, Concubines, and the Cult of Female Fidelity: Gender and Social Change in China, 1000–1400.* Cambridge, MA: Harvard University Asia Center, 2013.

———. "A Daughter Is a Daughter All Her Life': Affinal Relations and Women's Networks in Song and Late Imperial China." *Late Imperial China* 21, no. 1 (2000): 77–106.

———. *Powerful Relations: Kinship, Status, and the State in Sung China (960–1279).* Cambridge, MA: Council on East Asian Studies, Harvard University Press, 1998.

———. "Shifting Identities: Courtesans and Concubines in Song China." *Harvard Journal of Asiatic Studies* 62, no. 1 (June, 2002): 5–37.

Bradley, James. "Body Commodification? Class and Tattoos in Victorian Britain." In *Documenting Individual Identity: The Development of State Practices in the Modern World,* edited by Jane Caplan, and John Torpey, 136–55. Princeton, NJ: Princeton University Press, 2001.

Butler, Marcia. "Reflections of a Military Medium: Ritual and Magic in Eleventh and Twelfth Century Chinese Military Manuals." Ph.D. diss., Cornell University, 2007.

Caplan, Jane, ed. *Written on the Body: The Tattoo in European and American History.* London: Reaktion, 2000.

Caplan, Jane, and John Torpey, eds. *Documenting Individual Identity: The Development of State Practices in the Modern World.* Princeton, NJ: Princeton University Press 2001.

Ceresa, Marco. "Written on Skin and Flesh: The Pattern of Tattoo in China, Part One: Generalities." In *Studi in Onore Di Lionello Lanciotti,* edited by S. M. Carletti, M. Sacchetti, and P. Santangelo, 329–40. Naples: Instituto Universitario Orieentale, 1996.

Chaffee, John W. *Branches of Heaven: A History of the Imperial Clan of Sung China.* Cambridge, MA: Harvard University Asia Center, Harvard University Press, 1999.

———. *The Thorny Gates of Learning in Sung China: A Social History of Examinations.* Cambridge: Cambridge University Press, 1985.

Chen Feng 陈峰. *Beisong wujiang qunti yu xiangguan wenti yanjiu* 北宋武将群体与相关问题研究. Beijing: Zhonghua shuju, 2004.

———. "Shilun Song chu wujiang jingshen mianmao de zhuanbian" 试论宋初武将精神面貌的转变. *Hebei daxue xuebao (zhexue shehui kexue ban)* 25, no. 5 (2000): 14–19.

———. *Songdai junzheng yanjiu* 宋代军政研究. Beijing: Zhongguo shehui kexue chubanshe, 2010.

———. *Wushi de beiai: Beisong chongwen yiwu xianxiang yanjiu* 武士的悲哀: 北宋崇文抑武现象研究. Beijing: Renmin chubanshe, 2011.

Chen Xiaoshan 陈晓珊. "Beisong baojiafa zhiding yu shishi guocheng zhong de quyu chayi" 北宋保甲法制定与实施过程中的区域差异. *Shixue yuekan* 6 (2013): 49–56.

Chen Yuanpeng 陳元朋. "Shenti yu huawen—Tang Song shiqi de wenshen fengshang chutan" 身體與花紋–唐宋時期的文身風尚初探. *Xin xue shi* 1, no. 1 (March 2000): 1–44.

Cheng Long 程龙. *Beisong xibei zhanqu liangshi buji dili* 北宋西北战区粮食补给地理. Beijing: *Shehui kexue wenxian chubanshe*, 2006.

Cheng Minsheng 程民生. "Songdai bingli bushu kaocha" 宋代兵力部署考察. In *Zhongguo gudai shehui gaoceng luntan wenji: jinian Zheng Tianting xiansheng danchen yibai yishi zhounian* 中国古代社会高层论坛文集: 纪念郑天挺先生诞辰一百一十周年, 320–28. Beijing: Zhonghua shuju, 2011.

———. *Songdai renkou wenti kaocha* 宋代人口问题考察. Zhengzhou: Henan renmin chubanshe, 2013.

Chesneaux, Jean, and Lucien Bianco. *Popular Movements and Secret Societies in China, 1840–1950*. Stanford, CA: Stanford University Press, 1972.

Chia, Lucille. *Printing for Profit: The Commercial Publishers of Jianyang, Fujian (11th–17th Centuries)*. Cambridge, MA: Harvard University Asia Center for Harvard–Yenching Institute, Harvard University Press, 2002.

Chittick, Andrew. *Patronage and Community in Medieval China: The Xiangyang Garrison, 400–600 CE*. Albany: State University of New York Press, 2010.

Clark, Hugh R. "Scoundrels, Rogues, and Refugees: The Founders of the Ten Kingdoms in the Late Tenth Century." In *Five Dynasties and Ten Kingdoms*, edited by Peter Lorge, 47–77. Hong Kong: Chinese University Press, 2011.

———. "What's the Matter with 'China'? A Critique of Teleological History." *Journal of Asian Studies* 77, no. 2 (May 2018): 295–314.

Clendinnen, Inga. *Ambivalent Conquests: Maya and Spaniard in Yucatan, 1517–1570*. Cambridge: Cambridge University Press, 2003.

Collins, Patricia Hill. *Black Feminist Thought: Knowledge, Consciousness, and the Politics of Empowerment*. New York: Routledge, 2000.

Curry, Anne, and David Andrew Graff. "Introduction to Volume II." In *Cambridge History of War: Volume II, War and the Medieval World*, edited by Anne Curry and David Andrew Graff, 14–28. Cambridge: Cambridge University Press, 2020.

Dai Jianguo 戴建国. *Tang song biange shiqi de falü yu shehui*. 唐宋变革时期的法律与社会. Shanghai: Shanghai guiji chubanshe, 2010.

Davis, Angela Y. *Women, Race, and Class*. New York: Vintage, 1983.

Davis, Richard L. *Court and Family in Sung China, 960–1279: Bureaucratic Success and Kinship Fortunes for the Shih of Ming-chou*. Durham, NC: Duke University Press, 1986.

Deng Guangming 邓广铭. *Yue Fei zhuan (zengdingben)* 岳飞传（增订本）. 1963. Reprint, Beijing: Renmin chubanshe, 1983.

Deng Xiaonan 邓小南. "Tan Song chu zhi 'yu wuchen dushu' yu 'yong dushuren'" 谈宋初之"欲武臣读书"与"用读书人." *Shixue yuekan* 7 (2005).

Di Cosmo, Nicola. "Introduction." In *Military Culture in Imperial China*, edited by Nicola Di Cosmo, 1–22. Cambridge, MA: Harvard University Press, 2009.

———. "Violence in Inner Asian History." In *The Cambridge World History of Violen ce, Vol. II, 500–1500 CE*, edited by Matthew S. Gordon, Richard W. Kaeuper, and Harriet Zurndorfer, 19–37. Cambridge: Cambridge University Press, 2020.

Du Wenyu 杜文玉. "Nansong junzhi yanjiu" 南宋军制研究. *Weinan shizhuan xuebao* (*shehuike xueban*) 24, no. 2 (1994): 38–47.

Duara, Prasenjit. *Rescuing History from the Nation: Questioning Narratives of Modern China*. Chicago: University of Chicago Press, 1995.

Dutton, Robert Michael. *Policing and Punishment in China: From Patriarchy to "the People."* Cambridge: Cambridge University Press, 1992.

Ebrey, Patricia Buckley. *The Inner Quarters: Marriage and the Lives of Chinese Women in the Sung Period*. Berkeley: University of California Press, 1993.

———. "Women, Money, and Class: Ssu-Ma Kuang and Sung Neo-Confucianism Views on Women." Paper presented at the Papers on Society and Culture of Early Modern China 中國近世社會文化史論文集, Taibei, June 1992.

Egan, Ronald. *The Problem of Beauty: Aesthetic Thought and Pursuits in Northern Song Dynasty China*. Cambridge, MA: Harvard Asia Center, Harvard University Press, 2006.

Elvin, Mark. *The Pattern of the Chinese Past: A Social and Economic Interpretation*. Stanford, CA: Stanford University Press, 1973.

Fan Xuehui 范学辉. "Guan yu 'beijiu shi bingquan' ruogan wenti de zai tantao" 关于"杯酒释兵权"若干问题的再探讨. *Shixue yuekan,* no. 3 (2006): 38–48.

———. "Liangsong Sanya kao—yi yashu wei zhongxin" 两宋三衙考— 以衙署为中心. *Wen shi* 3, no. 108 (2014): 123–66.

———. "Songren benchao junzheng tizhi lunzheng shitan" 宋人本朝军政体制论争试探. *Shi wen zhe* 301, no. 4 (2007).

Fang Cheng-hua 方震華. "Military Families and the Southern Song Court—the Lü Case." *Journal of Song-Yuan Studies* 33 (2003): 49–70.

———. "Power Structures and Cultural Identities in Imperial China: Civil and Military Power from Late Tang to Early Song Dynasties (A.D. 875–1063)." Ph.D. diss., Brown University, 2001.

———. "Yangbing weimin—mubingzhi helihua lunshu zai songdai de jiangou" 養兵衛民— 募兵制合理化論述在宋代的建構. *Zhongyang yanjiuyuan lishi yuyan yanjiusuo jikan* 82, no. 1 (2011): 43–78.

Forage, Paul Christopher. "The Sino-Tangut War of 1081–1085." *Journal of Asian History* 25, no. 1 (1991): 1–28.

Foucault, Michel. *Discipline and Punish: The Birth of the Prison*. Translated by Alan Sheridan. New York: Vintage, 1995.

Fried, Morton H. "Military Status in Chinese Society." *American Journal of Sociology* 57, no. 4 (1952): 347–57.

Fu Changze 傅昌泽, "Qingxing sankao" 黥刑散考. *Qinghai minzu xueyuan xuebao (sheshui kexuebao)* 3 (1990): 97.

Fu Libai 傅礼白. "Songdai shumiyuan de shishi yu junshi juecequan de zhuanyi" 宋代枢密院的失势与军事决策权的转移. *Shixue yuekan*, no. 2 (2004): 37–46.

Ge Jianxiong 葛剑雄. "Songdai renkou xinzheng" 宋代人口新证. *Lishi yanjiu* 6 (1993): 34–45.

Gong Yanming 龚延明. *Yue Fei pingzhuan* 岳飞评传. Nanjing: Nanjing daxue chubanshe, 2001.

Graff, David A. "China, The Tang: 600–900." In *The Cambridge History of War: Volume 2, War and the Medieval World*, edited by Anne Curry and David A. Graff, 207–38. Cambridge: Cambridge University Press, 2020.

———. *Medieval Chinese Warfare, 300–900*. London: Routledge, 2002.

Gulik, Willem R. van. "Irezumi: The Pattern of Dermatography in Japan." Leiden, Netherlands: E. J. Brill, 1982.

Harrison, James P. "Chinese Communist Interpretations of the Chinese Peasant Wars." *History in Communist China*, edited by Albert Feuerwerker, 189–214. Cambridge, MA: MIT Press, 1968.

Hartwell, Robert M. "Demographic, Political, and Social Transformations of China, 750–1550." *Harvard Journal of Asiatic Studies* 42, no. 2 (1982): 365–442.

———. "Financial Expertise, Examinations, and the Formulation of Economic Policy in Northern Sung China." *Journal of Asian Studies* 30, no. 2 (1971): 281–314.

———. "Markets, Technology, and the Structure of Enterprise in the Development of the Eleventh-Century Chinese Iron and Steel Industry." *Journal of Economic History* 26, no. 1 (1966): 29–58.

———. "A Revolution in the Chinese Iron and Coal Industries During the Northern Sung, 960–1126 A.D." *Journal of Asian Studies* 21, no. 2 (1962): 153–62.

Higham, Robin, and David A. Graff. "Introduction." In *A Military History of China*, edited by David A. Graff and Robin Higham, 1–18. Boulder, CO: Westview, 2002.

Ho Koon-wan 何冠環. *Beisong wujiang yanjiu* 北宋武將研究. Hong Kong: Zhonghua shuju, 2003.

Hu Shaohua. "Revisiting Chinese Pacifism." *Asian Affairs, an American Review* 32, no. 4 (Winter 2006): 258–79.

Huai Jianli 淮建利. *Songchao xiangjun yanjiu* 宋朝厢军研究. Zhengzhou: Zhongguo guji chubanshe, 2007.

Huang, Donglan. "Shrines of Yue Fei—Spaces for Creation of Public Memory." *Chinese Sociology and Anthropology* 37, no. 2/3 (2004): 74–112.

Huang Kuan-chong 黄寬重. "Jia She shigong shuping—yi Nansong zhongqi huaidong de fangwu wei zhongxin" 贾涉事功述评—— 以南宋中期淮东的防务为中心. *Jinan xuebao (zhexue shehui kexueban)* 25, no. 1 (2003): 101–13.

———. *Nansong difang wuli: difang yu minjian ziwei wuli de tantao* 南宋地方武力：地方軍與民間自衛武力的探討. Taibei: Dongda tushu gongsi, 2002.

———. "Tang Song jiceng wuli yu jiceng shehui de zhuanbian—yi gongshou wei zhongxin de guancha 唐宋基层武力与基层社会的转变— 以弓手为中心的观察. *Lishi yanjiu* 1 (2004): 3–17.

Huang, Martin W. *Negotiating Masculinities in Late Imperial China*. Honolulu: University of Hawai'i Press, 2006.

Huang Qinglian 黃清連. "Tangmo Wudai de qingzu" 唐末五代的黥卒. In *Junshi zuzhi yu zhanzheng* 軍事組織與戰爭, edited by Huang Kewu 黃可武. Taibei: Zhongyang yanjiuyuan lishi yuyan yanjiusuo, 2002.

Hymes, Robert P. *Statesmen and Gentlemen: The Elite of Fu-chou, Chiang-hsi, in Northern and Southern Sung*. Cambridge: Cambridge University Press, 1986.

———. "Truth, Falsity, and Pretense in Song China: An Approach through the Anecdotes of Hong Mai." *Zhongguo shixue* 15 (2009): 1–26.

Ihara Hiroshi. "Numerical Indices that Can Reveal the Life of Song Commoners." In *Trading Networks in Early Modern East Asia*, edited by Angela Schottenhammer, 5–26. Wiesbaden, Germany: Harrassowitz, 2010.

Jenner, William John Francis. "Tough Guys, Mateship and Honor: Another Chinese Tradition." *East Asian History* 12 (December 1996): 1–34.

Johnston, Alastair I. *Cultural Realism: Strategic Culture and Grand Strategy in Chinese History*. Princeton, NJ: Princeton University Press, 1995.

Ji Yong 籍勇. "Songdai shibing yanjiu" 宋代士兵研究. Ph.D. diss., Hebei University, 2012.

Jiang Quanbao and Jesâus J. Sâanchez-Barricarte. "Bare Branches and Social Stability: A Historical Perspective from China?" *Frontiers of History in China* 6, no. 4 (2011): 538–61.

Jiang Xidong 姜锡东. "Beisong de bingyuan yu muzheng" 北宋的兵源与募征. In *Zhongguo Songshi yanjiuhui di shijie nianhui ji Tangmo Wudai Songchu xibei shi yantao hui* 中国宋史研究会第十届年会暨唐末五代宋初西北史研讨会, 71–87. Lanzhou: Xibei shifan daxue, 2002.

Kaegi, Jr., Walter Emil. *Byzantine Military Unrest, 471–843: An Interpretation.* Amsterdam: Hakkert, 1981.

Kaplan, Edward Harold. "Yueh Fei and the Founding of the Southern Sung." Ph.D. diss., University of Iowa, 1970.

Keegan, John. *The Face of Battle.* New York: Barnes & Noble, 1993.

———. *The First World War.* New York: Vintage, 2000.

Kim Sung Kyu. *Sōdai no seihoku mondai to iminzoku seisaku* 宋代の西北問題と異民族政策. Tōkyō: Kyūko Shoin, 2000.

Kitamura, Takahiro. *Tattoos of the Floating World: Ukiyo-E Motifs in the Japanese Tattoo.* Amsterdam: Hotei, 2003.

Koiwai Hiromitsu. 小岩井 弘光. *Sōdai heiseishi no kenkyū* 宋代兵制史の研究. Tokyo: Kyūko shoin, 1998.

———. "Sōdai no rōei ni tsuite" 宋代の老兵について. In *Jinbun gakkai kiyō/Kokushikan daigaku bungakubu jinbun gakkai en* 人文学会紀要/国士舘大学文学部人文学会編 10 (1989): 85–102.

Kracke, Edward A. *Civil Service in Early Sung China, 960–1067; with Particular Emphasis on the Development of Controlled Sponsorship to Foster Administrative Responsibility.* Cambridge, MA: Harvard University Press, 1953.

Kuhn, Dieter. *The Age of Confucian Rule: The Song Transformation of China.* Cambridge, MA: Belknap Press of Harvard University Press, 2009.

Labadie, John Richard. "Rulers and Soldiers: Perception and Management of the Military in Northern Sung China (960–Ca. 1060)." Ph.D. diss., University of Washington, 1982.

Lang, Kurt. "Military Organizations." In *Handbook of Organizations*, edited by James G. March, 838–78. Chicago: Rand McNally, 1965.

Lary, Diana. *Warlord Soldiers: Chinese Common Soldiers 1911–1937.* 1985. Reprint, Cambridge: Cambridge University Press, 2010.

Lei, Daphne, P. "The Blood-Stained Text in Translation: Tattooing, Bodily Writing, and Performance of Chinese Virtue." *Anthropological Quarterly* 82, no. 1 (2009): 99–127.

Lewis, Mark Edward. *The Early Chinese Empires: Qin and Han*. Cambridge, MA: Belknap Press of Harvard University Press, 2007.

Lin Ruihan 林瑞翰. "Songdai bingzhi chutan" 宋代兵制初探. *Taida lishi xuebao* 3 (1976): 101–18.

Liu, James T. C. 劉子健. "Yüeh Fei (1103–41) and China's Heritage of Loyalty." *Journal of Asian Studies* 31, no. 2 (February 1972): 291–97.

———. "Yue Fei: cong shixueshi he sixiangshi lai kan" 岳飛：從史學史和思想史來看 *Zhongguo xueren* 2 (1970): 43–58.

Liu Jin 刘缙. *Songdai zhengguijun junshi xunlian chutan* 宋代正规军军事训练初探. Ph.D. diss., Shaanxi Normal University, 2008.

Lo, Winston. *An Introduction to the Civil Service of Sung China: With Emphasis on Its Personnel Administration*. Honolulu: University of Hawai'i Press, 1987.

Lorge, Peter Alan. *The Asian Military Revolution: From Gunpowder to the Bomb*. Cambridge: Cambridge University Press, 2008.

———. "The Entrance and Exit of the Song Founders." *Journal of Song-Yuan Studies* 29 (1999): 43–62.

———. "From Warlord to Emperor: Song Taizu's Change of Heart during the Conquest of Shu." *T'oung Pao* 91, no. 4/5 (2005): 320–46.

———. "The Great Ditch of China and the Song-Liao Border." In *Battlefronts Real and Imagined: War, Border, and Identity in the Chinese Middle Period*, edited by Don J. Wyatt, 59–74. New York: Palgrave Macmillan, 2008.

———. "Military Institutions as a Defining Feature of the Song Dynasty." *Journal of Chinese History* 1, no. 2 (2017): 269–95.

———. *The Reunification of China: Peace through War under the Song Dynasty*. Cambridge: Cambridge University Press, 2015.

———. "State, Society and Trained Violence in China, 618–1500." In *The Cambridge World History of Violence, Vol. II, 500–1500 CE*, edited by Matthew S. Gordon, Richard W. Kaeuper, and Harriet Zurndorfer, 228–47. Cambridge: Cambridge University Press, 2020.

———. "War and the Creation of the Northern Song State." Ph.D. diss., University of Pennsylvania, 1996.

———. *War, Politics and Society in Early Modern China, 900–1795*. London: Routledge, 2005.

Louie, Kam. *Theorising Chinese Masculinity: Society and Gender in China*. Cambridge: Cambridge University Press, 2002.

Lü Zhixing 吕志兴. "*Songdai peixing zhidu tanxi* 宋代配刑制度探析." *Xinan shifan daxue xuebao (renwen shehui kexuebao)* 30, no. 1 (2004): 101–08.

Mann, Susan L. "The Male Bond in Chinese History and Culture." *American Historical Review* 105, no. 5 (December 2000): 1600–14.

Matten, Marc Andre. "The Worship of General Yue Fei and His Problematic Creation as a National Hero in Twentieth Century China." *Frontiers of History in China* 6, no. 1 (2011): 74–94.

McDermott, Joseph Peter. *A Social History of the Chinese Book: Books and Literati Culture in Late Imperial China*. Hong Kong: Hong Kong University Press, 2006.

McGrath, Michael Charles. "Military and Regional Administration in Northern Sung China (960–1126)." Ph.D. diss., Princeton University, 1982.

McKnight, Brian E. *Law and Order in Sung China*. Cambridge: Cambridge University Press, 1992.

———. *Law and the Military in the Sung*. Nangang: International Conference on Sinology Academia Sinica, 1986.

———. "Maximum Security in the Sung: the Facilities at Sramana Island." *Bulletin of Song Yuan Studies* 16 (1980): 8–22.

———. *The Quality of Mercy: Amnesties and Traditional Chinese Justice*. Honolulu: University Press of Hawai'i, 1981.

Meyer-Fong, Tobie S. *What Remains: Coming to Terms with Civil War in 19th Century China*. Stanford, CA: Stanford University Press, 2013.

Metzger, Thomas, A. "Chinese Bandits: The Traditional Perception Re-Evaluated." *Journal of Asian Studies* 33, no. 3 (1974): 455–58.

Mignolo, Walter D. *The Darker Side of the Renaissance: Literacy, Territoriality, and Colonization*. Ann Arbor: University of Michigan, 2003.

Miyakawa Hisayuki. "An Outline of the Naitō Hypothesis and Its Effects on Japanese Studies of China." *Far Eastern Quarterly* 14, no. 4 (1955): 533–52.

Morgan, Gwenda, and Peter Rushton. "Visible Bodies: Power, Subordination and Identity in the Eighteenth-Century Atlantic World." *Journal of Social History* 39, no. 1 (2005): 39–64.

Mote, Frederick W. *Imperial China, 900–1800*. Cambridge, MA: Harvard University Press, 1999.

Moyer, Mark. "The Current State of Military History." *Historical Journal* 50, no. 1 (2007): 225–40.

Mu Jing 穆静. "Wudai bingzhi kaolun" 五代兵制考论. Ph.D. diss., Dongbei shifan daxue, 2010.

Ning Ke 宁可. "Shibing cizi 士兵刺字." In *Ning Ke shixue lunji* 宁可史学论集, 629–34. Beijing: Zhongguo shehui kexue chubanshe, 1999.

Ousbi, Ian. *The Road to Verdun: World War I's Most Momentous Battle and the Folly of Nationalism*. New York: Doubleday, 2002.

Parker, Geoffrey. *The Military Revolution: Military Innovation and the Rise of the West, 1500–1800*. Cambridge: Cambridge University Press, 1996.

Plaks, Andrew H. *The Four Masterworks of the Ming Novel: Ssu ta ch'i-shu.* Princeton, NJ: Princeton University Press, 1987.

Poysden, Mark, and Marco Bratt. *A History of Japanese Body Suit Tattooing.* Amsterdam: KIT, 2006.

Pulleyblank, Edwin G. "The An Lu-Shan Rebellion in Late T'ang China." In *Essays on T'ang Society*, edited by Bardwell L. Smith and John Curtis Perry, 33–60. Leiden, Netherlands: Brill, 1976.

Qian Junling 钱俊岭. "Songdai jundui shangfa zhidu yanjiu" 宋代军队赏罚制度研究. Ph.D. diss., Hebei University, 2011.

Qian Mu 錢穆. "Zhongguo lidai zhengzhi deshi" 中國歷代政治得失. In *Qian binsi xiansheng quanji* 錢賓四先生全集, vol. 31, 105–13. Taibei: Lianjing chuban shiye gongsi, 1994.

Reed, Carrie E. "Early Chinese Tattoo." *Sino-Platonic Papers* 103 (2000): 1–52.

———. "Tattoos in Early China." *Journal of the American Oriental Society* 120, no. 3 (July-September 2000): 360–76.

Robinson, David. *Bandits, Eunuchs, and the Son of Heaven: Rebellion and the Economy of Violence in Mid-Ming China*. Honolulu: University of Hawai'i Press, 2001.

Ropp, Paul. "The Distinctive Art of Chinese Fiction." In *Heritage of China: Contemporary Perspectives on Chinese Civilization*, edited by Paul S. Ropp and Timothy Hugh Barrett, 309–34. Berkeley: University of California Press, 1990.

Rossabi, Morris, ed. *China among Equals: The Middle Kingdom and Its Neighbors, 10th–14th Centuries.* Berkeley: University of California Press, 1983.

Saitō Tadakazu. 齋藤忠和. *Sōdai boheisei no kenkyū: kinsei shokugyō heishi no jissō* 宋代募兵制の研究: 近世職業兵士の実相. Tokyo: Benseishuppan, 2014.

Sanmenxia Shi wenwu gongzuodui 三门峡市文物工作队. *Beisong Shaanzhou louze yuan* 北宋陕州漏泽园. Beijing: Wenwu chubanshe, 1999.

Scott, James C. *Domination and the Arts of Resistance: Hidden Transcripts.* New Haven, CT: Yale University Press, 1990.

———. *Weapons of the Weak: Everyday Forms of Peasant Resistance.* New Haven, CT: Yale University Press, 1985.

Shaw, George Bernard. "Preface." In *English Prisons under Local Government,* Beatrice Webb and Sidney Webb. London: Longmans, Green, 1922.

Shiba Yoshinobu. *Commerce and Society in Sung China*. Translated by Mark Elvin. Ann Arbor: Center for Chinese Studies, University of Michigan, 1970.

Smith, Paul Jakov. "Shuihu Zhuan and the Military Subculture of the Northern Song, 960–1127." *Harvard Journal of Asiatic Studies* 66, no. 2 (2006): 363–422.

———. *Taxing Heaven's Storehouse: Horses, Bureaucrats, and the Destruction of the Sichuan Tea Industry, 1074–1224*. Cambridge, MA: Council on East Asian Studies, Harvard University Press, 1991.

Sogabe Shizuo. 曽我部静雄. "Sōdai no shi-hai ni tsuite" 宋代の刺配について. *Bunka* 29, no. 1 (1965): 1–23.

Standen, Naomi. "Raiding and Frontier Society in the Five Dynasties." In *Political Frontiers, Ethnic Boundaries and Human Geographies in Chinese History*, edited Don J. Wyatt and Nicole Di Cosmo, 162–191. London: Routledge, 2003.

———. *Unbounded Loyalty: Frontier Crossing in Liao China*. Honolulu: University of Hawai'i Press, 2007.

Szonyi, Michael. *The Art of Being Governed: Everyday Politics in Late Imperial China*. Princeton, NJ: Princeton University Press, 2017.

———. "Making Claims about Standardization and Orthopraxy in Late Imperial China: Rituals and Cults in the Fuzhou Region in Light of Watson's Theories." *Modern China* 33, no. 1 (January 2007): 47–71.

Tackett, Nicolas. *The Destruction of the Medieval Chinese Aristocracy*. Cambridge, MA: Harvard University Asia Center, 2014.

———. "The Great Wall and Conceptualizations of the Border under the Northern Song." *Journal of Song-Yuan Studies* 38, no. 1 (2008): 99–138.

———. *The Origins of the Chinese Nation: Song China and the Forging of an East Asian World Order*. Cambridge: Cambridge University Press, 2017.

Takahashi Hiroomi. "Nansō Rin'an no kasō-min to toshi gyōsei" 南宋臨安の下層民と都市行政. *Ehime daigaku hōbungakubu ronshū jinbun gakka hen* 21 (2006): 119-–50.

Tan Su-cheng 譚溯澄. "Songdai zhi jundui" 宋代之軍隊. Ph.D. diss., National Chengchi University, Taiwan, 1972.

ter Haar, Barend. "Rethinking 'Violence' in Chinese Culture." In *Meanings of Violence: A Cross Cultural Perspective*, edited by Göran Aijmer and Jon Abbink, 123–40. Oxford: Berg, 2000.

Thompson, Edward Palmer. *The Making of the English Working Class*. London: Penguin , 1991.

Tsuji Masahiro. 辻正博. "Sō-hatsu no hairu to hai-gun" 宋初の配流と配軍. *Tōyōshikenkyū/tōyōshikenkyūkai* 52, no. 3 (1993): 331–61.

Von Glahn, Richard. *The Country of Streams and Grottoes: Expansion, Settlement, and the Civilizing of the Sichuan Frontier in Song Times*. Cambridge, MA: Council on East Asian Studies, Harvard University, 1987.

Wang Gungwu. "The Military Governors and the Decline of the T'ang Dynasty." In *The Making of China: Main Themes in Premodern Chinese History*, edited by Chun-shu Chang, 211–29. Englewood Cliffs, NJ: Prentice-Hall, 1975.

———. *The Structure of Power in North China during the Five Dynasties*. Kuala Lumpur: University of Malaya Press, 1963.

Wang Junying 王军营 and Chen Feng 陈峰. "Beisong jiceng shizu bianluan zhenglun" 北宋基层士卒变乱刍论. *Shaanxi shifan daxue xuebao (zhixue shihuike xuebao)* 41, no. 3 (2012):118–23.

Wang, Yuan-kang. *Harmony and War: Confucian Culture and Chinese Power Politics*. New York: Columbia University Press, 2011.

Wang Yunchang 王云裳. *Songdai jundui jingying wenti yanjiu* 宋代军队经营问题研究. Beijing: Zhonghua shuju, 2013.

Wang Yunhai 王云海 and Zhang Dezong 张德宗. "Songdai de youdipu bing" 宋代的邮递铺兵. In *Songshi yanjiu lunwenji yi jiu ba si nian hui biankan* 宋史研究论文集：一九八四年会编刊, edited by Deng Guangming 邓广铭 and Xu Gui 徐规, 324–34. Hangzhou: Zhejiang renmin chubanshe, 1987.

Wang Zengyu 王曾瑜. "A History of the Sung Military." In *The Cambridge History of China: Sung China, 960–1279*, edited by John W. Chaffee and Denis Twitchett, 214–49. Cambridge: Cambridge University Press, 2015.

———. *Huangyin wudao Song Gaozong* 荒淫无道宋高宗. Shijiazhuang: Hebei renmin chubanshe, 1999.

———. *Jinzhong baoguo: Yue Fei Xinzhuan* 尽忠报国: 岳飞新传. Shijiazhuang: Hebei renmin chubanshe, 2001.

———. *Songchao junzhi chutan (zengding ben)* 宋朝军制初探（增订本）. Beijing: Zhonghua shuju, 2011.

———. *Yue Fei he nansong qianqi zhengzhi yu junshi yanjiu* 岳飞和南宋前期政治与军事研究. Kaifeng: Henan daxue chubanshe, 2005.

Wilhelm, Hellmut. "From Myth to Myth: The Case of Yüeh Fei's Biography." In *Confucian Personalities*, edited by Arthur F. Wright and Denis Twitchett, 146–61. 1953. Reprint, Stanford, CA: Stanford University Press, 1962.

Wong Hon-chiu. "Government Expenditures in Northern Sung China (960–1127)." Ph.D. diss., University of Pennsylvania, 1975.

Worthy, Edmund Henry. "The Founding of Sung China 950–1000: Integrative Changes in Military and Political Institutions." Ph.D. diss., Princeton University, 1976.

Wright, David C. *From War to Diplomatic Parity in Eleventh-Century China: Sung's Foreign Relations with Kitan Liao*. Leiden, Netherlands: Brill, 2005.

Wu Pei-Yi. "Yang Miaozhen: A Woman Warrior in Thirteenth-Century China." *Nan nü: Men, Women, and Gender in Early and Imperial China* 4, no. 2 (2002): 137–69.

Wyatt, Don J. "Conspirators in Violence: The Imperial State and its Armies in Medieval China." In *The Cambridge World History of Violence, Vol. II, 500–1500 CE*, edited by Matthew S. Gordon, Richard W. Kaeuper, and Harriet Zurndorfer, 38–57. Cambridge: Cambridge University Press, 2020.

———. "Unsung Men of War: Acculturated Embodiments of the Martial Ethos in the Song Dynasty." In *Military Culture in Imperial China*, edited by Nicola Di Cosmo, 192–218. Cambridge, MA: Harvard University Press, 2009.

Yang, Li. "The Emperor's Generals, a Study of the Sanya Commanders in the Northern Song (960–1126)." Ph.D. diss. University of Arizona, 2004.

Yang Shao-yun. *The Way of the Barbarians: Redrawing Elite Boundaries in Tang and Song China*. Seattle: University of Washington Press, 2019.

You Biao 游彪. "Lun Songdai shibing taowang ji qi yingxiang" 论宋代士兵逃亡及其影响. In *Songdai yanjiu lunwenji yi jiu jiu si nian nianhui biankan* 宋代研究论文集一九九四年年会编刊, edited by Hu Zhaoxi 胡昭曦 and Qi Xia 漆侠, 98–118. Hebei: Hebei daxue chubanshe, 1996.

Young, Charles S. *Name, Rank, and Serial Number: Exploiting Korean War POWs at Home and Abroad*. Oxford: Oxford University Press, 2014.

Zeng Ruilong 曾瑞龙 and Zhao Yule 赵雨乐. "Tang Song junzheng biange shi yanjiu shuping" 唐宋军政变革史研究述评. In *"Tang song biange" lun de youlai yu fazhan* 「唐宋变革」论的由来与发展, edited by Li Huarui 李华瑞, 63–113. Tianjin: Tianjin guji chubanshe, 2010.

Zhang Guogang. "The Transformations of the Tang Military System and Social Changes in Medieval China." *Frontiers of History in China* 2, no. 3 (2007): 293–319.

Zhang Ling. "Changing with the Yellow River: An Environmental History of Hebei, 1048–1128." *Harvard Journal of Asiatic Studies* 69, no. 1 (2009): 1–36.

Zhang Ming 張明. "Liang Song shibing taowangfa xintan" 两宋士兵逃亡法新探. *Xibei daxue xuebao (zhexue shehui kexue bao)* 37, no. 3 (May 2007): 72–76.

———. *Songdai junfa yanjiu* 宋代军法研究. Beijing: Zhongguo shejui kexue chubanshe, 2010.

Zhao Dongmei 趙冬梅. *Wen wu zhi jian: Beisong wuxuanguan yanjiu* 文武之間: 北宋武選官研究. Beijing: Beijing chubanshe, 2010.

Zhu Dejun 朱德军. "Songdai xibei diqu taobing wenti de lishi kaocha—yi e zang heishuicheng wenxian wei zhongxin" 宋代西北地区逃兵问题的历史考察—以俄藏黑水城文献为中心. *Shaanxi daxue xuebao (zhexue shehui kexue ban)* 34, no. 4 (2011): 41–46.

Zhu Ruixi 朱瑞熙. "Songdai de cizi he wenshen xisu" 宋代的刺字和文身习俗. *Zhongguoshi yanjiu* 1 (1998): 102–08.

Zinn, Howard. *A People's History of the United States: 1492—Present*. 2001. Reprint, New York: Harper Perennial, 2005.

Žižek, Slavoj. *Violence: Six Sideways Reflections*. New York: Picador, 2008.

Index

Harvard East Asian Monographs

(most recent titles)

414. Chieko Nakajima, *Body, Society, and Nation: The Creation of Public Health and Urban Culture in Shanghai*
415. Pu Wang, *The Translatability of Revolution: Guo Moruo and Twentieth-Century Chinese Culture*
416. Hwansoo Ilmee Kim, *The Korean Buddhist Empire: A Transnational History, 1910–1945*
417. Joshua Hill, *Voting as a Rite: A History of Elections in Modern China*
418. Kirsten L. Ziomek, *Lost Histories: Recovering the Lives of Japan's Colonial Peoples*
419. Claudine Ang, *Poetic Transformations: Eighteenth-Century Cultural Projects on the Mekong Plains*
420. Evan N. Dawley, *Becoming Taiwanese: Ethnogenesis in a Colonial City, 1880s–1950s*
421. James McMullen, *The Worship of Confucius in Japan*
422. Nobuko Toyosawa, *Imaginative Mapping: Landscape and Japanese Identity in the Tokugawa and Meiji Eras*
423. Pierre Fuller, *Famine Relief in Warlord China*
424. Diane Wei Lewis, *Powers of the Real: Cinema, Gender, and Emotion in Interwar Japan*
425. Maram Epstein, *Orthodox Passions: Narrating Filial Love during the High Qing*
426. Margaret Wan, *Regional Literature and the Transmission of Culture: Chinese Drum Ballads, 1800–1937*
427. Takeshi Watanabe, *Flowering Tales: Women Exorcising History in Heian Japan*
428. Jürgen P. Melzer, *Wings for the Rising Sun: A Transnational History of Japanese Aviation*
429. Edith Sarra, *Unreal Houses: Character, Gender, and Genealogy in the* Tale of Genji
430. Yi Gu, *Chinese Ways of Seeing and Open-Air Painting*
431. Robert Cliver, *Red Silk: Class, Gender, and Revolution in China's Yangzi Delta Silk Industry*
432. Kenneth J. Ruoff, *Japan's Imperial House in the Postwar Era, 1945–2019*
433. Erin L. Brightwell, *Reflecting the Past: Place, Language, and Principle in Japan's Medieval Mirror Genre*
434. Janet Borland, *Earthquake Children: Building Resilience from the Ruins of Tokyo*
435. Susan Blakely Klein, *Dancing the Dharma: Religious and Political Allegory in Japanese Noh Theater*

436. Yukyung Yeo, *Varieties of State Regulation: How China Regulates Its Socialist Market Economy*
437. Robert Goree, *Printing Landmarks: Popular Geography and* Meisho zue *in Late Tokugawa Japan*
438. Lawrence C. Reardon, *A Third Way: The Origins of China's Current Economic Development Strategy*
439. Eyck Freymann, *One Belt One Road: Chinese Power Meets the World*
440. Yung Chul Park, Joon Kyung Kim, and Hail Park, *Financial Liberalization and Economic Development in Korea, 1980–2020*
441. Steven B. Miles, *Opportunity in Crisis: Cantonese Migrants and the State in Late Qing China*
442. Grace Huang, *Chiang Kai-shek's Politics of Shame: Leadership, Legacy, and National Identity*
443. Adam Lyons, *Karma and Punishment: Prison Chaplaincy in Japan*
444. Craig A. Smith, *Chinese Asianism, 1894–1945*
445. Sachiko Kawai, *Uncertain Powers: Sen'yōmon and Landownership by Royal Women in Early Medieval Japan*
446. Juliane Noth, *Transmedial Landscapes and Modern Chinese Painting*
447. Susan Westhafer Furukawa, *The Afterlife of Toyotomi Hideyoshi: Historical Fiction and Popular Culture in Japan*
448. Nongji Zhang, *Legal Scholars and Scholarship in the People's Republic of China: The First Generation (1949–1992)*
449. Han Sang Kim, *Cine-Mobility: Twentieth-Century Transformations in Korea's Film and Transportation*
450. Brian Hurley, *Confluence and Conflict: Reading Transwar Japanese Literature and Thought*
451. Simon Avenell, *Asia and Postwar Japan: Deimperialization, Civic Activism, and National Identity*
452. Maura Dykstra, *Empire of Routine: The Administrative Revolution of the Eighteenth-Century Qing State*
453. Marnie S. Anderson, *In Close Association: Local Activist Networks in the Making of Japanese Modernity, 1868–1920*
454. John D. Wong, *Hong Kong Takes Flight: Commercial Aviation and the Making of a Global Hub, 1930s–1998*
455. Martin K. Whyte and Mary C. Brinton, compilers, *Remembering Ezra Vogel*
456. Lawrence Zhang, *Power for a Price: The Purchase of Appointments in Qing China*
457. J. Megan Greene, *Building a Nation at War: Transnational Knowledge Networks and the Development of China during and after World War II*
458. Miya Qiong Xie, *Territorializing Manchuria: The Transnational Frontier and Literatures of East Asia*
459. Dal Yong Jin, *Understanding Korean Webtoon Culture: Transmedia Storytelling, Digital Platforms, and Genres*
460. Takahiro Yamamoto, *Demarcating Japan: Imperialism, Islanders, and Mobility, 1855–1884*
461. Elad Alyagon, *Inked: Tattooed Soldiers and the Song Empire's Penal-Military Complex*
462. Borje Ljunggren and Dwight H. Perkins, eds., *Vietnam: Navigating a Rapidly Changing Economy, Society, and Political Order*